THE AMERICAN CITY
AND
ITS CITIZENS

The Dream on the Move

By the same author:

Regional Geography: Theory and Practice, H.U.L., 1967
The Changing Nature of Geography, H.U.L., 1970
Introduction to Models in Geography, Longman, 1975
Human Geography From the Air, Macmillan, 1969
Settlements From the Air, Macmillan, 1971
Factors in Farming, Nelson, 1976
Simulation Games in Geography, (co-author), Macmillan, 1972
Correlation Techniques in Geography, (co-author), Philip, 1972
Networks in Geography, (co-author), Philip, 1973
Sampling Techniques in Geography, (co-author), Philip, 1975
Assignments in Geography, (co-author), Philip, 1978

THE AMERICAN CITY
AND
ITS CITIZENS

The Dream on the Move

Roger Minshull

The Book Guild Ltd
Sussex, England

The Book Guild Ltd
25 High Street,
Lewes, Sussex

First published 1996
© Roger Minshull, 1996
Set in Times
Typesetting by Acorn Bookwork, Salisbury

Printed in Great Britain by Bookcraft (Bath) Ltd., Avon.

A catalogue record for this book is
available from the British Library

ISBN 1 85776 101 4

CONTENTS

ACKNOWLEDGEMENTS

Fig 1.1,2.1 and 2.2 reproduced with kind permission of Prentice-Hall, New Jersey. Sources: Berry, B.J.L., *Geography of Market Centers and Retail Distribution* and Berry, B.J.L & Horton, F.E., *Geographical Perspectives on Urban Systems* (1970)

Figure 3.1 reproduced with kind permission of Penguin. Source: Schaeffer, K.H. & Sclar, E, *Access For All* (1975)

Figure 5.1a reproduced with king permission of Lane Magazine and Book Co., California. Source: Editors of Sunset Books, *Los Angeles* (1968)

Figure 5.1b reproduced with kind permission of Sam Bass Warner Jr. Source: Sam Bass Warner, *The Urban Wilderness: A History of the American City*, University of California Press (1972). Copyright (c) 1972 Sam Bass Warner Jr.

Figure 6.1 reproduced with kind permission of HarperCollins Publishers. Source: Sinclair, R. & Thompson, B., *Detroit* (1977)

Figure 7.1 reproduced with kind permission of McGraw-Hill, New York. Source: Smith, D.M., *The Geography of Social Well-Being in the United States* (1973)

Figure 8.1 reproduced with kind permission of University of California. Source: Brian J. Godfrey, *Neighbourhoods in Transition: The Making of San Francisco's Ethnic and Nonconformist Communities.* Copyright (c) 1988 The Regents of the University of California.

Figure 9.1 reproduced with kind permission of HarperCollins Publishers. Source: Conzen, M.P. & Lewis, G.K., *Boston* (1976)

Figure 10.1 reproduced with kind permission of Doubleday, a division of Bantam Doubleday Dell Publishing Group, Inc. Source: Garreau, J., *Edge City* (1991)

Figure 11.1 reproduced with kind permission of The University of Chicago Press. Source: Mayer, H.M & Kohn, C.F., *Readings in Urban Geography* (1959); and Dr David Herbert. Source: *Urban Geography*, David & Charles (1972)

1

THE CONCENTRATED CITY

In 1620 there were no cities in that part of North America now occupied by the United States and Canada. There were settlements, but the villages of the Amerindians in the eastern woodlands, on the northern High Plains and in the irrigated valleys of the southwest — some with Spanish missions already attached to them — had predominantly rural functions. Moreover, the villages of the Iroquois, the Mandans and the Hopi were not the beginnings of the gigantic cities like New York, Chicago and Los Angeles which today rival the ancient Japanese cities in size and complexity. When Rome, Paris, Cologne and London were many centuries old, the first posts and stones of the American cities which outgrew and outrivalled them had not been placed on the ground.

A study of American cities, then, first involves some of the most rapid urban growth ever recorded: from nothing to population centres of fifteen, possibly twenty million. (see tables 1.1 & 1.2). Secondly, part of the story is of massive immigration, rapid urbanisation and overwhelming industrialisation. But the study also involves continuous change, not just in the size and functions of those cities, but also in the geography, the layout and spatial arrangement of the peoples and their activities in these vast urban areas, resulting in a complex pattern. Equally importantly, the analysis reveals the total man-made environment which has developed as these urban systems grew in size and complexity, producing the conditions, both advantageous and problematical, in which the large majority of Americans presently live.

Writing in England, one is consciously addressing the issue from a British and, to a lesser extent, a European point of view. Through films, novels, newspapers, magazines and television the lay person with an interest in America is already aware of the appearance and functions of many parts of cities like Boston, Miami, Houston, San Francisco and others, in addition to those already mentioned above.

1

Table 1.1 National and International Rankings of US Cities

Note that the populations are calculated on a different basis from all the other tables in this book. The world cities are defined as continuously built-up-areas with at least 5,000 people per square mile.

World Rank	City	Pop. 1991	US Rank
1	Tokyo	27,245,000	
2	Mexico City	20,899,000	
3	Sao Paulo	18,701,000	
4	Seoul	16,792,000	
5	New York	14,625,000	1
13	Los Angeles	10,139,000	2
27	Chicago	6,529,000	3
47	Philadelphia	4,003,000	4
48	San Francisco	3,987,000	5
56	Miami	3,471,000	6
68	Detroit	2,969,000	7
76	Dallas	2,787,0900	8
80	Washington DC	2,565,000	9
82	Boston	2,476,000	10
88	Houston	2,329,000	11
United Kingdom			
17	London	9,115,000	
46	Manchester	4,030,000	
92	Birmingham	2,162,000	

Source: Statistical Abstract of the US 1992

Not so familiar, however, is the rapid growth; and perhaps least familiar — plus the most difficult for someone who has not been able to explore the American urban landscape — is the sheer size of those great sprawls. The continuously built-up-area of greater New York spreads across three states: New York, New Jersey and Connecticut. Greater Chicago covers an area larger than Lincolnshire, the second largest county in England, while one could drop London into Los Angeles five times, and still have space round the edges to add a few small towns.

Table 1.2 Metropolitan Trends in Population

Metropolitan area	1970 total (1,000)	1980 total (1,000)	1990 Total (1,000)	Rank	Under 18 yrs. old (percent)	65 yrs. old and over (percent)	Percent change 1970–80	Percent change 1980–90
Albany–Schenectady–Troy, NY MSA	811	836	874	48	23.3	14.2	3.1	4.6
Albuquerque, NM MSA	316	420	481	77	26.1	10.5	33.1	14.4
Allentown–Bethlehem–Easton, PA-NJ MSA	594	635	687	58	23.1	15.2	6.9	8.1
Appleton–Oshkosh–Neenah, WI MSA	277	291	315	114	26.7	11.9	5.2	8.2
Atlanta, GA MSA	1,684	2,138	2,834	12	25.9	7.9	27.0	32.5
Atlantic City, NJ MSA	235	276	319	112	22.7	16.2	17.8	15.6
Augusta, GA-SC MSA	291	346	397	91	27.9	9.9	18.8	14.7
Austin, TX MSA	360	537	782	52	25.3	7.4	48.9	45.6
Bakersfield, CA MSA	330	403	543	68	31.5	9.7	22.1	34.8
Baltimore, MD MSA	2,089	2,199	2,382	18	24,1	11.7	5.3	8.3
Baton Rouge, LA MSA	376	494	528	71	28.6	8.9	31.6	6.9
Beaumont–Port Arthur, TX MSA	348	373	361	102	27.6	13.1	7.4	-3.2
Binghamton, NY MSA	268	263	264	127	24.0	14.2	-1.8	0.4
Birmingham, AL MSA	794	884	908	46	25.4	13.2	11.3	2.7
Boston–Lawrence–Salem, MA-NH CMSA	3,939	3,972	4,172	7	22.2	12.4	0.8	5.0
Boston, MA PMSA	2,887	2,806	2,871	(X)	20.8	12.9	-2.8	2.3
Brockton, MA PMSA	163	183	189	(X)	25.5	11.3	12.4	3.6
Lawrence–Haverhill, MA-NH PMSA	301	339	394	(X)	26.4	11.6	12.7	16.1
Lowell, MA-NH PMSA	225	243	273	(X)	26.0	9.7	7.8	12.3
Nashua, NH PMSA	100	143	181	(X)	26.9	7.9	42.5	26.7
Salem–Gloucester, MA PMSA	263	258	264	(X)	21.0	14.9	-1.7	2.4
Brownsville–Harlingen, TX MSA	140	210	260	129	35.3	10.6	49.4	24.0
Buffalo–Niagara Falls, NY CMSA	1,349	1,243	1,189	33	23.6	15.2	-7.9	-4.3
Buffalo, NY PMSA	1,113	1,015	969	(X)	23.3	15.2	-8.8	-4.6
Niagara Falls, NY PMSA	236	227	221	(X)	24.9	15.2	-3.5	-2.9
Canton, OH MSA	394	404	394	93	25.3	14.4	2.7	-2.6
Charleston, SC MSA	336	430	507	73	27.6	8.6	28.1	17.8
Charleston, WV MSA	257	2707	250	134	23.8	14.9	4.8	-7.1
Charlotte–Gastonia–Rock Hill, NC-SC MSA	840	971	1,162	34	24.7	10.9	15.6	19.6
Chattanooga, TN-GA MSA	371	426	433	82	24.8	13.0	15.0	1.6
Chicago–Gary–Lake County, IL-IN-WI CMNSA	7,779	7,937	8,066	3	26.1	11.4	2.0	1.6
Aurora–Elgin, IL PMSA	277	316	357	(X)	29.8	9.2	13.8	13.1
Chicago, IL PMSA	6,093	6,060	6,070	(X)	25.4	11.8	-0.5	0.2
Gary–Hammond, IN PMSA	633	643	605	(X)	27.9	11.8	1.5	-5.9
Joliet, IL PMSA	274	355	390	(X)	29.6	9.0	29.4	9.7
Kenosha, WI PMSA	118	123	128	(X)	26.8	12.6	4.4	4.1
Lake County, IL PMSA	383	440	516	(X)	27.6	8.4	15.1	17.3
Cincinnati–Hamilton, OH-KY-IN CMSA	1,613	1,660	1,744	23	26.7	11.8	2.9	5.1
Cincinnati, OH-KY-IN PMSA	1,387	1,401	1,453	(X)	26.8	12.1	1.0	3.7
Hamilton–Middletown, OH PMSA	228	259	291	(X)	26.2	10.2	14.4	12.6
Cleveland–Akron–Lorain, OH CMSA	3,000	2,834	2,760	13	24.8	13.9	-5.5	-2.6
Akron, OH PMSA	679	660	658	(X)	24.4	12.9	-2.8	-0.4
Cleveland, OH PMSA	2,064	1,899	1,831	(X)	24.6	14.6	-6.0	-3.6
Lorain–Elyria, OH PMSA	257	275	271	(X)	27.4	11.6	7.0	-1.4
Colorado Springs, CO MSA	236	309	397	90	27.6	8.0	31.1	28.3
Columbia, SC MSA	323	410	453	79	25.0	9.3	27.0	10.6
Columbus, OH MSA	1,149	1,244	1,377	29	25.1	10.0	8.2	10.7
Corpus Christi, TX MSA	285	326	350	105	30.8	10.2	14.5	7.3
Dallas–Fort Worth, TX CMSA	2,352	2,931	3,885	9	27.3	8.0	24.6	32.6
Dallas, TX PMSA	1,556	1,957	2,553	(X)	27.2	7.7	25.8	30.4
Fort Worth–Arlington, TX PMSA	795	973	1,332	(X)	27.3	8.6	22.4	36.9
Davenport–Rock Island–Moline. IA-IL MSA	363	384	351	104	26.7	13.7	6.1	-8.8
Dayton–Springfield, OH MSA	975	942	951	44	25.3	12.4	-3.4	1.0
Daytona Beach, FL MSA	169	259	371	96	19.7	22.8	52.7	43.3
Denver–Boulder, CO CMSA	1,238	1,618	1,848	22	25.6	9.2	30.7	14.2

3

Table 1.2 *continued*

Metropolitan area	1970 total (1,000)	1980 total (1,000)	1990 Total (1,000)	Rank	Under 18 yrs. old (per-cent)	65 yrs. old and over (per-cent)	Percent change 1970–80	Percent change 1980–90
Boulder–Longmont, CO PMSA	132	190	225	(X)	23.0	7.6	43.8	18.8
Denver, CO PMSA	1,106	1,429	1,623	(X)	25.9	9.4	29.1	13.6
Des Moines, IA MSA	340	368	393	94	25.6	11.7	8.2	6.9
Detroit–Ann Arbor, MI CMSA	4,788	4,753	4,665	6	25.8	11.6	-0.7	-1.8
Ann Arbor, MI PMSA	234	265	283	(X)	21.6	7.5	13.1	8.9
Detroit, MI PMSA	4,554	4,488	4,382	(X)	26.1	11.8	-1.5	-2.4
El Paso, TX MSA	359	480	592	66	32.6	8.2	33.6	23.3
Erie, PA MSA	264	280	276	124	25.9	13.8	8.1	-1.5
Eugene–Springfield, OR MSA	215	275	283	119	24.5	13.1	27.8	2.8
Evansville, IN-KY MSA	255	276	279	121	25.4	14.0	8.5	1.0
Fayetteville, NC MSA	212	247	275	8	125	28.0	6.1	16.6
Flint, MI MSA	446	450	430	84	28.0	10.2	1.1	-4.4
Fort Myers–Cape Coral, FL MSA	105	205	335	110	19.6	24.8	95.1	63.3
Fort Pierce, FL MSA	79	151	251	133	20.9	23.6	91.7	66.1
Fort Wayne, IN MSA	335	354	364	100	27.9	11.5	5.8	2.7
Fresno, CA MSA	413	515	667	59	31.3	10.4	24.5	29.7
Grand Rapids, MI MSA	539	602	688	57	28.6	10.5	11.6	14.4
Greensboro–Winston-Salem–High Point, NC MSA	743	851	942	45	23.0	12.2	14.6	10.6
Greenville–Spartanburg, SC MSA	473	570	641	62	24.3	12.1	20.4	12.4
Harrisburg–Lebanon–Carlisle, PA MSA	510	556	588	67	23.4	13.9	9.0	5.7
Hartford–New Britain–Middletown, CT CMSA	1,000	1,014	1,086	36	22.8	13.3	1.4	7.1
Bristol, CT PMSA	70	74	79	(X)	23.0	12.9	5.6	7.8
Hartford, CT PMSA	711	716	768	(X)	23.1	13.2	0.7	7.3
Middletown, CT PMSA	74	82	90	(X)	21.3	12.1	10.6	10.7
New Britain, CT PMSA	145	142	148	(X)	21.9	15.1	-2.1	4.2
Honolulu, HI MSA	631	763	836	51	24.5	11.1	20.9	9.7
Houston–Galveston–Brazoria, TX CMSA	2,169	3,100	3,711	10	28.9	7.3	42.9	19.7
Brazoria, TX PMSA	108	170	192	(X)	29.3	7.8	56.6	13.0
Galveston–Texas City, TX PMSA	170	196	217	(X)	27.6	10.5	15.3	11.1
Houston, TX PMSA	1,891	2,735	3,302	(X)	28.9	7.1	44.6	20.7
Huntington–Ashland, WV-KY-OH MSA	307	336	313	115	24.5	14.4	9.7	-7.1
Indianapaolis, IN MSA	1,111	1,167	1,250	31	26.3	11.1	5.0	7.1
Jackson, MS MSA	289	362	395	92	28.1	10.5	25.4	9.2
Jacksonville, FL MSA	613	722	907	47	26.0	10.9	17.9	25.5
Johnson City–Kingsport–Bristol, TN-VA MSA	374	434	436	81	22.3	14.6	16.1	0.6
Kansas City, MO-KS MSA	1,373	1,433	1,566	25	26.4	11.6	4.4	9.3
Killeen–Temple, TX MSA	160	215	255	131	28.2	8.0	34.3	19.0
Knoxville, TN MSA	477	566	605	65	22.9	13.3	18.8	6.9
Lakeland–Winter Haven, FL MSA	229	322	405	87	24.1	18.6	40.8	26.0
Lancaster, PA MSA	320	362	423	85	26.5	13.1	13.2	16.7
Lansing–East Lansing, MI MSA	378	420	433	83	25.6	9.0	10.9	3.1
Las Vegas, NV MSA	273	463	741	53	24.5	10.5	69.5	60.1
Lexington–Fayette, KY MSA	267	318	348	106	23.9	10.3	19.1	9.7
Little Rock–North Little Rock, AR MSA	381	474	513	72	26.5	11.4	24.5	8.1
Los Angeles–Anaheim–Riverside, CA CMSA	9.981	11,498	14,532	2	26.6	9.8	15.2	26.4
Anaheim–Santa Ana. CA PMSA	1,421	1,933	2,411	(X)	24.4	9.2	36.0	24.7
Los Angeles–Long Beach, CA PMSA	7,042	7,477	8,863	(X)	26.2	9.7	6.2	18.5
Oxnard–Ventura, CA PMSA	378	529	669	(X)	27.4	9.4	39.8	26.4
Riverside–San Bernardino, CA PMSA	1,139	1,558	2,589	(X)	29.8	10.8	36.8	66.1
Louisville, KY-IN MSA	907	956	953	43	25.2	12.6	5.5	-0.4
Macon–Warner Robins, GA MSA	235	264	281	120	27.2	10.8	12.4	6.6
Madison, WI MSA	290	324	367	99	22.7	9.3	11.5	13.5
McAllen–Edinburg–Mission, TX MSA	182	283	384	95	36.6	10.0	58.1	35.4
Melbourne–Titusville–Palm Bay, FL MSA	230	273	399	89	21.9	16.6	18.7	46.2
Memphis, TN-AR-MS MSA	834	913	982	41	27.8	10.3	9.5	7.5

4

Table 1.2 *continued*

Metropolitan area	1970 total (1,000)	1980 total (1,000)	1990 Total (1,000)	Rank	Under 18 yrs. old (percent)	65 yrs. old and over (percent)	1970–80	1980–90
Miami–Fort Lauderdale, FL CMSA	1,888	2,644	3,193	11	22.7	16.6	40.0	20.8
Fort Lauderdale–Hollywood–Pompano								
Beach, FL PMSA	620	1,018	1,255	(X)	20.4	20.8	64.2	23.3
Miami–Hialeah, FL PMSA	1,268	1,626	1,937	(X)	24.2	14.0	28.2	19.2
Milwaukee–Racine, WI CMSA	1,575	1,570	1,607	24	26.4	12.4	–0.3	2.4
Milwaukee, WI PMSA	1,404	1,397	1,432	(X)	26.3	12.5	–0.5	2.5
Racine, WI PMSA	171	173	175	(X)	27.8	12.0	1.3	1.1
Minneapolis–St Paul, MN-WI MSA	1,982	2,137	2,464	16	26.3	9.9	7.8	15.3
Mobile, AL MSA	377	444	477	78	28.0	12.5	17.7	7.5
Modesto, CA MSA	195	266	371	97	30.6	10.8	36.7	39.3
Montgomery, AL MSA	226	273	293	117	27.4	11.4	20.7	7.3
Nashville, TN MSA	699	851	985	40	25.1	10.6	21.6	15.8
New Haven–Menden, CT MSA	489	500	530	69	22.6	14.1	2.4	5.9
New London–Norwich, CT-RI MSA	243	251	267	126	23.5	12.4	3.4	6.4
New Orleans, LA MSA	1,100	1,257	1,239	32	27.9	11.0	14.3	–1.4
New York–Northern New Jersey–Long Island,								
NY-NJ-CT CMSA	18,193	17,540	18,087	1	23.0	13.3	–3.6	3.1
Burgen–Passaic, NJ PMSA	1,358	1,293	1,278	(X)	21.7	14.5	–4.8	–1.1
Bridgeport–Milford, CT PMSA	444	439	444	(X)	23.2	14.7	–1.2	1.2
Danbury, CT PMSA	136	170	188	(X)	24.4	9.9	24.8	10.3
Jersey City, NJ PMSA	608	557	553	(X)	22.1	13.7	–8.4	–0.7
Middlesex–Somerset–Hunterdon, NJ PMSA	852	886	1,020	(X)	21.9	11.3	4.0	15.1
Monmouth–Ocean, NJ PMSA	670	849	986	(X)	23.6	17.3	26.7	16.1
Nassau–Suffolk, NY PMSA	2,556	2,606	2,609	(X)	23.3	12.4	2.0	0.1
New York, NY PMSA	9,077	8,275	8,547	(X)	23.0	13.0	–8.8	3.3
Newark, NJ PMSA	1,937	1,879	1,824	(X)	23.5	12.5	–3.0	–2.9
Norwalk, CT PMSA	128	127	127	(X)	21.1	12.3	–0.7	0.5
Orange County, NY PMSA	222	260	308	(X)	27.6	10.4	17.1	18.5
Stamford, CT PMSA	206	199	203	(X)	20.8	14.1	–3.6	1.9
Norfolk–Virginia Beach–Newport News, VA MSA	1,059	1,160	1,396	28	26.4	9.0	9.6	20.3
Oklahoma City, OK MSA	719	861	959	42	26.6	11.1	19.8	11.4
Omaha, NE-IA MSA	556	585	618	63	27.8	10.6	5.2	5.7
Orlando, FL MSA	453	700	1,073	37	24.4	10.9	54.4	53.3
Pensacola, FL MSA	243	290	344	107	25.7	11.3	19.2	18.9
Peoria, IL MSA	342	368	339	108	26.4	13.8	7.0	–7.3
Philadelphia–Wilmington–Trenton, PA-NJ-DE-MD								
CMSA	5,749	5,681	5,899	5	24.3	13.3	–1.2	3.9
Philadelphia, PA-NJ PMSA	4,824	4,717	4,857	(X)	24.4	13.5	–2.2	3.0
Trenton, NJ PMSA	304	308	326	(X)	22.5	13.0	1.2	5.8
Vineland–Millville–Bridgeton, NJ PMSA	121	133	138	(X)	26.0	13.5	9.5	3.9
Wilmington, DE-NJ-MD PMSA	499	523	579	(X)	24.6	11.6	4.8	10.6
Phoenix, AZ MSA	971	1,509	2,122	20	26.2	12.5	55.4	40.6
Pittsburgh–Beaver Valley, PA CMSA	2,556	1,423	2,243	19	21.8	17.3	–5.2	–7.4
Beaver County, PA PMSA	208	204	186	(X)	23.3	16.9	–1.9	–9.0
Pittsburgh, PA PMSA	2,348	2,219	2,057	(X)	21.7	17.4	–5.5	–7.3
Portland–Vancouver, OR-WA CMSA	1,047	1,298	1,478	27	25.7	12.0	23.9	13.9
Portland, OR PMSA	919	1,106	1,240	(X)	25.1	12.2	20.3	12.1
Vancouver, NY MSA	128	192	238	(X)	28.4	10.7	49.6	23.8
Poughkeepsie, NY MSA	222	245	259	130	23.9	11.4	10.2	5.9
Providence–Pawtucket–Fall River, RI-MA CMSA	1,065	1,083	1,142	35	22.8	15.1	1.7	5.4
Fall River, MA-RI PMSA	152	157	157	(X)	23.4	16.8	3.2	(Z)
Pawtucket–Woonsocket–Attleboro,								
RI-MA PMSA	301	307	329	(X)	24.1	14.2	2.2	7.2
Providence, RI PMSA	612	619	655	(X)	22.1	15.1	1.0	5.9
Provo–Orem, UT MSA	138	218	264	128	37.7	7.0	58.3	20.9

5

Table 1.2 *continued*

Metropolitan area	1970 total (1,000)	1980 total (1,000)	1990 Total (1,000)	1990 Rank	1990 Under 18 yrs. old (percent)	1990 65 yrs. old and over (percent)	Percent change 1970–80	Percent change 1980–90
Raleigh–Durham, NC MSA	446	561	735	54	22.5	8.9	25.7	31.2
Reading, PA MSA	296	313	337	109	23.3	15.6	5.4	7.7
Reno, NV MSA	121	194	255	132	23.1	10.3	59.9	31.5
Richmond–Petersburg, VA MSA	676	761	866	49	24.3	11.3	12.6	13.7
Rochester, NY MSA	962	971	1,002	39	25,0	12.4	1.0	3.2
Rockford, IL MSA	272	280	284	118	26.4	12.6	2.7	1.5
Sacramento, CA MSA	848	1,100	1,481	26	26.2	10.8	29.8	34.7
Saginaw–Bay City–Midland, MI MSA	401	422	399	88	27.5	12.1	5.2	–5.3
St Louis, MO-IL MSA	2,429	2,377	2,444	17	26.3	12.8	–2.2	2.8
Salem, OR MSA	187	250	278	122	26.4	14.4	33.9	11.3
Salinas–Seaside–Monterey, CA MSA	247	290	356	103	27.5	9.8	17.4	22.5
Salt Lake City–Ogden, UT MSA	684	910	1,072	38	35.5	8.4	33.1	17.8
San Antonio, TX MSA	888	1,072	1,302	30	29.0	10.3	20.7	21.5
San Diego, CA MSA	1,358	1,862	2,498	15	24.5	10.9	37.1	34.2
San Francisco–Oakland–San Jose, CA CMSA	4,754	5,368	6,253	4	23.1	11.1	12.9	16.5
Oakland, CA PMSA	1,628	1,762	2,083	(X)	24.3	10.7	8.2	18.2
San Francisco, CA PMSA	1,482	1,489	1,604	(X)	18.9	13.3	0.5	7.7
San Jose, CA PMSA	1,065	1,295	1,498	(X)	24.0	8.7	21.6	15.6
Santa Cruz, CA PMSA	124	188	230	(X)	23.8	11.3	52.0	22.1
Santa Rosa–Petaluma, CA PMSA	205	300	388	(X)	24.7	13.4	48.3	29.5
Vallejo–Fairfield–Napa, CA PMSA	251	334	451	(X)	27.4	10.2	33.2	34.9
Santa Barbara–Santa Maria–Lompoc, CA MSA	264	299	370	98	23.2	12.3	13.0	23.7
Sarasota, FL MSA	120	202	278	123	15.7	32.2	68.0	37.3
Scranton–Wilkes-Barre, PA MSA	696	729	734	55	22.3	18.2	4.7	0.7
Seattle–Tacoma, WA CMSA	1,837	2,093	2,559	14	24.6	10.7	14.0	22.3
Seattle, WA PMSA	1,425	1,608	1,973	(X)	23.8	10.7	12.8	22.7
Tacoma, WA PMSA	412	486	586	(X)	27.2	10.5	17.8	20.7
Shreveport, LA MSA	296	333	334	111	28.7	12.2	12.5	0.4
Spokane, WA MSA	287	342	361	101	26.4	13.3	18.9	5.7
Springfield, MA MSA	528	515	530	70	24.2	14.7	–2.4	2.8
Stockton, CA MSA	291	347	481	76	29.6	11.1	19.3	38.4
Syracuse, NY MSA	637	643	660	61	25.2	12.4	1.0	2.6
Tampa–St Petersburg–Clearwater, FL MSA	1,106	1,614	2,068	21	20.4	21.6	46.0	28.2
Toledo, OH MSA	606	617	614	64	28.3	12.4	1.7	–0.4
Tucson, AZ MSA	352	531	667	60	24.9	13.7	51.1	25.5
Tulsa, OK MSA	526	657	709	56	26.8	11.6	25.0	7.9
Utica–Rome, NY MSA	340	320	317	113	24.5	15.7	–6.0	–1.1
Visalia–Tulare–Porterville, CA MSA	188	246	312	116	33.1	10.8	30.5	26.9
Washington, DC-MD-VA MSA	3,040	3,251	3,924	8	23.5	8.6	6.9	20.7
West Palm Beach–Boca Raton–Delray Beach, FL MSA	349	577	864	50	19.6	24.3	65.3	49.7
Wichita, KS MSA	417	442	485	75	27.8	11.9	6.2	9.7
Worcester, MA MSA	400	403	437	80	23.8	14.2	0.8	8.4
York, PA MSA	330	381	418	86	24.4	13.2	15.7	9.6
Youngstown–Warren, OH MSA	537	531	493	74	24.8	15.8	–1.1	–7.3

X Not applicable.   Z Less than .05 percent.

Source: US Bureau of the Census. *1980 Census of Population, Supplementary Report, Metropolitan Statistical Areas*, (PC80-S1-18); press release CB91-66; and *1990 Census of Population and Housing*, Summary Tape File 1A.

In Europe now we have skyscrapers, we have suburban sprawl, we have drive-ins, urban motorways, hypermarkets and Big Macs. Many Europeans believe that our urban civilisation is developing the same way as the American; or copying it in fact. It is more likely that such features are superficial and that the complete American urban system is the result of different factors, different dynamics from those operating in Britain and Europe. A study of the American city certainly has important lessons for those concerned with the future of our European cities; but there is much which is unique to the North American continent. Therefore, what follows is offered first for its intrinsic fascination in its own right. If it proves useful in another context too, then that will be a bonus.

One fact makes the study of the American city easer than, say, the study of 'The European City'. In the latter case, the cities are so old, had such different types of locations, origins and functions, have experienced such different histories and purposes in the possession of different peoples under different political systems, that in spite of the common, but most complex, European culture, several separate studies would be needed. But Anglo-American cities are less than four hundred years old, have remarkably similar sites and origins, were developed by a self-selected group of Europeans with shared aims and methods. This short history, then, with identical early functions developed by people, at first, with a narrower range of cultural baggage from Europe, has produced cities across three thousand miles of the continent remarkable not for their diversity, but for their fundamental similarity. With the very important exception of Los Angeles, then, to be considered in Chapter Five, while one may indulge the old regional geographer's interest in the contrasts between London, Paris and Rome, one can much more reliably combine the studies and discover common factors in the growth, functions, layout and problems of New York, Houston and St Louis, and can realistically attempt to understand the American city.

Other than Los Angeles, the big cities of the United States originated at waterfront locations. This was partly for communication with the home countries in Europe, particularly Britain, but more importantly because these were all established primarily as commercial centres at a time when land transport was still slow, difficult and expensive. Water transport by sailing ship, barge, and raft made sites on the coast, on lakes or on rivers essential for settlements whose first and most important function was trade. The enormous cities we see now started on greenbank sites in the seventeenth and eighteenth centuries as wharves, quays, jetties and piers closely overlooked by a cluster of warehouses, offices, and the first homes of the entrepreneurs.

7

Los Angeles is the only multi-millionaire exception to this generalisation, and there are fewer than a dozen exceptions of cities of a million people or under. Five cities originated in connection with local resources. Spokane (177,000 in 1990) started as a sawmill in 1871. Two began as centres to supply surrounding gold mining communities, Sacramento (369,000) from 1849, Denver (468,000) after the Pike's Peak gold rush in 1858. Birmingham (266,000) grew up during the Civil War to produce steel and armaments for the Confederacy using local iron ore and coal, while Phoenix (983,000), although in existence as a railroad town in 1887, did not start to flourish until the completion of the Roosevelt Dam in 1911.

The railways became important for all five of these cities, and each in turn became a focus of radiating lines after the 1870s, consolidating its function as a central place as well as a primary producer. Two major cities are more clearly the products of the railways alone. Dallas (1,007,000) developed after the arrival of the railway in 1870. Atlanta was earlier: the Western Atlantic Rail Road terminated on the site in 1836. In 1847 the new small town was re-named Atlanta after the word Atlantic in the company's title.

The last four cities may be said to be the results of unique events. Maryland donated land for Washington DC (607,000) where building started in 1791 and which became the capital in 1800. Similarly, a piece of land in central Indiana was chosen for the state capital, Indianapolis (731,000), in 1820.

At noon on 22 April 1889 a shot was fired. Settlers raced into former Indian Territory. Among the plots of land they staked out that afternoon was the site of Oklahoma City (445,000). Earlier, in 1847, less than 150 people came to the western foothills of the Wasatch Mountains where Salt Lake City (160,000) now stands, and where Brigham Young is reported to have said, 'this is the place'. Apart from these major special cases, a commercial waterfront site was the rule.

The eastern shore of the Shawmut peninsula, the southern tip of Manhattan island, the great meander on the Delaware, the mouth of the Chicago river, the banks of the Mississippi, Lake Pontchartrain, the Embarcadero on San Francisco Bay were chosen as the sites for the early trading centres which were to become multi-millionaire cities within two or three centuries. There are engravings of San Francisco and of Boston, drawn in their first few years by people sitting on the grassy hills above the quays (in Boston's case on a hill later removed to fill Back Bay) showing the tightly grouped cluster of warehouses and wooden homes nestling against the bare masts of the sailing ships. An engraving of South Street in Manhattan shows dozens of sailing ships on one side of the street, the street itself covered in merchandise, and the only stone buildings of New York at the time, the offices and homes of the merchants and bankers, on the other side. Similarly, one of the first photographs of Chicago shows the mouth of the river clogged with sailing ships, one early steam tug, and a single enormous warehouse on the point where the river joins Lake Michigan.

The sites, the function, and the type of transport gave very similar forms to the cities originating within a relatively short time of each other. The sites were chosen where sufficiently deep water could be found against a firm shore, in reasonable shelter, with access to the local trade routes or the developing economic area. Those sites varied from the drumlin-studded Boston Bay to the natural levees on the silt-clogged Mississippi. But whether the cluster of huts was to become Boston or St Louis, whether the settlement was started by French trying to cut off the English, or English trying to get away from other English, the early settlements' livelihoods depended on trade.

Some American cities are so new that in fact the first buildings were put on the ground after the beginning of the Steam Age, but most of those of any size today were established when people depended on sail power on the water and horse power on the land. Water transport was quicker and cheaper than transport on land. Transport depending on horses, mules and oxen to pull heavy, narrow-wheeled carts on rutted, unsurfaced roads was relatively so expensive that it kept the movement of goods on land to the absolute minimum. Goods were often moved much further than the straight-line distance between origin and destination in order to move them the shortest distance on land, even if this meant a much longer journey by water. For example, one trade route from Cincinnati to New York went down the Ohio, down the Mississippi, through the Gulf and up the Atlantic coast. Similarly, many Forty-niners went round the Horn rather than overland to California. Moreover, if one could not afford a carriage or a horse on land, one walked. Many historians refer to the small cities of the time as the Walking City: all the functions had to be within walking distance of each other, and within an area over which land transport of the goods was practicable and economical.

The direct result of this was that the American city, in its infancy, was clustered and concentrated. European cities often did have similar forms at the time, for the same reasons. But often their layout was not as tightly concentrated because so many different factors had already operated over many centuries. The larger European cities often had other functions by the eighteenth century, connected with the State, the Church, defence, and the glorification of rulers, which were made manifest in their palaces, cathedrals, fortifications, triumphal avenues, parks and the rest. In their early days most American cities had a much more single-minded population and consequently a tighter concentration.

If one walked to the office, the warehouse, the exchange, the dock, the workshop, the store, or to school, then the shorter the distance one walked on a dusty track or a muddy street blocked with merchandise and covered with horse faeces, the better. If the desirable location for the warehouse, the office and the bank was as close to the ship or barge as possible, then the desirable location for one's house was, for the same reason, as close to the office or bank as possible. So the wealthiest people in the very early days of the Walking City had their houses built within as short a distance of the place where they made their money as they could. The poorer people had their more modest homes further away, while the lowest-paid workers put up their shacks on the edge of town.

In most American cities this spatial arrangement — the rich in the centre, the middle class in the next ring outwards and the poor furthest from the centre — did not last very long. But the Walking City was one in which the residential areas, small as they were, were arranged to minimise the walking distance for those who could afford the costs, the land and property prices, or the rent, in the most desirable and therefore the most expensive land close to, and focused on, the original docks or quays. As in Britain earlier, the buildings at the heart of these small, concentrated, commercial settlements often had several functions. The activities of the shipper, the banker, the insurer or the merchant were therefore often in the same wooden building as the warehouse and the residence.

The second major function to be added to that of trading in the growing concentrated port town was manufacturing. This was based not on deposits of raw materials, or on water power sites, but on the operations of the port. Here, raw materials were passing through, or could be brought in. The very fact that the town had started as a centre of transport and communication, however small and local, meant that fuel and materials could be assembled, goods supplied to the local market or sent out, and market information obtained from the shippers. Moreover, labour was available in the new, growing towns, and the trade provided capital to start the first factories and mills. But a conflict began to develop in what might have appeared to be a perfect symbiotic relationship; again, the most profitable, and therefore the most desirable, sites for the new manufacturing were where the materials were transhipped from barge to wagon, from cart to hold. The best sites for the factories were seen to be as close as possible to the wharves and quays.

10

The early factories in Boston, New York, Philadelphia, Chicago, St Louis and the other waterside towns which were to become millionaire cities in a century, crowded up to the waterfront sites and the commercial cores, emphasising the increasing concentration round the original focus of the port. There was a difference here between the cities of the eastern seaboard which had become established before the invention of the steam engine, tug, ship and railway, and those west of the Appalachians which grew up — indeed were often founded — after the steam engine was perfected. Whatever the slight differences in early history, usually only to be seen in different street patterns now, the major long-term results were remarkably the same from Philadelphia to San Francisco. The new factories, wood, brick, sheet metal and smokestacks, crowded up to the young town centres, shouldering in like bullies round a timid child. While eating ice cream in a transformed Ghirardelli Chocolate factory near one of the old wharves in San Francisco it may be virtually impossible to visualise this now, but the ruins of such location and crowding were still depressingly much in evidence in Philadelphia in the 1980s. Most convincing, and much more dramatic than old gazetteers and maps, are the etched prints of the time which show such things as the chimneys of the McCormick Reaper Company factory where the Loop now is in Chicago; or massive industrial areas and the long marshalling yards of the New York Central and Hudson River Railroad Company on Manhattan Island, still with fields up towards the Bronks's farm.

Once three equally important elements were successfully in place, these urban systems grew and flourished. The three were: steam ships and barges on the water; the warehouses, factories and commercial organisations on the banks; and the railways radiating into the hinterlands. The people of the east coast cities thoroughly understood this as they rivalled each other to push railways inland and draw trade to their own city away from those of their rivals. That was as vital to them as the spread of the midwestern networks was to Chicago. Then, for the order of a century, up to the 1940s, not only did those American commercial and industrial centres grow faster than any cities anywhere before, but they shared a remarkably similar development and resulting urban layout and structure from one end of the country to the other. One reason for the rapid growth is that even the earliest city did not have its first hut until the seventeenth century, and most in the interior not until the nineteenth; there was much catching up to do. More importantly, these cities of all but the northeastern seaboard put down their first foundations after the beginning of the industrial revolution in Britain and parts of Europe. The combined forces of rapid industrialisation, massive immigration, and a slower but eventually significant urbanisation (the proportion of the total population living in urban areas) as farming mechanised, resulted in cities of 15 million people and more in less than 150 years.

While land transport remained difficult, slow, and therefore expensive, there was increasing demand for land in the centre of the city. Most people trying to make a buck in Chicago, Baltimore or Topeka perceived that they could make it quickest at the centre. This perception at that time is the important fact. It may be splendid at this remove in space and time to show that a business could have made a bigger profit from a cheaper site, but the vast majority of American city entrepreneurs did not believe that until the 1950s. The geographical evidence was before them: there was the dock on New York harbour, Lake Michigan, or the Mississippi. There, a few steps away, were the massive warehouses. There, across the street, were the smoking chimneys and the freight yards. Here were the banks, the realtors, the insurers and the early stores. Those early entrepreneurs could see money being made before their eyes: this must be the place. Given that the first and second functions of most of what are now the largest American cities were trade and manufacturing, this is where the growing numbers of entrepreneurs saw their opportunities. Where to locate the new warehouse, factory or shop? Some worked it out; most followed the crowd. It came to the same thing. If Elmer was turning a profit at the mouth of the Chicago river, or the southern end of Manhattan Island, then those were the places to be.

As success followed success and encouraged others, more and more individuals, more and more companies, wanted sites on or very close to the waterfront. Mark Twain recommended land as a good investment, saying that as it is always going to be there, and that as they ain't making any more of it, then it must rise in value. Many more enterprises wanted city-centre land, particularly at the waterfront, with rail access, or on a main street, than there were sites available. The weakest went to the wall; more correctly the poorer individuals and institutions were pushed out to the edge. Those who could pay got the prime central sites, and those who could not pay so much for a finite commodity in rapidly increasing demand got second and third best, further and further out from the centre. Sometimes, of course, the hopefuls got it wrong, and paid more rent for a prime central site than they could make from manufacturing or trading on it. But the evident fact is that the vast majority got it right often enough to produce the kind of flourishing, concentrated American city which had emerged by the time of the First World War.

When more people wanted land than there was land to spare, those happy few who owned it were in paradise. Who would have bought some waterlogged grass by the side of a lake which the French had just given up in 1799? The actual demand for land was translated into dollars per square foot for sale or rent. Land values at the centre, particularly at the docks, along the railways and canals, and at major street intersections took off like rockets, and soon rose out of sight. After thirty years of familiarity with case studies of small parcels of land, one still finds the billions of dollars involved hard to believe. A map of land values in Topeka, Kansas, with the city centre next to the crossing of the Kansas river shows that in the 1950s values along 6th Street ranged from $1000 as one approaches the business district to over $200,000 per square foot at the junction with Kansas Avenue. More impressive is a graph of the same values. The curve has a gentle gradient until only a few blocks from the centre, then it shoots up almost vertically through the top of the paper. A three-dimensional computer representation of these land values looks as if a structure a hundred times higher than Nelson's Column, but with similar proportions, had been built at Sixth and Kansas.

By the mid-nineteenth century demand for the land, which had been translated into rocketing land values, could not be satisfied by the creation of more space in the city centre with the technology of the time. The early geographical responses were outward movements, resulting in changes of land use facilitated by progress in the methods of transport. It is emphasised here that the demand for city centre space in the concentrated city and the desire to live in the suburbs were forces, involving thousands of corporations and perhaps millions of people, which existed decades before the developing technologies made achievement of those things possible. The Walking City kept the urban area compact and concentrated; but the Walking City was changing. Horse buses introduced in mid-century in cities like Chicago carried more people than carriages and wagons had, but on the muddy streets they were no faster. The horse-trams (horsecars) which were running by the 1860s on rails laid in the streets were noticeably faster because of the reduced friction. Electric trams (trolley-cars) were not perfected and put into use until the 1890s. Like the horse-trams, they both speeded up journeys and made commuting from the ever-receding edge of town a practicable proposition for hundreds of thousands of people. Although trams were the most successful means of mass transport in most American cities, as in British and European cities, several other systems were tried. Cable-cars operated in places like Chicago as well as in San Francisco, where a few survive. Others tried steam locomotives pulling trains of cars at street level.

The functions of the successful and the unsuccessful systems were all the same: to move people to and from the docks, wholesale districts, industrial areas, shops and commercial enterprises which remained prosperous and concentrated at one focal point, the downtown area centred on the Central Business District, the CBD. It was a spatial system which worked but which, whatever the persistence of its major elements for more than a century, was constantly in a state of change. Most noticeably, the built-up urban area grew at a rapid pace. The Back Bay of Boston was filled in to make more land; there were fourteen miles of Manhattan to move into; Chicago had most of the Midwest at its disposal. Wooden houses, often prefabricated in the new sawmills, went up very quickly along alternately muddy and dusty unpaved streets. Often the rival train and tram companies raced to put lines into these raw new residential areas. Just as often they bought land, put in the tram, trolley and cable-car routes, and created new residential areas on the edge of town as the wooden homes followed.

The commercial and industrial centres of the cities gained the space they needed for most of the second half of the nineteenth century by growing outwards, shouldering other functions out of their way. The earliest houses and apartments, already filtering down from the original families to immigrants from Europe, were often torn down to make more space for new railway yards, silos, elevators, factories, warehouses, offices and stores. The central commercial areas of New York, Philadelphia, Pittsburgh, Chicago, St Louis and San Francisco became so big that specialist areas could emerge. The speed of growth is emphasised by the fact that as the distinct manufacturing, wholesale, transport, retail, professional, commercial, administrative and recreational areas became established in the centres of the cities just named, other cities like Detroit, Los Angeles, Houston and Miami were not even up and running.

Eventually, in the largest cities with the highest-order functions, three concentric zones could be discerned downtown. These were the core and the frame of the CBD and then the transition zone between them and the residential areas. The core was the expensive location for:

- retailing
- offices
- the best hotels
- consumer services
- banks and financial functions
- theatres
- the prestige galleries and concert-halls
- professional and business services
- local and regional government functions.

14

This was the area of most intensive land use, with a highly concentrated daytime population using functions all clustered within easy walking distance.

The frame surrounding the core was a zone of lower intensity land use, the location for functions which had to be close to the core to serve it, but which needed more space and could not pay the high rents of the centre. Located there were:

- wholesaling
- warehousing
- parking
- car sales
- car servicing
- bus stations
- railway stations
- docks
- institutions
- the cheaper hotels
- schools and colleges
- hospitals
- manufacturing
- the less prestigious and wealthy galleries, museums, etc.

These functions were more dispersed and needed to be served by public transport. For some access to major routes in and out of the core was as important as proximity to the core. Functions in the frame often tended to cluster at transport nodes.

Beyond the frame of the Central Business District then was the transition zone where frame functions overlapped with residential structures. As the city and the CBD grew, the core and frame pushed outwards and the oldest houses and apartments were demolished to provide more land for commercial and institutional functions. The centre was pushing out because it had nowhere else to go as it grew, although the desire to locate in the centre for the best chance of success was still strong. But as the Walking City became the Tracked City, and the Wheeled City, many people began to realise that they could, at last, live away from the noise, smells and overcrowding of the centre. The middle-income middle classes started to move out into the new houses of the streetcar suburbs, selling or renting their former homes to the new immigrants. The richer people, in the days before Cadillacs, Mercedes, Lexuses and Rolls-Royces, built large villas on the edge of town, having the money for the longest train and trolley rides, and more time to get to the office or store.

15

Thus the first revolutionary change in the layout of most American cities, in the nineteenth century, was a complete reversal of the roughly concentric residential pattern of the time. The days of living on Beacon Hill next to the action in downtown Boston, with the poor Irish out on the edge, had gone. By the last quarter of the century the common pattern was for the rich to live in what were then the suburbs, and for the poor to live in the centre where most of them still walked to work.

By the 1890s some of the steam trains, not commercially viable in the few avenues in which they were tried, had literally got off the ground. Commuter rail travel was developing in America much as in Britain, but a few cities, notably New York and Chicago, also put railways up in the air. One serious problem with the networks of trams and cable-cars in American cities was the gridlock where lines intersected at the right-angled junctions of streets and avenues. Unlike horses and carts earlier, or cars and lorries later, trolley-cars could not dodge round one another like two London cabs. Nor, being at the same level, could one jump over the other. Elevated railways were the successful answer to the problem. Complete railway systems were constructed in the air on steel columns. They looked fine, even impressive, built up the centres of the wide avenues in the big cities. But photographs of the New York elevated railways built along the narrower streets show trains rattling and clattering along within inches of the upper windows of both offices and cheap apartments on Manhattan and Long Island. The urban noise and pollution were made even worse, but the trains were unimpeded as they crossed the streets and avenues on their viaducts with the trolleys and horse-drawn traffic passing underneath. In this way the American city had started its vertical growth.

Although several cities had elevated railways, just as San Francisco is identified with the cable-car, Chicago is identified with the El. The elevated tracks from north, west and south focused on the area just south of the mouth of the Chicago river, to move people to and from the CBD. Where the tracks came together in that most densely built-up and intensively used part of the city, they were built into a rectangle of lines completely enclosing the CBD. The El thus encircled and enshrined the downtown area of Chicago in its heyday, forming the Loop.

In 1885 a balloon ride over lower Manhattan would have given a view very similar in some important respects to a balloon ride over Paris. In the view of New York there are more vessels on the East River than on the Seine, sailing ships and steam tugs, as well as barges. The docks can be seen at the end of Wall Street and along the bank of the

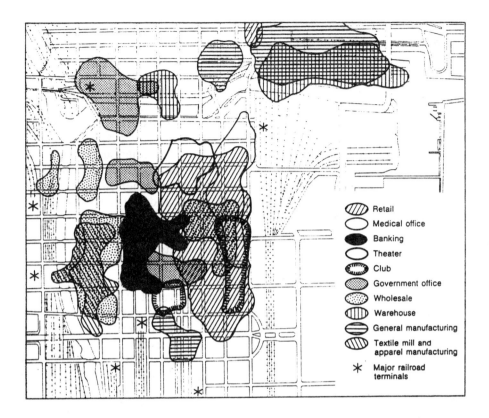

Figure 1.1 The Central Business District of the Concentrated City
Chicago's CBD near the mouth of the Chicago river, 1960. Note the banking district
at the centre, and the manufacturing at the edge.
Source: Yeates, M.H. & Garner, B.J., *The North American City*, Harper and Row, New York,
1971, p. 360

Hudson, but there is only one bridge, that across to Brooklyn. The
view of the two built-up-areas is remarkably similar. In Paris the
churches and public buildings stand up above the apartment blocks.
In New York in 1885 one can see the trees of Battery Park, the ramp
up to Brooklyn Bridge, the European pattern of radiating streets
south of the Bowery contrasting with the gridiron pattern up towards

the then-new Central Park. The two most common features are the church spires standing above the five and six-storey offices, shops, hotels and homes. For anyone sailing into New York harbour in 1885, the city had no special American-style skyline.

In contrast, a European sailing into New York harbour on a Cunard liner fifty years later might well have thought, from that perspective, that Manhattan was covered completely with what were perceived by then to be a purely American phenomenon: skyscrapers. Aerial photographs of American cities up to the mid-twentieth century, however, show clearly that the tall buildings were originally clustered and localised in one very small area of each city, and that that area had a very special location.

Just as the invention of the car and the development of roads eventually made it possible for people to achieve their desire to live in the suburbs, so a series of other inventions and technological developments made it possible for American businesses to make more land, or at least much more floor space, in the heart of the CBD. Many achievements had to accumulate during the second half of the nineteenth century: the production of structural steel, reinforced concrete, fireproofing of buildings, electric lighting, the electric lift, air conditioning, water pumps, water closets, the telegraph and the telephone, to name the most important. Some simplistic accounts give the impression that as soon as economic demand arose for more floor space, tall buildings were immediately erected in American cities. But the reality is that demand existed long before the technology was perfected to satisfy it. The demand developed in cities which still had wooden buildings, unpaved streets and earth closets. A skyscraper with wooden cladding, gas lighting, water carriers going up and down stairs, messengers moving information on foot, and workers going to and from privies in the back yard would have matched something from a Hieronymus Bosch painting.

Demand and technology came together in Chicago in 1890 when one building was completed which was so tall, so special, that it was given the nickname 'Skyscraper'. An important element was the skill of the architect who not only gave us a new architectural form but also overcame the severe problems of the foundations. Many features of that first skyscraper were significant. It was the Home Insurance Building, and provided commercial premises built at great cost to make money in commerce. It was constructed next to the Loop, located in the downtown area in the belief that that location would help maximise profits for the company. The essence of that skyscraper was to meet the demand for more office space in the overcrowded, concentrated, but still very successful city centre.

18

Chicago is located on glacial debris, the moraines and outwash deposits which have dammed up the waters of Lake Michigan, closed its former outlet to the Mississippi and diverted the waters of the Great Lakes towards the St Lawrence River. The low buildings of nineteenth-century Chicago were stable enough on the glacial sands and clays. But skyscrapers, with their deep foundations, can find no solid footing in the waterlogged sands bordering the Chicago River, so many of them have had to be floated most ingeniously on concrete rafts. Some years after it was built, two extra storeys were added to the Home Insurance Building. Perhaps this was to maintain its position as the tallest building. We do not know because, sadly, this most historic American edifice has been knocked down. What we do know is that the building which was so impressive when it went up that it was called a Skyscraper was a mere eleven storeys tall.

As the technology improved, skyscrapers got taller and taller and spread to other American cities. As the purpose was to cash in on the demand for floor space in the core of the CBD, the early skyscrapers completely covered each plot of land on which they were built, their walls rising vertically towards the sky. As skyscrapers were built in downtown New York, Wall Street and the nearby streets and avenues became deep, narrow, gloomy canyons between the towering buildings. By 1912 the street-level situation had become so bad that New York brought in the Sky-Angle Law by which new skyscrapers had to be stepped back the higher they were built, in an attempt to let a small amount of sunlight reach the sidewalks, at least for a short time each day. This tended to result in skyscrapers with tops like pyramids. A more recent solution to the problem is to build a skyscraper on only part of the plot of land, leaving space around it at street level.

Within a couple of decades skyscrapers were built in the downtown areas of most of the other big commercial and industrial cities. Notable exceptions in the first half of the twentieth century were San Francisco, where the earthquake danger resulted in regulations to limit the height of buildings, and Los Angeles, where there was little demand for such property. An inaccurate story has been repeated many times that the first skyscrapers were built in New York, where their foundations could go down to the granite bedrock, because of a supposed serious lack of space on Manhattan. The bedrock may make building easier in New York than in Chicago, but maps and aerial photos of Manhattan in the early 1930s, before the Empire State Building was completed, show two things. First, there was plenty of space on the island when skyscraper building was in its second boom period, and second, that the skyscrapers were then tightly clustered at the southern tip of Manhattan in the downtown area centred on Wall Street.

A few American cities, notably New York and Boston, now have two distinct and separate clusters of skyscrapers. New York started building them in Midtown in mid-century, and Boston in Back Bay a decade or so later. This was partly as a result of the different functions of the areas — banking and insurance versus corporate head offices and consumer services — partly as a result of these cities' roles as major regional centres, and partly as an attempt to prevent over-concentration and congestion in one part of the city, as will be seen later.

By the end of the twentieth century, of course, skyscrapers have been built all over the world, in all parts of urban areas, and for many different purposes, so that their original precise location and function have become obscured. After their spread to the downtown areas of all but two or three of the largest American cities, skyscrapers started to be built in small towns too. It is baffling to see small Midwestern and particularly High Plains towns — where the centre, the tree-covered suburbs, and the open surrounding country-side can all be encompassed in one view — with a little cluster of unnecessary skyscrapers in the middle. There is no question of excessive demand for commercial space in such locations. One can conclude only that it is a matter of fashion, pride, or urban prestige — if New York, Denver and Atlanta have skyscrapers, then Podunk must have some too.

Prestige is certainly a major factor in the building of so many skyscrapers in the downtown areas of all the big cities in the second half of this century. San Francisco and Los Angeles have caught up since techniques of building earthquake-proof towers have been developed. In the early days the prestige of the different corporations was reflected in the elaborate architecture of their headquarters. The result was the Woolworth Building, AT&T, the Chrysler Building and the like. There was rivalry of architectural styles between different corporations within one city. By the 1930s a competition more in keeping with the idea of piling as many floors on top of each other as possible emerged as the Empire State Building was completed and was claimed to be the tallest building in the world. The rivalry widened from the urban to the national scale when the John Hancock Building overtopped the Empire State. Then the World Trade Center overtopped the John Hancock. Later Chicago recaptured the blue riband when the Sears Building overtopped the World Trade Center. But in one sense the World Trade Center, also located at the southern end of Manhattan Island, brought the race to something approaching a dead end. The architectural imagination involved in the building puts everything in Europe into the shade: the perfection of minimalism, it consists of eight vertical walls and two flat tops.

San Francisco then took another direction in this urban rivalry. Down near the Embarcadero, again the original dock site, and again a commercial building, there arose the Transamerica skyscraper. It resembles an attenuated pyramid with the fins from a hydrogen bomb stuck on the sides. Once seen it is always remembered and recognised, unlike hundreds of larger skyscrapers all over the United States. Without the use of any lettering, just as the Eiffel Tower says Paris, the Transamerica says San Francisco. If a TV news or documentary programme wants instantly to convey the location to its viewers, then the White House, the Palace of Westminster or the Eiffel Tower will do the trick. It is much more difficult to convey visually that the location is, say, Frankfurt, hence the new Messeturm. The task is impossible for Tokyo so far. But do you recognise the John Hancock Building in Boston? Can you distinguish it from the John Hancock Building in Chicago? The two horns help. Can you, at a quick glance, distinguish the Sears Building in Chicago from the Natwest Tower in London? Do you care whether you can or not, the way the owning corporations care about their prestige? In this connection it has been suggested that the new generations of skyscrapers have three other functions on top of that of providing maximum floor space on prime sites. One, that they provide or enhance corporate identity; two, that they inherently express the rivalry of American cities, especially when they compete to win the head offices of national and multinational firms; and three, that in their size, cost, architectural excellence (sic) and recognisability, they are to American cities what the medieval cathedrals were to the major cities of Europe.

Like the growth of the docks and the industries, and the rapid radiation of half a dozen different transport systems, the upward surge of the skyscrapers bore witness to the rapid, vigorous, healthy growth of gigantic cities in an unbelievably short time. The industrialisation outpaced anything in Europe. The immigration not only transferred millions of people from Europe to America, it transferred them from the rural parts of countries like Ireland, Italy and Poland to the centres of some of the world's largest and newest metropolitan areas. The urbanisation within America itself eventually threatened to leave parts like the Dakotas virtually uninhabited. Moreover, the bridges, the cable railways, the countless variety of buildings, the railways in the sky and the towers reaching up into the clouds were at one and the same time physical expressions of the vast and rapid production of unparalleled wealth, of confidence, and of hope.

21

As the residential areas grew and spread further from downtown, the number, location and type of clusters of commercial enterprises, professional and city services became more and more complex. No longer could all such things be clustered at the centre and serve the whole inhabited area. Most geographical studies have concentrated on the retail functions in this development and the terminology coined in relation to those in the American city will have to be used here to avoid confusion. But the other services, local government functions and other activities will be considered here alongside the retail features which are usually emphasised in the models.

As residential areas were built too far from the city centre for people to walk to the shops and offices and other services, or to consider it worth paying for public transport to reach them, entrepreneurs seized the opportunities to open businesses in what, until then, were only residential areas of the growing city. In this way a ring of smaller shopping and professional service centres was developed, not by planners, but by hundreds of individuals and small firms, to serve the people with low-order functions for ordinary daily and weekly needs close to their homes. This ring of centres was far enough away from the CBD to avoid direct competition with identical services there and thus, by the same token, close to the more outlying residential areas of the time from which the residents would readily use the closer, more convenient, new local service centres. These shops and other family businesses located predominantly at major crossroads, or where a busy street crossed a main avenue, repeating on a smaller scale the accessibility of the CBD.

As time went on, two changes were seen in the half dozen or so shopping or 'bright lights' areas. First, they grew as more shops and local services joined them, following a process similar to that which added more and more businesses to downtown. Secondly, as these centres grew, attracting more residents from a wide area for a longer time each visit, higher-order functions joined those providing the basic necessities which had started the process. Then, as these first handful of service centres grew in size, in variety of their functions and in the specialisation of their higher-order services, so they rose in rank and made it possible for a second generation of small, low-order centres to emerge around and between them. In this way, as the city population grew and residential densities increased, largely as a result of private enterprise responding to perceived needs and opportunities, a hierarchy of service/shopping centres was developed all over the built-up-area of the increasingly large Concentrated City. These centres had retail, professional, social and local administration elements, although the names given by geographers tended to emphasise

22

the retail functions. In most large American cities by the middle of this century usually five ranks in the hierarchy were recognised, with the CBD at the top:

- Central Business District
- Regional Centres
- Shoppers Goods Centres
- Convenience Centres
- Neighbourhood Centres.

The word centre in such a context now usually refers to a glassed-in mall with an atrium and other revivalist post-modern architectural features. But these centres being described here, studied by Berry and others, were shops and offices along ordinary streets and avenues complete with traffic, smog, cats and dogs, out in the sun and the rain. The retail functions are shown in (Yeates and Garner) where it should be pointed out for clarity that as one reads up the hierarchy, only the functions entering for the first time are spelled out; but each rank also has *all* the functions of the lower ranks.

The service hierarchy had five characteristics worth emphasising although they are implicit in the table and the map.

1. There was a smaller number of centres at each higher rank, rising to the single CBD.
2. Each higher rank included all the lower-order services of the lower rank or ranks.
3. The larger centres, fewer in number, were further apart within the built-up-area.
4. Each higher rank, with more specialised services, requiring a higher threshold, served and drew on a larger part of the total residential area.
5. The CBD contained all ranks of services and served not only the city but a large region beyond the suburbs as well.

Most of the main features of the hierarchy of shopping centres within the residential matrix of the big cities resembled, in the theory of their size, function, location and spacing, the features of Central Places (villages, market towns, regional cities) postulated by Walter Christaller. The service centres distributed over the city have many similarities with central places distributed over a large region such as southern Germany or European Russia. These service centres are very well explained by a variation of Central Place Theory, the idea of centres of different sizes and functions spaced at increasing distances

23

apart to serve people for higher and higher order functions according to the time and effort they are prepared to put in to reaching them. But, as with Christaller's theory, in real life the urban centres, any more than the towns in a region, do not show the very regular spacing, the regular steps in size, and, in particular the number of centres at each rank as the theory seems to demand.

The maps and the data available for actual cities in the USA from the mid-twentieth century (when this development reached its peak before declining as thresholds were lost to the suburbs), suggest that the numbers in the hierarchy were something of the order shown below, on the left. For comparison, Berry's map of Chicago in 1960 shows the numbers on the right.

NORM	RANK	CHICAGO Circa 1960
1	Central Business District	1
6	Regional Centres	7
18	Shoppers Goods Centres	18
36	Convenience Centres	27
100	Neighbourhood Centres	110

Three factors were operating to produce this fairly regular distribution of service centres within the rapidly expanding residential areas. First, many residential areas were finding themselves too far from the CBD, while the residents needed access to those services which they used most frequently, such as food shops, schools, doctors and bars, nearby. In the free enterprise system, of course, these would not have been provided unless there had been *effective* demand, and this was expressed in the numbers of people with enough dollars to pay for the goods and services.

Secondly, each shop, office or other function needed a surrounding area with enough people with effective demand to support it. This minimum number of customers, clients, patients, audience, etc. within reasonable travelling time and distance of the service is known as the threshold population of that service. The larger a population above the threshold in a given area, the more likely the business is to start in the first place, thrive and remain. Later, as people left for the suburbs, populations dropped below necessary thresholds and many of the service centres have now consequently disappeared. A neighbourhood grocery store could work on a small threshold in a tiny part of the city. A furniture store needed, say, a sixth of the city, while a very high-order specialist jeweller would need to rely on trade from surrounding small towns as well as the city itself.

As table 1.3 shows, there were four main types of activities in and around these service centres dispersed throughout the residential areas:

1. social services and activities organised by the residents
2. professional services
3. retail services
4. local government and local administration best provided on a small area basis.

Regular as the pattern of such urban service centres might be in theory, several factors interrupted the regularity of distribution in many cities. The nature of the site had an effect in places like hilly San Francisco, and around the capes, bays and rivers of Boston or the islands of New York. The regular street plans of the Midwest and the High Plains facilitated a neater pattern than did the irregular plans in the South and on the East Coast. Less obviously, not only were service centres distributed in geographical space, with hills, rivers, canals, railways, industrial areas, parks and the like interrupting the theoretical pattern, but those service centres were also distributed in social space. Thus they tended to be closer together in areas of high population density, other things being equal, and where the middle classes had plenty of disposable wealth. They tended to be further apart in areas of low population density, and in the areas with poorer people.

The net result for the Concentrated City was a range of centres, with retail, professional, administrative and social functions, of varying sizes, varying degrees of importance with higher and lower orders of functions, at different distances apart according to the terrain and the socio-economic composition of the residential population. These clustered centres were normally, but not exclusively, to be found where streets crossed, or where a street crossed an avenue. But most cities also showed ribbon development along the busiest streets, and particularly along the main routes in and out of the city.

A model used to illustrate the spatial arrangements can, in fact, be misleading, and a word of caution is appropriate here. A diagram of a circus tent is often used in the model, the canvas surface representing the residential areas while the tops of the poles supporting the canvas represent the service centres. However, in the circus tent the tops of the poles holding up the middle of the tent, the roof over the audience, and then the sides, get lower and lower from the centre to the edge. This can give the misleading impression that the service centres also decreased in size and the order of their functions from the CBD to the edge of the city. This was not the case. Inspection of the maps of the real service centres in actual cities, such as Brian Berry's map of Chicago, shows that moving out from the centre one did not progress simply down the hierarchy. In real life the Regional Centres were well away from the CBD. Consequently, moving from downtown towards the outer suburbs, one was much more likely to pass through a sequence such as:

- A Neighbourhood Centre
- A Convenience Centre
- A Shoppers Goods Centre
- A Regional Centre
- A Shoppers Goods Centre
- A Convenience Centre
- Another of the many neighbourhood centres.

If the city were big enough, one might repeat the sequence, or part of the sequence, before leaving the Concentrated City with its complex hierarchy of service centres.

As with retail functions, while the city rapidly grew and expanded over a large area, manufacturing spread well beyond the original dock sites. Transport has always been a major location factor for manufacturing within the built-up-area, and the new railways began to provide accessible sites away from the sea, lakes and rivers. Much more recently urban motorways, interstate highways and airports have done the same thing. The increasing numbers of new factories were located at a variety of sites with good transport facilities throughout the city and, later, throughout the suburbs.

Alan Pred, in a series of studies, has given a comprehensive account of the location of manufacturing within the American city. The factors which influence the sites and locations within the built-up area are different in emphasis, if not always in kind, from the classic location factors which influence where manufacturing locates within a region or country. Within the city, a small area compared to, say, the northeast or the Midwest, variations of capital, labour, markets, raw materials, fuel and power become of marginal importance in helping to decide the location. The key factors inside the city are land, particularly suitable sites at the right price, communications, particularly transport of materials and finished goods, in a phrase, sites with good access. But as one is considering thousands of firms in any one large American city, then factors like linkages between firms playing different roles in the manufacturing process (e.g. car makers and

Table 1.3 Services in Urban Commercial Centres

Retail	Local administration
Shops	Schools
Stores	Libraries
Bars	Police stations
Restaurants	Fire stations
Pool-halls	Local government offices
Dance-halls	Post offices
Car sales and service	Lower law courts
Gas stations	
Oil and coal supplies	

Services	Social organisations
Doctors	Churches
Dentists	Other religious buildings
Accountants	Political clubs
Realtors	Social clubs
Solicitors	Ward offices
Banks	Sports facilities
Insurance	National Guard armouries
Savings and Loan	
Vaudeville theatres	
Cinemas	
Commercial hotels	
Barbers	
Hairdressers	
Morticians	
Hospitals	

component makers now that 'just in time' delivery is vital) where firms need to co-operate, and external economies to be obtained by similar firms grouping together to share common services such as marketing, advertising and wholesaling become of equal importance.

In a country like the USA, state and federal governments have had considerable influence on the location of several types of manufacturing in different parts of the continent. One thinks of the drive to attract manufacturing to southern states after the Second World War, and the power of US senators, the military-industrial complex and NASA to award large contracts to firms in favoured regions, giving them employment these would not have obtained in a genuinely free market. Within the city, local government control has similarly been influential in deciding where manufacturing has, and has not, located. The various zoning laws and regulations have been another type of factor helping to determine the pattern of distribution within the American city.

Alan Pred analysed what, in contrast to the original cluster at the port, can appear to be a chaotic scatter of industrial areas all over the city — and now the suburbs — into seven types of location, with the mix and the emphasis of location factors different in each case. Pred recognises:

1. Industries with the whole city as their market. These originally located near the CBD but have now moved to much more accessible sites in the suburbs.
2. Industries dependent on external economies. These were also originally located at the centre, but are now grouped together in industrial parks.
3. Industries using local materials for local markets. These are dispersed throughout the urban area.
4. Industries making very high-value products. These are found in small nucleations at major highway intersections and at airports.
5. Industries dependent on research and special expertise. These tend to be clustered on highway locations, increasingly in the suburbs rather than the city. Many are located near universities and research and development organisations.
6a. Industries with distant raw material supplies and/or markets. These are located on major routes in and out of the city.
6b. Industries with bulky raw materials and/or products. These are still located at waterfront locations, but not necessarily the original sites. They are often further from the centre now at deeper water and on cheaper land.
7. Industries with wide markets and bulky products. These have, according to Pred, always sought suburban locations.

While this analysis can help to tidy up a very complex picture, the continued growth of the major cities has meant that formerly separate small towns, each with their own pattern of manufacturing, have been engulfed. More recently big American cities have grown until cities have merged together, particularly on the east coast and in the Midwest. In these cases the distribution of manufacturing within the total built-up-area is a composite pattern made up of the originally separate results of decision-making around each of a number of separate centres. Moreover, as with all other urban features, especially in America, the situation is not static.

Many years ago I picked up a photograph taken in a back street in Manhattan. The camera is pointing between five-storey buildings on each side, over the roof beyond towards taller buildings further away lit by weak sunshine filtered through the city's haze. For me the picture epitomises the early, very concentrated city. About half a mile away is an ornate, stepped, early skyscraper, a tall commercial building downtown. A bit nearer to the viewer is a factory, perhaps a clothing factory of the garment district. Nearest to the camera are apartment blocks festooned with iron fire escapes. At the time the photograph was taken they were probably the homes of recent arrivals in the city, possibly immigrants. In that one photograph we see that city concentric, compact and concentrated.

In its second spatial arrangement, then, the large American city was concentrated because of the continued focus on one original site in the belief that this was the only location for most types of enterprise to be profitable. It was compact and congested because, for most of the first century and a half, it was the Walking City and the Tracked City where space was at a premium and distance had to be minimised. That it was concentric in its residential layout is more problematical, but Burgess was probably right. Several generations of British students have learned the Burgess concentric model of city layout — CBD at the centre surrounded by concentric zones (rings) of the transition zone, the working-class areas, the middle class, and the wealthy commuters furthest out from the centre. Park, Burgess and McKenzie (the reference is under Park), who were sociologists, walked the streets of Chicago in the early 1920s and described what they saw. And what they saw was a commercial city, brand new but already being torn down to be rebuilt again and again. They saw an industrial city where factories and grain silos rubbed shoulders with the skyscrapers; the 'City of the Big Shoulders', as Carl Sandburg named it in one of his poems. Above all they saw Irish, Germans, English, Italians, Sicilians, Lithuanians, Letts, Greeks, Albanians, Poles, Russians and the rest streaming off the ships and trains to look for work in a private enterprise labour exchange known as the slave market.

The WASPS – white, Anglo-Saxon protestants – were already moving out of the way of this influx and the rich had gone out into Cook County. Burgess and his two companions described Chicago by means of their concentric model in 1924. The model did not fit Boston, New York and Philadelphia, the older cities of the eastern seaboard, as well as it did the cities of the Great Lakes and the Midwest, but for the present purpose, mindful both of its origin and of its time, the concentric model will serve here for the moment. But one element must be added to the diagram of concentric zones.

Superimposed on that diagram one must visualise the radiating lines of the trolley routes, the cable-car lines and the tracks of the El. The concentrated city was also the commuting city, entirely dependent on mass transport. People commuted to the centre to work, to produce the wealth each day, and commuted outward, even if not very far by modern standards, each night. There are three essentials of the concentrated urban system summed up in the Burgess model. First, the elements of the system: the port, the CBD, the retail and cultural areas at the centre, then the concentric immigrant, middle-class WASP, and exclusive suburban zones around these.

Second, connecting these elements and enabling them to function together as a single spatial system, were the rivers, canals, railways, cable-car routes, trolley tracks, elevated railways and streets. The streets first serving horses and carts, later cars and trucks. The transport networks enabled the separate elements to interact.

Third was the *raison d'être* behind all this. None of it happened by chance, or as the result of some blind determinism, as many geographers once professed to believe. It would have been impossible for so many cities to develop in a way so similar that is uncanny to many Europeans familiar with the different elements, growth and functioning of, say, Oxford, Florence and Paris. The reasons, the driving forces, the purposes of making a living and finding somewhere to live, of establishing so many cities in such a short time and working out a *modus vivendi* drove most of the urban systems and gave them their similar structure.

There was very little planning either in the classical or the modern sense. Washington, an exception for several reasons, was laid out in a European ceremonial style. There were grandiose schemes for Chicago such as the Burnham Plan, but in the event, most of the planning was complete once a gridiron of streets and avenues had been laid out and concessions to the streetcar developers had been sold. In a few cities half a dozen radiating avenues were added for good measure, but that was it. It may well have been the nearest to free-market development we will see. So an urban economic and social spatial system developed within the limits of the technology of the time, to meet perceived ends. A type of concentric and highly concentrated spatial system emerged — and it is important to remember that for a time that concentrated commuting system worked very well. In fact, it worked too well for its long-term survival.

Two different types of factor were operating which resulted in insurmountable problems in the long run. One was the set of inevitable changes as time went on, in perceptions, in aims and, above all, in technology. The other type of factor, often overlooked, is simply that in the United States not enough cities were created and established during the period. Those that were successfully established too quickly became too big. With the unprecedented industrialisation, immigration and urbanisation, not enough separate centres were initiated to provide easily for the needs of such a large and rapidly growing population which wanted to live and work in very big cities. Consequently, each city which did exist, because of the forces in operation, grew until it was too large to function as the kind of system described above. The American cities of the 1930s were much smaller than the urban sprawls of the 1990s, but they became too big for the systems and forces operating at the time. In particular, each city became too big to continue to operate with absolutely everything focused on one CBD in the centre of one compact downtown area.

On one day in 1910 Chicago ground to a stop. The urban system was overloaded. It was only temporary but it was symptomatic of what was to come. The fact was front-page news. Chicago was so clogged up and things were so still that even the slow photographic plates of the time could be exposed without anything moving and blurring the picture.

Traffic jams are not caused by the internal combustion engine and the car. When the planners try to take your car off you and put you on a computer-controlled, driverless mass-transit monster, show them the photograph taken in Chicago in 1910. Traffic jams are caused by people: by too many people trying to move in the same area at the same time, whatever the vehicles. In particular, they are caused by too many people trying to get to the same place at the same time. The Romans probably had traffic jams when something good was on at the Colosseum or the Hippodrome. The traffic jams in Chicago in the 1910s and 1920s were the result of trams — the photographs show trams, trolley-cars, nose-to-tail in all directions. Among the chaos are a few horses and delivery carts, and one or two early cars. But trams brought Chicago to a halt in 1910 just as deregulated buses are bringing Sheffield to a halt in the 1990s. Eventually the concentrated, concentric commuter system began to fail because too many people tried to move in and out of the single central area where all the action was taking place. Too many people were dependent for getting to their work, to the shops, and to most forms of recreation in the trolleys and elevated trains, but not, not yet at least, in cars.

2

THE SUBURBAN SOLUTION

Before elections in America, as in Britain, politicians have frequently promised impressively higher public spending and enticingly lower taxes. Just as frequently, the suckers have rushed to vote for them. It is like telling two children that if they sit on a see-saw both ends will go up at the same time. After the election the disillusioned public finds that the laws of economics do not work that way, and neither do the laws of physics: one end of the see-saw has to be down while the other is up.

By the end of the twentieth century we have the evidence that, secretly, a large majority of the population believed in another complete contradiction — that they could all live in the country *and* all enjoy the benefits of the metropolis at the same time. Until the 1920s most people in Britain and America could not test this. They could not even get on the see-saw to find out the hard way that if one end goes up the other must come down; that for each gain there must be a corresponding trade-off. Making this truth more difficult to perceive was the fact that the first very lucky few who achieved suburban living did appear to get the cake and keep the ten cents too.

The idea of living in the country while working, shopping, being educated and entertained in the city may have come from Europe. During the nineteenth century strong encouragement for the idea certainly arrived in America from Britain, but it was equally certainly taken up most enthusiastically there. As in Britain, the first suburban communities were by-products of railway building. Specifically suburban and commuter lines were built later, when a profit beckoned, but once the first inter-urban lines were complete, a station on a line just beyond the built-up area in an attractive location could quickly become the focus of a new community. Unlike Britain, in the United States beyond the eastern seaboard there were no farming villages to provide attractive focal points. Round some major cities like Chicago the alternative was for rich people to establish golf courses and country clubs as focal points for their new settlements. At the turn of the century the rich both wanted, and could afford, to live in the country, but for nearly everything else they expected to use the city. Sinclair Lewis's Babbitt took the train downtown to the office each day, worked on making his fortune, boozed and buffooned with the boys, and went back to his earthly paradise only in the evening.

Babbitt and his buddies needed the wealth, as well as the extra leisure which money can buy, to achieve their dream. At first the virgin land on which they built their wooden villas and fieldstone country clubs was cheap. But the buildings themselves were elaborate, ostentatious and expensive. The cost of daily travel added up, as any commuter knows, and the cost of deliveries to the tradesmen's entrance all added to the bottom line. As the city grew, pushing the most desirable locations further and further from downtown, country living cost that small group dear, both in the considerable time spent commuting and in the cost of maintaining a lifestyle which more and more became a matter not so much of pleasure as of prestige.

The British protagonists, and the American boosters — optimistic promoters of their own cities — who took up the idea enthusiastically, promoted suburban living for all the best reasons. Perhaps prestige and power were implicit for those who knew the codes. The boosters emphasised the attractions of fresh air, space, green fields, trees, peace, safety and quiet. Implicit also was the idea that one would have as neighbours well-heeled people with values similar to one's own. The enthusiasts pointed out the advantages of getting away, if only for the evening and the weekend, from smoke, grime, noise, crowds, clanging trolleys, dark streets and the congestion of the city. Again, the fact that one would be escaping the Great Unwashed, the floods of immigrants in particular, needed no articulation.

Adopting the ideas of the pleasures and benefits of rural life and Garden Cities from Britain, American newspapers, journals and businessmen promoted them strongly. Plans were published for ideal homes. Journals offered more than enough ideas on how to furnish and equip the wooden mansions. Lumber companies widely advertised their house designs, new country homes for those with taste and money; or just money. The strategy worked because the desire was already there. It had been there long before it could be fulfilled. The boosters breathed on it and started to turn it into reality. The railways and the longer trolley-car routes at last made it physically possible and the small, select suburban communities, originally for those rich people who did not want to live in the city, started to grow into something else. By the 1920s they were sufficiently common,

33

numerous and well-established for Burgess and Park to put the suburban commuter zone, the outermost residential zone to which all others aspired, into their urban residential model.

Both by design and because of the constraints of the transport systems of the time, the numbers of suburban commuters were small. While fresh air, countryside and space were the types of attractions most often stressed, the remoteness, exclusiveness and the prestige of those communities out beyond the edge of the concentrated city were equally vital; they were the goal of Jay Gatsby's dream. As Burgess and Park realised, most American urban residents, immigrants included, aspired to move outward to better, newer homes; but those who had managed to move out really did not want the others to follow. That really would defeat the object of the exercise: the other end of the see-saw would go down instead of both staying up. When everybody is somebody, nobody is anybody.

It is clear that the desire to live on the edge of town had been there for a long time among the majority of peoples who flocked to the mushrooming American cities, but that for the first century and a half for the majority this was not possible. Most people had to live in the apartments and houses which they could afford, within time and cost distances from work. Until the time of the Second World War most of that work was concentrated in the city centres, and until after the First World War, the right kind of transport was not available.

In 1989, the centenary, the Germans and the French argued about which of them had invented the car. But of far greater importance is the demonstrable fact that the Americans adopted the car much more enthusiastically than either of the putative inventors; and while for many decades Europeans kept the car as a hand-made luxury, American manufacturers soon started to make cars cheaply for mass markets. The cliches about Ford have been repeated too often. Henry was by no means the only entrepreneur working and thinking hard in Michigan. The mass production of affordable cars was more the result of business rivalry than of Ford's monomania. Furthermore, those who take the trouble to read the histories will see that the many companies which in one way or another joined to become General Motors did as much as Ford to develop the mass-produced car, and it was cut-throat competition between all the manufacturers which brought the price down.

The net result was that cars were available in large numbers to the middle-income middle class in America some four or five decades before we saw a similar situation in Britain and Europe. For a time the trouble was that, thanks to people like McAdam, Blind Jack of Knaresborough the surveyor, and Lloyd George, we had surfaced roads and the Americans did not. Road building and the grading and surfacing of streets, let alone rural roads, proceeded much more slowly in America than in Europe. Strangely, the depression of the 1930s, which hit the car industry very severely, resulted in action which was to benefit it beyond measure after the Second World War. As one of the many schemes of Roosevelt's New Deal, in order to give people work, put money in their pockets and get the economy working again, what were then called Parkways were constructed in several American cities. While Los Angeles built the first motorway, the Pasadena Freeway, eastern cities, again influenced by European ideas including the German autobahns, used the cheap New Deal labour to build landscaped roads out towards the suburbs. They were paved dual carriageways with wide central reservations and verges and they were intended to be lined with trees.

As with the skyscraper, inventions and technological developments were accumulating steadily to meet a pent-up demand. The car, pneumatic tyres (some historians name the urban area in the car age the rubber city) steel saloon 'safety' bodies, automatic transmissions, hydraulic brakes, freeways and parkways formed a single transport system. Many of the highway features which the British and Europeans now take for granted, like roundabouts, traffic lights and double lines, were American inventions. Another set of developments was also accumulating at the same time. The mail-order prefabricated house already existed, available from places like Chicago, via a Sears Roebuck catalogue. To these were added: central heating, air conditioning, wall insulation, showers, deep freezers, fridges, electric cookers, washing machines, dish washers, waste disposers, things not seen in Britain in any quantity until many decades later. There was a revolution waiting to happen, signalled by a development on Long Island.

There, as America came out of the Depression, just a few years before Pearl Harbor, a company called Levitt combined an improvement in rapid prefab construction called balloon-frame building, with the latest labour-saving devices in the kitchen, to make the dream houses of the future at a price Levitt knew the mass of the middle class could afford. Moreover, that speculative venture on greenfield sites just to the east of New York City was laid out not on the rectangular grid system of most American cities, but in the form of crescents, closes, avenues, circles and other street-plan features of English Garden Towns and suburbs. Levitt should be celebrated in the same way and in the same context as Ford. He mass-produced not only houses but virtual towns in the way Ford and General Motors mass-produced cars. Levittown on Long Island was the first. From the air it looks now like a British council-house estate, but the houses were for sale and the development *is* the size of a town. Many more Levittowns have been built all over the United States and many other firms followed the lead from the late 1940s onward.

All the factors detailed above came together immediately after the Second World War. Small numbers of people had been moving to the suburbs for decades. The desire and the demand were certainly there, but had been unfulfilled for so long. The mass production of cars had made the potential commuting possible, and Levitt and many others were now able to produce the brand new housing. Before the war, the federal government had guaranteed mortgages for middle-class, middle-income people in approved areas of safe, sound new housing. Now, after the war, the Veterans' Administration extended that guarantee to all returning servicemen. The mass movement of American urban residents to the suburbs began in earnest.

The new homes were built on greenfield sites at the edge of the built-up-area, along the attractively curving crescents and closes; and they were built at densities lower than those of the houses and apartments in the city. The new suburbs neither waited for tram lines, elevated railways or bus routes to be pushed out from the city, nor were they dependent on the promise of such for the future. The pre-war city necessitated high density residential areas crowded along mass transit routes. A house or apartment had value according to how far one had to walk to the trolley stop or the El station, and that could not be very far. (Try walking the streets in New York on a hot July day when the humidity is unbelievable to anyone from Europe. Try getting through the snowdrifts in January, and the point is made.) The new suburbs were built for the car. Their low-density planning provided the back yards (gardens), tree-lined streets, relative space and air which had been advertised and recommended for so many decades. Many Europeans, circling over Long Island as they come in to Kennedy Airport, will have seen the tens of thousands of tiny back-yard swimming pools in the eastern suburbs of New York, like a rash of pale blue measles on the landscape. Those suburbs were made to be spacious for their time. They were designed for the car and, again with their low densities, have always been dependent on the car. In very few places are the residential densities high enough financially to justify putting in mass passenger transport systems. So, with a family to start and raise after the war, a new Chevy on hire purchase, a balloon-frame house with a mortgage insured by Uncle Sam, fresh air and space for the 2.4 kids, middle-class Americans needed little more encouragement to make for the suburbs. And just in case they did, Levitt offered a free Bendix washing machine in every home.

36

Before 1935 the big downtown and midtown Manhattan retailers had opened ten stores in the suburbs. Between 1935 and 1940 they opened ten more. On the east coast the trend which was to spread to the Pacific and later into the Sunbelt had started. But between 1945 and 1950 those same retailers opened over fifty stores: in New York State north of the Bronx, over on the Jersey side, in Connecticut, and particularly on Long Island. One of the most effective pieces of simple cartography shows the shores of Lake Michigan, the administrative boundary of Chicago, and the land of the surrounding area. On that map (Figure 2.1) simple plus signs each show where ten new stores had opened. These plus signs are well dispersed over Lake County, Cook County and Du Page County, the new middle-class residential areas where the stores opened in the decade to 1955. The same map uses minus signs to show where ten stores closed down during the same period. All but one or two of the minus signs are within the city limits. Even more, the cartographer had to draw so many of those minus signs representing ten closed stores in the Loop and on the near West side that all the short lines have run together in one solid black map of urban decline in the city centre.

Density in the centre: dispersal in the suburbs. New growth in one type of location as that end of the see-saw went up, counterbalanced by the inevitable decline in the old location as the other end went down. The first mass movement was of middle-class people into the new residential suburbs; the second move was of retailing. As owners lost trade inside the city and saw it growing in the suburbs, at first they opened branches in the new residential areas. But later they moved out of town completely. The last one to leave switched off the lights: Macy's closed in Manhattan in 1992.

Some of the early developments just after the war, both residential and retail, while suburban in their characteristics, were still built within the city limits. In such cases there was no loss of people, trade or revenue from the city. As time went on, of course, three other features became apparent. First, as hundreds of thousands of people continued to move and houses were built for them, those houses were located at the edge of the built-up-area. The American city became like a tree adding a new outer ring each year. So very quickly the original post-war suburbs were no longer really suburbs as the edge of the city moved further and further out and they were left behind.

Secondly, in most cases, the continuously built-up-area spread beyond the city limits. There were exceptions such as Los Angeles but, in the main, people, jobs and revenue were moving beyond the city's control. Thirdly, as the newer and newer suburbs engulfed small settlements which had once been satellites to the cities, the suburbs

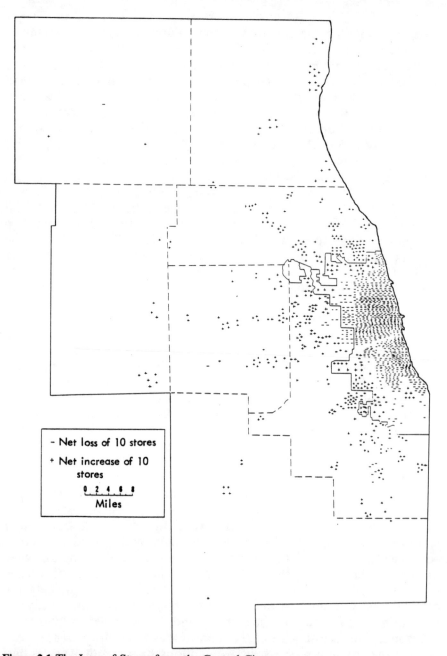

Figure 2.1 The Loss of Stores from the Central City
Movement of retail stores out of Chicago between 1948 and 1958.
Source: Berry, B.J.L. & Horton, F.E. *Geographical Perspectives on Urban Systems,*
Prentice-Hall, Englewood Cliffs, New Jersey, 1970, p. 471.

38

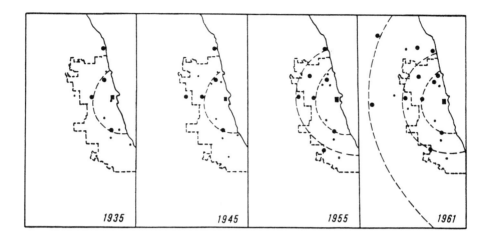

Figure 2.2 The Spread of Retail Centres in the Suburbs
The widening dispersal of an increasing number of shopping centres in the growing suburbs of Chicago between 1935 and 1961.
Source: Berry, B.J.L. & Horton, F.E., *Geographical Perspectives on Urban Systems*, Prentice-Hall, Englewood Cliffs, New Jersey, 1970, p. 473.

were built at lower and lower densities, each decade using up more space for the same number of people and activities.

From this point onwards, the word suburbs will be used to mean specifically those built-up-areas beyond the original city limits. Once the built-up-area spread into one or more different political units, significant changes took place, to have, in many cases, a devastating effect on city centres by the last decade of the twentieth century.

In the period since 1945 suburban growth in America has been such that new nomenclature has been coined to describe certain aspects of it. The real phenomenon in the real world is the continuously built-up-area, say from the Empire State building out into Connecticut, or from the Sears Building out into Kane or even De Kalb County. The Bureau of the Census now refers to the original city at the centre of this urban sprawl as the Central City. For the whole area, including Central City, suburbs and the engulfed former separate towns, there is now the name Metropolitan Statistical Area, the MSA. This is made

39

up of all the administrative units which completely contain the continuously Built-Up-Area, or BUA. Beyond this, sometimes as much as one hundred miles from Times Square or the Loop, is a wider zone from which people commute into the MSA. This wider area in exurbia, focused on the city and functionally connected to it, is the Daily Urban System, the DUS. So:

- Central City
- MSA
- BUA
- DUS

are abbreviations which will be very useful here and in later chapters.

In more detail, the arrangement and nomenclature is as follows. From 1949 the groupings of administrative units were called Standard Metropolitan Areas, SMAs. From 1959 they were called Standard Metropolitan Statistical Areas, SMSAs and from 1983 have been called Metropolitan Statistical Areas, MSAs. However, if a very large urbanised area of more than a million people contains units which meet Office of Management and Budget criteria, each of those units becomes a Primary Metropolitan Statistical area, PMSA. A built-up area of more than a million people which contains two or more PMSAs is now known as a Consolidated Metropolitan Statistical Area (CMSA), rather than just MSA.

There may now be up to three official Central Cities in an MSA or CMSA plus other cities of over 50,000 population not officially designated. An MSA must have at least one Central City of 50,000 plus, and a minimum population in the BUA of 100,000. The county containing the Central City is called the Central County, and any other county with at least half its population in the BUA becomes officially part of the MSA. Note that the criteria are somewhat different for New England. Further detail is given in the appendix of the Statistical Abstract of the US published annually in Washington DC.

Examples using 1990 Census figures:

CLEVELAND – AKRON – LORAIN CMSA
Cleveland PMSA	1,831,000 population
Akron PMSA	658,000
Lorain-Elyria PMSA	271,000

CLEVELAND Ohio PMSA
| Cuyahoga County | 1,412,000 Cleveland 506,000 |
| Geauga County | 81,000 |

| Lake County | 215,000 |
| Medina County | 122,000 |

MEMPHIS MSA

Shelby Co. Tennessee	826,000 Memphis 610,000
Tipton Co. Tennessee	36,000
Crittenden Co. Arkansas	50,000
De Soto Co. Mississippi	68,000

Note that Memphis MSA spreads into three states.

When the first of the still small number of motels were introduced to Britain they were located in all sorts of strange, out of the way places. The British knew what they looked like but did not know what they were for because we did not have the conditions which gave rise to them. The motels — motor hotels — were among the first of an ever-growing number of suburban characteristics specifically designed for life in which the private car is as essential as a pair of legs. The motel in its logical place is located at intervals along the long-distance routes across the continent, or at the edge of the town and the edge of the city. In the days of the concentrated city one arrived by train in Grand Central Station in the downtown area and stayed next door in a city-centre hotel. Now one arrives at the city by car, or by plane at the airport where one hires a car, then one drives to the parking lot of the motor hotel on the edge of town where one leaves the automobile outside the door to one's room.

One still has to walk three or four steps into the room, but at a drive-in movie one did not even need to get out of the car. The car windscreen faced the silver screen, and the loudspeaker, the hot dogs and the Coke came in through the driver's window. Then came drive-in banks, drive-in churches and, inevitably, drive-in hamburger chains and the rest. Some of these functions, over-adapted to the car, are dated now, and some were never central to life in the suburbs, but two points should be emphasised: one, that life in the low-density, widely spaced suburbs is genuinely impossible without cars; and two, that more and more of the built environment is designed for and intended to be used only by people in cars, with no provision made for pedestrians.

The early Levitt houses often had a picture window as the main feature facing the street. In the bungalows built now, the two-, three- and four-car garage doors are the main features seen by other motorists passing by. The big suburban stores do not have windows full of goods facing the street any more; they have blank curtain walls facing ever larger car parks. Shopping malls similar to but usually larger than Brent Cross, Meadowhall and Metroland are the norm now, and will be examined in detail later. They are the major focal points in the larger suburban areas. But for a long time a characteristic of the sprawling American suburbs was their lack of any focal points. Not only were the houses and schools dispersed, but for several decades many of the other functions which followed the middle class out of the city were dispersed too. Thus Pop drove off in one direction to park at work, Mom drove off in a different direction to drop the kids off at school, drove in a third direction to the supermarket, in a fourth direction to, say, park at the beautician. Later the family would drive in fifth and sixth directions to different and widely separated locations for sports and entertainment. Very different from the old days when one went downtown for most of these things.

The many directions involved, and the distances which had to be covered, meant that it was essential to go by car. As a result, each factory, each school, each supermarket, mall, doctors' practice, hospital, poodle parlour, sports facility and movie complex needs, and has, its own integral car park. In the newest locations one can park in one place and visit shops, movie and restaurants inside one mall, but in most of the places with older facilities and in many of the new, it is just too far to walk from one non-residential building to another. One uses the car from parking lot to parking lot to parking lot to parking lot all day.

People started and continued to move to the suburbs. Then retailing started and continued to move to the suburbs. The third overlapping wave of movement outwards was that of manufacturing. In the 1950s the US government inaugurated the Interstate Highway System, the first complete network of first-class roads north–south and east–west across the continent. They did this by matching State road-building funds with federal dollars, provided the new roads were constructed to Interstate standards. As the network grew and neared completion many cities also built by-passes at various distances from their centres to link up the Interstates so that traffic would not have to pass through their centres. Concurrently, and partly affected by this, although also affected by the growth of air traffic, railways in the United States were in decline. They lost most of their passenger traffic to cars and planes but much of their freight traffic too, to trucks.

Much goods transport, excluding the bulky raw materials still carried by rail and the high value smaller items carried by air, was captured by the huge articulated trailers pulled by the brightly painted, chromium-plated tractors. So, as the railways were in decline and the heavy trucks were either excluded from the congested city centres or wasted too much time getting there, factories inside cities were becoming less accessible. But the new highways were cutting through the new suburbs or circling round close to their outer edges. Manufacturers began to think of new locations away from the docks, the railway yards and the cramped conditions of their original city centre sites.

The suburbs had several types of attractions. They had space, cheap land for single-storey factories where the production lines could be laid out on one level instead of zig-zagging up and down the multi-storeyed loft buildings in the city. The cheap land also offered more space for storing raw materials and finished goods, wide parking lots for the workers and even landscaping to make the enterprises look attractive. Added to all this was the very important factor that rates and local taxes in the counties beyond the city limits were always much lower than in the expensive Central City itself.

New factories started to be built in the suburbs by the sides of the new roads. Direct access to the increasingly important road network was an added bonus to the factors outlined above. Land near Interstate interchanges became premium sites. As with department stores, often the first new factories were branches of firms in the city as the businesses of these expanded. More recently the trend has been for firms to close down in the city and move completely into the suburban sites. In the last couple of decades brand new manufacturing enterprises have not even considered the Central City as a possible location but have established themselves on the edge of the built-up-area from the start. Route 128 in the 1950s round Boston became the classic example of a type-location for firms moving to the suburbs. Silicon Valley on the southern edge of San Francisco is a well-known example of a more recent type of almost exurban location.

In different urban areas, and for different industries, naturally other factors have reinforced the influences. For example, food processing industries have moved nearer to their major markets in the suburbs while industries have been zoned, like with like, so that heavy industry causing gas, liquid and noise pollution is kept as far as possible both from desirable residential areas and from different industries which could suffer from proximity. High-tech light industries, compatible with each other and with residential amenities, are usually grouped into the many industrial parks. The prior existence of colleges and universities with research facilities is often a location factor for the new high-tech firms which never contemplated the city centre.

Other functions once characteristic of, sometimes unique to, the downtown area moved out subsequently, starting at different times and moving at different speeds. Most of the wholesaling functions, benefiting from the cheap extra space, once many of their customers were in the suburbs, followed retailing and manufacturing. New schools had to be built in the suburbs, as did churches and hospitals. Sometimes higher education stayed at focal points in the cities, but many universities and colleges moved out. Broadway theatres, and prestige galleries, museums and concert-halls in several big cities, survived in the downtown areas for decades, but their patrons were moving further and further away. At the same time cinemas, theatres, libraries, museums, art galleries and the less prestigious cultural amenities, along with most sporting activities, put up very good new buildings in the outer suburbs. Finally, many financial services and the head offices of corporations were relocated to new office parks sited by the Interstates and the variety of parkways, tollways, turnpikes and freeways criss-crossing the suburban sprawl.

Most reluctant to move were those types of function which still derive some prestige — or believe they derive some prestige — from being downtown, often in a well-known skyscraper. Location downtown, especially at a focal point in the CBD where one could be found easily, was still believed to have a financial advantage, particularly for firms connected with the money markets. That may have been true until the 1980s, but within the last decade even the firms which made Wall Street famous have started to move from the CBD and out of New York altogether. There is a loss in two ways. Not only have all these functions moved out, but they have tended to disperse as well. The process has not been one of, say, the transfer of Chicago's downtown functions *en bloc* from the Loop to Evanston, but the dispersal of those functions to many parts of the suburbs. They have almost, but not quite, been scattered to the four winds, to a handful of smaller centres. In total, greater New York, greater Chicago and the rest, may have many, many more shops, factories, schools, colleges, theatres, cinemas, libraries, hospitals, financial offices and service functions than they had in their original downtown areas in the 1930s, but these are now scattered over an enormous, low-density landscape. Merely finding them is a very difficult trick for a stranger in town.

This problem may be reduced in time. The new tendency is for like to group with like, in the industrial park, in the office park, both often near a local airport, the high-tech and R&D park, the university campus, the multiplex cinema and, of course the shopping mall. But these single-function areas or parks are still scattered throughout the suburbanised areas the way corner shops were spread out in the old compact city, rather than all together in the modern equivalent of a single downtown. The sheer size of some of the suburban sprawls greatly aggravates this problem. Each decade the edge of the built-up area has been ever further from the old CBD. Each decade the new area built on has exceeded the area built on the decade before, as residential densities become lower and lower. For every million people moving outwards in each inter-census period, double, treble, even quadruple the land area has been required. In a continent as big as North America, an area very roughly 40 times that of the British Isles with only 5 times the population, this is not serious at the national level. The really serious problem is at city level where each MSA is such a huge urbanised area in which to live and, crucially, where most of the people and most of the revenue-producing activities are located and dispersed beyond the Central City limits.

There is little in Britain or Europe to compare with such large suburbs, such enormous, complex urban areas. From Santa Monica to Riverside is some 90 miles, the same distance as from the western end of Portsmouth to the eastern end of Hastings. From the Loop to the edge of the BUA beyond Aurora is the sort of distance from Charing Cross to north Oxford; the extent of greater New York from Manhattan to the fringe on Long Island would take one from the fens east of Lincoln to the hills north of Manchester. Randstad and our conurbations do not really compare in size.

Over the second half of the century, the suburbs have changed in several ways, and they are still growing. The older, inner suburbs are compact, sometimes on a grid pattern, and are already being renewed. The newer suburbs further out are much more open and show a much greater variety of street patterns. In general, the further one goes from the Central City, the newer the houses, the lower the density and the more irregular the pattern. Houses once on greenfield sites may now be ten or twenty miles from the countryside as the edge of the suburban sprawl moves outwards. The houses, of course, have had to stay where they are, but over the decades the people have moved again and again. What further complicates the picture in the United States is that people also move from city to city much more readily and much more often than they do in Britain and Europe. But, given that for any one city, until the rise of the Sunbelt, movement out of one BUA was roughly balanced by movement in, net movement within one BUA has been steadily outwards.

Rich people have been able to move most often and most easily, if they so wanted. As the suburbs have grown and as people once able to see farmland from their windows saw only 'ranches', duplexes, condos and split-levels, those who could afford moved out yet again, like pioneers always seeking the frontier. They moved to the edge, to the new homes with the larger back yards, larger garages, and houses with more gadgets, while their former homes filtered down to less affluent families following on behind. The average family with 2.4 children moved, in the decades since the war, on average, every seven years.

With their idiosyncratic skyscrapers, it is just possible to recognise the downtown areas of some Central Cities, but the suburbs of different American cities, seen from any angle, look very much the same. If a photo looking up to a skyscraper beyond a loft building could epitomise the concentrated city, then an aerial photograph is essential to help one grasp the key components of the suburban landscape. The greater the height from which the aerial picture is taken the better, for one needs to be able to see many square miles to begin to get an idea of the sheer size of the largest of these urban areas, and to be sure that enough of the many scattered functions are framed in one picture to give a representative view.

An aerial view of some newer suburbs may well show some remaining patches of farm land. In some places the square fields of the old quarter-sections have not been built on, usually because the owner is waiting for the price to rise. Cutting across the view, often cutting across the old gridiron pattern of the original land-survey plots, is a six-lane motorway, either leading to the Central City or curving round it. As often as not a clover-leaf or more complicated intersection gives a feature to relieve the monotony of the landscape. In the newer residential areas the street patterns deliberately curve and wind and are beginning to obscure the straight lines of the old grid. This is especially the case where mature trees are brought in by the private landscapers and sold to the homeowners to provide instant Arcadia.

All these features are recognisable at once to a European looking at the air photo. But here is a flat-topped building with a big yard round it. Over there is a bigger, single-storey, flat-topped building with an even bigger yard round it containing hundreds of short, parallel white lines. Are they factories? That idea comes to mind most readily by comparison with buildings one actually knows. Are they schools? Perhaps. Are they hospitals, banks, offices, motels, warehouses, art galleries, cinemas or even brothels? Usually one has to drive right up to the blank exterior walls under the flat, or fake mansard, roofs to find out. With the more discreet cases, when the small brass plate says something like 'AMZ Inc.' one has to try to get inside before one can be completely sure. The local people know, of course, but for the stranger trying to find one of these functions here it is not like going to Oxford Street for the big stores or Charing Cross Road for the bookshops; for the visitor to the large American city it can be more confusing than trying to find one's way in Marrakesh or Samarkand.

By the 1980s more than half the people in American urban areas, and the majority of the wealth-producing activities, were located in the suburbs. These people and functions may well be inside the same continuously built-up-area as that in which they started, but now they are, importantly as far as the census and economic matters are concerned, outside the administrative boundary of the Central City. Within fifty years, with this move of over half of the city's people and functions, there has been a locational and distributional revolution. As a result, there have also been urban financial and political revolutions too.

In the former concentrated city, a particular location was chosen: the Embarcadero, the mouth of the Chicago river, the great bend of the Delaware, or the tip of Manhattan. Then the cities which grew at those advantageous sites worked very well as spatial systems until they became so big that they became grossly overcrowded and were in danger of being brought to a standstill. In contrast, the move to the suburbs involved many choices of types of locations, rather than of a specific point. The suburbs were a *type* of area into which people, shops, factories, offices and the rest moved as much to get away from something as to locate *for* a specific reason. For a time, too, the suburban system worked well until, again, the very success started to defeat its own purposes. As new suburbs grew, the old suburbs were not suburbs any more; they became monotonously and busily urban. Moreover, as more and more high-order functions left the Central City, particularly as the very highest order functions left downtown and CBD, there was no longer everything in that single focal point on which the suburbanites could depend.

A British tourist going to the USA for the very first time in the 1990s and seeing central Manhattan, the Loop or downtown Dallas in all its glory may find this impossible to believe. But increasingly the showpiece skyscrapers are becoming shams, as will be shown in a later chapter. But not only have the suburbs lost the services of a single, functioning downtown, as the high-order functions have moved out, they have gained the high prices, congestion and other big-city evils which they moved to escape in the first place. In the long term, flight is not proving to be a particularly good solution.

The suburbs have gained some of the rich, most of the middle-income middle-class, nearly all the manufacturing, services, retail and wholesale trades. Above all they have received the majority of people with political power and the bulk of the wealth-producing enterprises. In the process they have lost the semi-rural environment which so often was put forward as their *raison d'etre*. They have lost, too, the excitement of the big city. Most suburban residents no longer need to

47

go into the centre for any purpose; and an increasing number of Americans are afraid to do so. Going to a Broadway theatre in a guarded coach and then being shipped straight back to the safe suburbs is not the same as living in the city and being able to stroll around Broadway and Times Square. In the 1990s there has been a continuous series of reports of tourists being mugged and killed, not only in New York and Los Angeles, but in places Europeans once thought to be much safer, like Miami and Orlando.

At first sight it might be assumed that the Central City must have gained so much from this process of suburbanisation. If overcrowding and congestion almost stopped it working, then suburbanisation must have had a great benefit in reducing those pressures and problems, leaving the centre free to work as in the good old days. But, as has been outlined above, too much has gone from the Central Cities. Not just people, but leaders, not just the middle class, but middle-income money, taxes and spending power. The factories with their air and water pollution have mostly gone, but so has the work for the blue-collar and unskilled classes, for the black people and the immigrants. Above all the revenue from industry and business has gone from the city treasury.

Hidden in the urban sprawl of the BUA stretching from the original downtown twenty, forty, sometimes sixty miles is an invisible line. That line is the administrative boundary of the original city, now the Central City of the MSA. One of the most important points in the argument outlined in these first two chapters is that too much of the urban wealth and political power has moved outside that line. At first acquaintance, greater New York, greater Chicago, or any other city is one huge urban unit. Disguised by the continuity of buildings across that line is the fact that in most cases this is not so.

In the bad old days, in the Chicago run by the Bosses for example, when everything was under its control within the city limits, the political machine was unendingly criticised for its corruption. Politicians bought votes off gullible immigrants, the Irish, for example, to retain power. But the machine in fact had its uses and benefits. The poor people went on selling their votes because in return they got practical help from local ward politicians, especially to find jobs. However corrupt the machine may have been, all the wealth was produced within the city limits, and most of it was spent within the city limits. Even if it was spent by a corrupt city hall primarily for the public benefit of the rich and powerful, the poor, by living in the same place, could not help but benefit to an extent too. Just enough wealth was indirectly redistributed to the poor to keep the system working.

48

Crudely and simply, the urban area is now two separate systems. Within the continuously built-up-area they are isolated by that invisible line. Most of the wealth is created in the suburbs and most of it is then spent there. The rest goes more often to the state capital — Albany, Harrisburg, Springfield or Lansing — than to the Central City. The net result is that the old city centres which gave the full-blooded drive for the creation of so many millionaire cities in less than two centuries have been in financial crisis for decades. Many of them are now permanently on the brink of bankruptcy. The proud cities described in Chapter One were often areas of decline and debt, beset by major problems by the 1970s. Some of those problems were common to all very big cities throughout the world. Some were the result of sheer size and rapid growth. But many were unique to the United States and can be attributed to that revolution which moved so many and so much out into the suburbs in the second half of the twentieth century. The people on the see-saw did seem to gain everything in the suburbs. It really did look as if one could get the infrastructure and keep the tax dollar as well. Capitalism and free enterprise seemed to be working just fine. But the other end of the see-saw has gone down inside the city, and we see that the pivot is on that invisible, but so far immovable, city boundary line.

3

CENTRAL CITY PROBLEMS

When considering the problems of the large American cities, for the moment the central showpiece areas of recent renewal in the brand new downtowns are specifically excluded. Depressing as this chapter may be, this is not a book about urban problems, nor a demand for something to be done; a survey of urban problems would require a much larger volume, and most of the items would be common to other cities in the world. The attention here is on the major problems of American Central Cities in the late twentieth century, particularly those resulting from the circumstances outlined in the preceding chapters.

In the 1960s, an era we look back on with some nostalgia now, attention began to be focused on the growing problems of the central areas of the largest American cities. One dramatic cartoon has a viewpoint looking vertically downwards between a dozen closely packed skyscrapers towards a tiny citizen in the canyon below, screaming for help. The neon signs on the roofs of the skyscrapers are not advertising Coke and jeans, instead they proclaim:

- Upper-Income Flight to the Suburbs
- Low-Income Migration to Cities
- Tax Squeeze
- Shortage of Recreation Areas
- Crime Rise
- Rise in proportion of Juvenile and Aged Groups
- Housing Ghettos
- Overcrowded Schools
- Transportation Jams
- Pollution
- Exodus of High-Wage Industries.

These phrases are not deathless prose, they do not inspire one to immediate action, but then the cartoonist had so much to convey in one picture that he had to be concise. Some of the items in this list look familiar to British eyes. One or two, like the shortage of recreational areas, do not look too alarming, and some of the problems in 1966 were nothing compared to the proportions they have reached now. The first and last items, however, were and are crucial.

A year later, in his book *The Northeastern United States*, Lew Alexander listed as the main problems of the very big cities of that region:

- the competition for space
- obsolescence and the need for rehabilitation and renewal
- new transportation requirements
- the search for water supplies and recreation areas
- the need for electric power
- the rise of technological unemployment
- the political impact of population shifts.

(His items six and seven have been transposed to give the last one greater emphasis.)

Some of these major problems have developed as the result of the cities growing in size and complexity. But sheer size of the population and area alone are not enough to create some of the other problems. Large urban areas with millions of people are found in other parts of the world. But when one realises that the sophistication in infrastructure and government have not kept pace with the growth or the changing needs, and that they have not been adapted to the formation of megalopolises, then one sees that some of the problems may be unique in America.

The urban area from Boston to Washington was first called Megalopolis, the very big city, by Jean Gottmann in the 1950s. In labelling this as one continuous urban area he gave very much the wrong impression to Europeans. It is not urban as we understand the term. Gottmann defined 'urban' as those areas having at least one urban function per mile of main road. By that definition most of England is one megalopolis. Travelling from New York to Boston, in some parts of New England it is very difficult to believe that one is in the middle of a megalopolis. Nevertheless, the concept is important because it highlights what has happened in the United States on a particularly mammoth scale. There are places where, as their suburbs grew, one city joined up with another. We see such conjunction of half a dozen towns and cities in the Ruhr, in Holland, and in such areas as the West Midlands and West Yorkshire. We call them conurbations. But a different name in the United States makes a lot of sense because their conurbations are on a vastly larger scale. The West Midlands conurbation is of the order of 50 miles across and houses perhaps seven million people. In contrast Boswash, Boston–Washington, measures some 500 miles from end to end and houses some 50,000,000 people. Later, cities in the Midwest spread until their suburbs joined together and Chipitts, Chicago–Pittsburgh, appeared on the maps. There are supposed to be two or three others and, certainly, if MSAs continue to grow they will join together. The existence of Sansan, San Francisco–San Diego, particularly just south of Bakersfield, is the hardest to believe in, although they may well have joined up by now.

As the lists at the beginning of this chapter suggest, some severe problems do derive simply from the fact of people in the most technologically advanced, wealthy society, living in such large agglomerations. Fifty million people living and working in Boswash need food and raw materials every day. Moving that much food is a fantastic achievement. Using a British yardstick will give a measure of this. If each person happened to consume only a pint of milk a day, that amounts to six and a quarter million gallons, every day. Then there is the bread for burger buns, potatoes for French fries, mayo, Coke...

The tonnage of raw materials for industry, paper for commerce, etc. is harder to visualise and calculate. Then most of the finished goods have to be distributed and are moved out. After all the milk and cookies have been eaten, 50,000,000 people go to the toilet several times a day, grind their household waste down the drains, put all their burger cartons and Perrier bottles in the trash cans. Meanwhile the factories are pumping carbon monoxide, carbon dioxide, lead, sulphur and other multi-coloured and foul-tasting compounds into the air and pouring hundreds of different pollutants into the rivers, lakes and bays. As a result, in the Midwest many rivers have been officially classified as fire hazards, as dead, or both.

Add to the above very brief outline of the daily ebb and flow of inputs and outputs, the increasing demands for water and electric power. Fuels either have to be moved in from further and further away, or power grids have to draw in energy from a wider and wider area. New York depends on much of the northern Appalachians for its water. When supplies proved inadequate in southern California, Los Angeles first turned to the lower Colorado River, then to northern California, thirdly to the Snake-Columbia basin, and now has a grid system which pipes in water all the way from Canada. Again these big megalopolitan areas concentrate resources on a surprisingly small number of gigantic centres, for such a large continental area.

While there is no question that the big concentrated cities in the first half of this century had the infrastructure to enable the urban system to function fairly well, that infrastructure was never planned as a whole. It grew piecemeal, and by the 1950s was proving to have severe limitations for continued growth and sustained long-term operation. The physical structure of the Central Cities, by the very fact that they were the oldest parts of the urban areas, was becoming worn out, decayed and obsolete. Drains, water systems, cables and urban central heating systems as in New York were reaching the end of their useful life. Sidewalks needed re-laying, roads needed widening, bridges needed re-building. While buildings were torn down and rebuilt again and again on the most profitable commercial sites by private firms, much city property, schools, hospitals, police stations, fire stations and the like were getting into a parlous state of disrepair. The oldest residential property, that in the innermost rings of the inner city, close to the CBD and the rest of downtown, was often abandoned by its owners when no more rents could be extracted and there was no longer any money for maintenance and repair.

City services similarly came under increasing pressure from the 1960s onwards. Four large groups of working people, teachers, the police, firemen and garbage collectors feature again and again in the disputes with city halls in the last two or three decades as there became more and more for them to have to do, in ever-deteriorating properties, with declining resources, and threats to freeze or even cut their pay. But other groups, not as large, nor as widely publicised, were in the same sinking ship and together added to the millions of people involved: social workers, probation officers, weights and measures officials, building safety inspectors, sewage workers, road maintenance teams, park attendants and prison officers were all needed in increasing numbers just at the time when funds to pay them started to decline.

Two examples, one physical, the other governmental, will serve to show how the organisation of the Central Cities and their surrounding suburbs tended to aggravate an already serious situation. Both the outline of the close connection between the development of transport and the growth of the urban area, in Chapter One, and the experience of any person who commutes to work daily in our kind of Western society, one hopes, will result in agreement that any large urban area needs an ordered transport system, whatever the type of vehicles involved. One can argue *ad infinitum* what these vehicles should be: underground trains, elevated trains, trams, buses, cars or bicycles. But if people are to live separately, and at a distance from work, school, shops, services and recreation, then an efficient and well-organised transport system — one stresses the system, not the vehicles — is indispensable.

In addition to all the well-known and often-rehearsed problems of transport which apply even to tiny towns like Lincoln and Cambridge, what has also bewildered and exasperated many experts studying the transport of American urban areas (not to mention the commuters), is that these gigantic, complex urban areas do not have unified transport systems. As the built-up-area spread beyond the city limits, one might have expected the urban infrastructure systems to continue into the suburbs. Very often they did no such thing. For example, as Washington merged with Baltimore, Baltimore merged with Wilmington, Wilmington with Philadelphia, Philadelphia with Trenton, Trenton, Jersey City, New York, then Bridgport, New Haven, Hartford, Worcester and Boston all joined to become the original megalopolis, one might have expected, at least hoped for, some reorganisation of the infrastructure. In many cases there has not even been co-operation. If this sounds unbelievable to those more familiar with European cities, read what Lew Alexander has to say on the matter. One can drive from one end of Boswash to the other, given time and patience, but the opponents of the car and the advocates of mass transit cannot point to any kind of co-ordinated system which serves the whole area in an efficient way.

London began the system which later developed into the Underground in 1862. Paris started to drop the Metro under its streets in 1900. In fact, a number of companies did build separate subways under Manhattan early this century, but those separate lines, mainly under Manhattan, still confuse those who take the interconnections of the Underground and the Metro for granted. Apart from New York, American cities did not start to build underground systems until the 1970s, and then only to serve the downtown areas. In a few cities like Washington and Boston two or three lines in each have been completed to date. Other cities such as Seattle and Detroit have put in highly visible and much publicised elevated monorails, but again there are few lines and they serve only the inner areas. These systems give those cities some prestige, and a cosmopolitan look, but they do not scratch the surface of the massive transport problem.

In addition to the sheer numbers of people who would have to be moved, there is another factor in the spatial revolution of American cities in the second half of the twentieth century which makes the organisation of one transport system for the whole BUA even more difficult to achieve. When trolleys, cable-cars and elevateds were in their heyday such a system could work because in the morning most people needed to go downtown, and in the evening they needed to

54

travel the same route back home. A feasible radial system focused on downtown could be built, was built, and for a time worked. But the majority of people don't work downtown any more. In an extreme case, an American citizen may live in almost any location in a built-up-area of thousands of square miles, and may work at any other single point absolutely anywhere else in that BUA. *Reductio ad absurdum*, a transport system would have to connect every single point in the BUA with every other point; not a complete technical impossibility, but only cars on streets come near to it in practice.

The daily tide in and out of the CBD was labelled commuting. The unbelievably complex pattern of journeys to work, school, shops, etc. between thousands of points anywhere in the BUA nowadays is referred to as cross-commuting. A diagram of traditional commuting is easy to draw. Arrows point inwards to one centre for the morning flow, their heads showing the direction, their shafts almost representing the mass transit lines. In the evening they point outwards like the spokes of a wheel. I once tried to draw a diagram of cross-commuting. I gave up when the arrows I had drawn in every direction made a terrible mess on the paper. Soon after I had to admire a cartographer who had drawn such a map very well for Cleveland. The shaft of each arrow started at the place of residence and ended at the place of work. The well-drawn map, which was still just clear enough to give the right impression, looked like cross-hatching going out of control. But those who did not know it was a map might have thought it was a drawing of the Indians' arrows at the moment of crisis during Custer's last stand at the Little Big Horn.

One of the most ambitious and best-known urban transport schemes of the last few decades is the Bay Area Rapid Transit system (BART) centred on downtown San Francisco. Like the others, essentially it aims to bring people into the centre from the suburbs, although the complete circuit around the bay obscures this function at first glance. San Francisco and the other American cities which are putting in modern subways and monorails are not just putting in the modern versions of the obsolete radial commuter systems; there is also the need to provide access to the expensive developments of urban renewal, as will be detailed in the next chapter.

BART links places like Sausalito, San Rafael, Richmond, Berkeley, Oakland, Hayward, Palo Alto, Redwood City and San Mateo with the Central City of the MSA, San Francisco, by means of a loop and half a dozen radial lines in and out of the suburbs. The lines run above ground along most of the routes, but dip underground beneath the densely built-up-area of the Central City. Like most of the other systems, BART has been an expensive failure. It took much longer to build than predicted, needed ever-increasing amounts of capital, and has made an operating loss since the first lines opened. Not enough people use the lines, so it has not achieved its prime purpose of enticing people to move off the roads into modern, fast, comfortable, clean, high-tech trains. But at least BART attempts to be a single system embracing all three elements of the MSA: the Central City, the widely scattered suburbs and the other cities round the bay.

If, to this purpose of MSA mass transit schemes, we add the needs: to provide one unified transport system for the whole BUA; to serve all parts of the urban area, to facilitate cross-commuting; to maintain downtown as the focal point; and to make a profit, then BART and the other systems have largely failed. Some of the aims are probably impossible to achieve. Too many lines would be needed to serve all parts of Boswash, Chipitts or Sansan. Cross-commuting in such large areas poses problems infinitely greater than those which the Chicago El managed to solve. Most people don't need to go downtown on a regular basis any more; above all they don't want to wait in the rain, change trains and walk the last half mile to work when they can get in their cars in their own garages, drive across town to work, park in the basement of the office building in which they work, then take an express lift to the office floor.

Much less visible but, in the end, much more fundamental than the transport problem, is the confusion of administrative units which continues to bedevil the MSAs. This description of the big cities so far may well have given the impression of one central administrative unit surrounded by one other circular suburban administrative unit. In fact the reality is not even as simple as one central unit surrounded by even a dozen suburban units which need to join up, get their act together and run the whole BUA as a single system.

The true situation is best analysed at four levels in order to comprehend the vast number of different bodies involved. Even within the Central City, say Chicago or New York, there is a bewildering number of separate local government authorities and administrative units at the lowest level. Within the administrative area of the city, apparently run by one elected body, are a score of other boards, authorities and departments. An example of the smallest units is the fire districts, followed by school board areas, units for garbage collection, libraries, parks, then slightly larger areas for health, housing and public welfare, the police precincts, larger areal units still for things like hospitals, transport and urban renewal, up to the largest administrative units for water supply and pollution control.

These separate boards, councils, districts and authorities came into being at different times over the past two hundred years as the need for them arose, and each one has its own elected officials, its own right to raise taxes, and its own unique area of jurisdiction. The confusion resulting from this piecemeal historical growth becomes only too apparent when one draws the boundaries of these authorities on a large-scale plan of only part of the city. When, in succession, one draws a line round the area each of the fire districts, school boards, parks administration and all the others listed above the visible reality is that no two areas are the same size and in only exceptional cases, say along rivers, do their boundaries coincide. Well, the United States is a modern, highly developed country, full of intelligent, well-educated people; they can sort that problem out in a couple of weeks. Chapter after chapter in books on urban geography shows the disbelief of writers that this chaotic situation persists decade after decade; that and frustration that nothing is, or perhaps can, be done about it. The reason is that each board keenly defends its right to be elected, its right to raise money, its right to go its own way. In a word, each board jealously protects its own power. This is a constitutional matter and will take a long, long time to resolve, particularly as the will to co-operate does not seem to be in the air.

If the city boundary hides a mass of conflicting, small local boards, the line around the MSA gives another deceptive diagram to one looking from the outside. An MSA exists only on a map and in the census records, it is not a single administrative unit which works together on the ground. The people at the Bureau of the Census observed the BUA spread beyond the city limits and sprawl over many administrative units in the counties beyond. Realising that the complete built-up area is *tending* to operate as a single Daily Urban System, the bureau collects data and presents it in a convenient form for these incipient systems. But that collection and presentation of data in a convenient way, as if the DUS were one single unit, does not actually make it into one administrative unit in real life.

At this second level of analysis, a medium-sized example will illustrate the point. The city of Boston is the Central City of an MSA. Route 128 circles round in the west, some ten to twelve miles from downtown on the Shawmut peninsula. The western edge of the boundary of the MSA is some 30 miles from the skyscrapers on Shawmut, the southern edge some 30 miles away near Duxbury. Within that line, in the area one thinks of as the modern Boston, are 80 separate municipal authorities. As early as 1970 the continuously built-up-area surrounding the Central City of Boston had spread across 25 municipalities *outside* the then line of the MSA, which has to be updated every so often. By now the outer suburbs have spread some 50 or 60 miles from the original quays and Faneuil Hall.

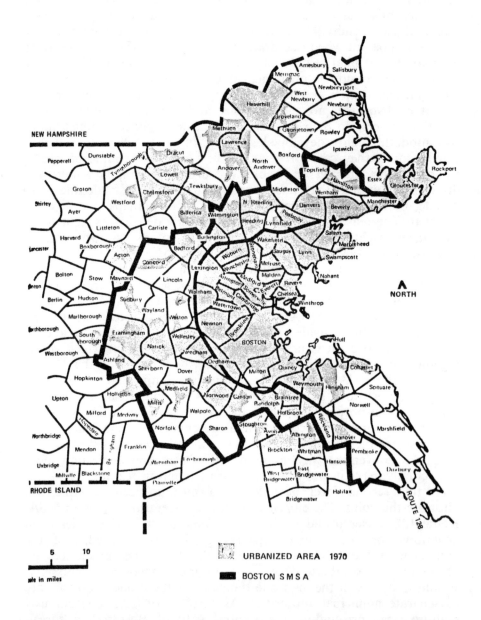

URBANIZED AREA 1970

BOSTON SMSA

Figure 3.1 The Complexity of Administrative Units Within and Beyond the SMSA
Note Route 128, the city of Boston at the head of the bay, and the built-up-area
spreading beyond even the SMSA by 1970.
Source: Schaeffer, K.H. & Sclar, E., *Access For All*, Penguin, 1975, pp. 82–83

58

Yet another kind of complication can be seen at the third level upwards, in the case of New York. New York City is divided into five boroughs: Manhattan, the Bronx, Queens, Brooklyn and Richmond. Within these is the plethora of fire districts, school boards, police precincts and the like discussed above. Beyond these five boroughs is an even larger number of municipalities in the MSA than there is around Boston. But the urban system in New York's case is administratively much more complex. Across the Hudson River, for all practical, functional economic purposes, the cities of Newark, Jersey City and Elizabeth are part of the Central City. But Newark, Jersey City and Elizabeth are not even in the same state: they are in New Jersey. The MSA of New York/Newark is so complex in fact, that three zones are recognised around the core of the central seven boroughs. Six more separate major administrative units form the inner ring, round from Union County in New Jersey to Nassau County in the state of New York on Long Island. Similarly, there are ten counties in the intermediate ring and three more in the outer ring. In all, these many different administrative units cover an area in which some eighteen million people live in what may be referred to loosely as greater New York.

But this case is special in another way. It must be remembered that the fifty states of the United States are, in many ways, analogous to fifty separate countries. Each state has much in common in its position in the union with a nation state in Europe. Each has its own government and makes its own laws, and these fifty 'countries' of what is thought of as one nation can, to the European travelling there for the first time, be disconcertingly different from each other. To understand the problem at this third level of the tiers of administration, for greater New York, then, imagine the whole BUA were in Europe. Greater New York spreads over the three states of New Jersey, New York, and Connecticut. In the European context this is equivalent to a city twice the size of Paris being one-third in France, one-third in Germany, and one-third in Holland — *before* the existence of the EU. Co-operation between the three states is minimal.

NEW YORK, NORTHERN NEW JERSEY, LONG ISLAND, NY-NJ-CT CMSA

Population 1990	18,193,000
BERGEN-PASSAIC	1,358,000
BRIDGPORT-MILFORD	444,000
DANBURY	134,000
JERSEY CITY	606,000

MIDDLESEX-SOMERSET-HUNTERDON	852,000
MONMOUTH-OCEAN	670,000
NASSAU-SUFFOLK	2,556,000
NEW YORK	9,077,000
NEWARK	1,937,000
NORWALK	128,000
ORANGE COUNTY	222,000
STAMFORD	206,000

SOURCE: Statistical abstract of the US 1992

By 1990 the built-up-areas of seven cities — Chicago, Cincinnati, Huntington-Ashland, Memphis, New York, Washington and Wilmington — had spread into parts of three states. Philadelphia extends now into parts of four: Pennsylvania, Delaware, Maryland and New Jersey. At the fourth level of complication are the megalopolitan areas.

The seeds of these administrative problems existed from the beginning. Hard as it may be to believe, even less has been done to solve them than has been done to solve the transport problems. While the growth of the enormous suburbs aggravated the administrative, transport, and other problems of the urban infrastructure, it was not inevitable that the Central Cities, and particularly the inner-city areas, should become such problem zones. The middle class had left the city, for all practical purposes, as had much retailing and manufacturing. Substantially, this movement tended to leave blue-collar working-class families in the majority in the inner cities. Given enough work for them, and given reasonable public services, there was no reason why the blue-collar white people, the recent immigrants, and the black people should not have followed the WASPs to the suburbs in their turn.

However, some of the processes bringing about these changes continued until they had passed breakpoints, points of no return, and now other factors have come into play to affect those processes and to change the urban system, penalising those left in the centre. Very soon it became clear that more jobs were leaving American Central Cities than were people. Corporations could afford to move — often it was financially imperative for them to move as city taxes increased — but usually the blue-collar workers, and especially black people, could not afford to move and follow the jobs to the suburbs. For a time, in some cities, reverse commuting existed. Poorer people who lived in the inner-city areas commuted *outwards* each morning and inward in the evening. In the end, however, the Central Cities became areas of the highest unemployment in America as jobs moved too far from the centre.

For many jobs provided by the city authorities, particularly those employing large numbers of people, a higher education is essential. Teachers need a degree and/or teaching certificate, while the police, firemen and other services have to pass the Civil Service exam. The net result of these understandable requirements is that many jobs which are available in the city are closed to the local people with the poorest education. The norm now is for teachers, police personnel, firemen and the like, middle-class, middle-income people, to live out in the suburbs and to travel in to the city only to work. Not only are their salaries paid in the city then spent in the suburbs, but many of these civil service workers can retire on half pay after only twenty years' service, further draining the urban money chest. (Dennis Smith and Tom Walker give fascinating accounts of this type of life.)

As more and more of the jobs have either moved out of the city, or become so high-tech and sophisticated that the workers require much skill and training, the least able have been left behind in the inner city with less and less of the kind of work they can do available to them. To compound the problem, other disadvantaged people have moved in to join them. Of the original residents of the concentrated city, those who moved to the suburbs tended to be middle-class, educated, skilled and ambitious. As time has gone on, those left behind tend to be those with manual skills, the least education, less ambition and the least enterprise. Moreover, during the last three decades, millions of the least successful people in American society have moved into the inner cities to join those already there. The first large wave of such people after suburbanisation began were the rural poor displaced by the massive mechanisation and re-organisation of American agriculture in the 1960s. They moved into the cheapest, oldest housing near the city centres, complete strangers to urban life and living. Studies such as the detailed ones for Indianapolis show that most of them have not moved out since.

By the 1970s, the effects of the Immigration Act of 1965 were also beginning to show results in the inner cities. The Act, which opened immigration to all but a very few nations, resulted in the influx of what are often called the 'New Immigrants' from Asia, as opposed to the old immigrants from Europe. Certainly the succeeding decades have seen many middle-class Asian families locate directly in suburban areas, but the majority of the first new immigrants, like the Europeans before them, made for the big city centres.

As will be argued in a later chapter, the black people of the Central Cities had an extra obstacle to making it to the suburbs. In addition

61

to the blue-collar problems mentioned above, they were deliberately kept out of many residential areas. For some three decades they were effectively confined to the inner-city ghettos. Add to these groups the rootless poor from other places who ended up in a few particular cities like New York (which offered better welfare services than most), and it becomes clear that the inner city areas, both by the loss of some sections of the complete spectrum of society, and the gain of more than their fair share of the poorer, most disadvantaged groups, had an increasing accumulation of social problems as suburbanisation progressed.

The parts of the inner cities where the majority of the least fortunate of these people are concentrated are labelled by researchers, politicians and others as areas of Residential Blight, or Social Blight — bland labels for far too much misery. The areas, defined by the data collected, are residential areas where, per thousand of the population, there are very high rates of:

- unemployment and underemployment
- families on welfare
- single-parent families
- school drop-outs
- untrained, unskilled people
- burglaries
- muggings
- arson
- drug abuse
- drug-related crimes
- prostitution
- mental disorders
- suicides
- notifiable diseases
- tuberculosis
- malnutrition
- repossessions for debt.

The list is not exhaustive, but this is enough to make the point and paint a picture. As often as not, the attitude of educated white Americans, usually from the suburbs, could be expressed along the lines of: 'no wonder there are slums in the inner city, what can you expect when so many idle, mental, criminal freeloaders get together in one place?' Cause and effect seem to have been reversed to those brought up in a society with a stronger socialist element. It is possible that many of the people in the inner city become like that because of where and how they are forced to live, not the other way round.

Whatever the cause, whatever the effect, the problem is there now, in the 1990s. Americans, including politicians, will debate the reasons more openly, revealing their prejudices, than we are used to in Britain. Perhaps we have a different attitude in a country which once had a welfare state; although as we lose ours, the Clinton administration may move towards one in America. Even then, in America it is not taken for granted that someone will have to do something about social blight. In the nation of free enterprise one is free to pursue wealth and the good life; but one is, by the same token, perfectly free to fail. Then the attitude to failure is: you blew it; you had your chance and didn't make it — tough! If one succeeds, nobody resents it — they hope to do the same. But if one fails, it is nobody else's fault — and nobody else's responsibility either. You are not expected to distribute largesse when you succeed, so don't expect a handout when you fail, because it must have been your own fault. In such a context, of course, the inner cities can not automatically look for, or expect, help from beyond their own boundaries and resources.

In the lists, such as those above, of the specific problems which constitute the social blight of the inner cities, three key items are rarely mentioned. Single-parent families and under-resourced schools mean not only that approved role models are lacking for the next generation. Of much more serious import is the fact that the present residents of the Central Cities have very few able leaders. They certainly no longer have the kind of leaders seen in the 1960s. As a result, it is not only the schoolchildren and teenagers who sink into anomie and alienation; often the adults do too. Apparently contradicting this assertion is the fact that so many Central Cities have had black mayors in the last quarter century. But check what those mayors have done; check what they have achieved for the people who voted for them. The record is thin and not very impressive. At the end of the twentieth century many of the largest cities in the USA have populations within their boundaries which are over fifty per cent black. When the condition of the black people in the city has been considered in detail in a later chapter it will be clear that this single factor of race makes it even more unlikely that substantial help will come from beyond the city boundary. The mayors may have the will, but they have not the resources to do very much.

Until very recently all but the most famous and successful black people had been effectively kept out of the suburbs. Throughout the short history of the American city, traditionally the newcomers: rural poor, immigrants from Europe, black people from the South have been allowed into only the oldest, poorest, cheapest housing at first; in other words, into the innermost residential rings. Now the problems are compounded by declining property values, property often owned by absentee landlords and badly maintained. Eventually the dilapidated properties are abandoned and become the refuges for the homeless squatters and the meths and drug addicts. The old residential property accumulates even more cockroaches and rats than when it was continuously inhabited by the poor, and also becomes a fire hazard. In the end the impoverished city authorities are faced with the extra cost of pulling it down.

Piled on top of the demands for extra welfare, probation services, remedial centres, drug rehabilitation centres, tuberculosis wards and the like, is the extra cost of policing the city where so many people cannot find work. Inevitably, a higher proportion of people in the city than in the suburbs turns to crime (see table 9.5). When a child sees an honest young man leave school and fail to find work again and again, while he sees the neighbourhood drug dealer with fine clothes and a big car, then the child who is no fool must soon see where his best career prospects lie. In short, role models have changed.

The dilapidation is there for all to see in the streets of Boston, Philadelphia and St Louis. One hears that it is worst in the inner ends of the ghettos from the few white students and reporters who bother, or are brave enough, to go to see. The bibliography lists books of photographs, some from as early as the 1960s, which show distressing conditions inside the homes as well as in the streets. One bright day in the 1980s we had been in the Lower East Side of Manhattan and decided to go to Greenwich Village not far away. As it was such a nice day, foolishly, we decided to walk. In the middle of Manhattan in broad daylight, every few yards along our route men and women slowly rose up from their lying positions on the sidewalk, obviously preparing to ask for, or demand, money. It was eerie and very frightening. (Fortunately a man in a car rescued the dumb limeys who were studying the city too closely.)

The problems, and the details of the resulting human misery, could too easily be expanded out of proportion. Moving the other way, they boil down to the fact that the demands on the Central Cities have been increasing over exactly the same period of time that their revenues and their leadership, in the widest sense, have been in decline. All-embracing transport systems need to be built, the infrastructure needs to be renewed, and much of the fabric of the inner city needs to be repaired. In the long run it would make more sense to advocate work for the unemployed so that they can then both look after themselves and become part of an increasing market for flourishing industry. But in the short term resources are needed desperately for remedial help. This need, as has been shown, grew as more and more of the taxpayers and more and more of the wealth-producing activities left the cities, and left those particular problems behind.

New York City was the first to reach the edge of bankruptcy. In 1975 the then-mayor, Abe Beame, announced that if New York did not get financial help by August it would not be able to pay its debts due in that month. There were special reasons why New York was first, and why its financial crisis was so acute, as will be shown in Chapter Five, but the city of New York was only the first of dozens of the largest cities in the United States to come to the brink of bankruptcy in the period since 1975. In that year, when New York was so much in the news, *Time* magazine ran a health check on other cities in October. Philadelphia reported a $19 million deficit. Dallas, San Diego and Milwaukee had just managed to stay in the black by cutting services and raising taxes. Cutting services increases the problems for the future, and raising taxes pushes more of the revenue-producers over the boundary into the lower tax areas of the suburbs (see tables 9.1–9.4).

Time reported that Chicago, Detroit and Baltimore had managed to get what New York had tried for and failed — financial help from their respective state governments. Chicago had its schools, hospitals, parks and welfare bills paid for by the state of Illinois, in effect by people in the suburbs as well as in other towns in the State. In Michigan the state raised the non-resident taxes in Detroit; that is, it taxed those who worked in the city but lived in the suburbs. Ohio helped Baltimore by running its airport, financing school construction and paying one-third of the police budget. Indianapolis achieved a similar result by boundary re-organisation to take in more of the suburban areas as part of the city. This latter move has been a common move in Britain but has been extremely difficult and rare in the United States.

Los Angeles was reported to have no financial problems in 1975, in fact a $61 million surplus, but this surplus was for Los Angeles County, not a city in the same sense as Philadelphia. Of Houston, *Time* said, 'officials foresee no future budgetary problems'. That was in 1975. In 1989 Beth Anne Shelton and her colleagues published their excellent analysis of the city, once a growth point in the Sunbelt, but by the 1980s in trouble. The full title they gave their book is *Houston: Growth and Decline in a Sunbelt Boomtown*. One way or another, most of the big cities have managed to avoid the headline crises which made New York so notorious. The net result is that belts have been tightened, some, but not all, presidents since Gerald Ford have made

65

some federal funds available, and the situation has continued to deteriorate further and further as even more people and commercial enterprises have left town. Some cities have been in the news because riots or excessive crime have drawn the attention of the media. But many cities prefer to keep quiet about their financial difficulties in order not to scare any business away.

In 1978 Cleveland too came to the edge of bankruptcy. The water supply system needed to be renewed completely. Fire service and police force budgets were cut. Boston followed in 1981. The salaries of the fire service, police and teachers were cut. In 1983 Buffalo was reaching a similar stage, although in that city's case the reaction was to blame Ronald Reagan rather than the long-term trends which were affecting most Central Cities, especially in the Rustbelt of the old industrial northeast. By 1984 in Chicago the financial constraints were such that the school budget was reported as less than a tenth of its value in 1974, the year before the Big Apple revealed something wrong with the core. Gang wars were becoming commonplace and Chicago tried to impose a 10.30 p.m. curfew for all youngsters under the age of 17. In such an enormous city, with reduced resources for the police, that could never work, never mind the constitutional implications. In 1988 15,000 homeless people were reported on the streets of Washington DC and 80,000 on the streets of New York. By comparison, in the notorious, terrible early 1930s, there were 6,000 homeless in New York during the crisis of the Depression.

In the days when all the people who lived and worked in one city were within that city's political boundaries, the wealth generated in that city was available for the infrastructure and services of the whole urban area. But a spatial revolution has taken place, starting slowly at the end of the nineteenth century, gathering pace in the twentieth, and rapidly nearing completion after the Second World War. By 1980 over half of the population of the top fifteen MSAs lived in the suburbs, and the proportion of cities and people has gone on increasing. Normal technological developments, especially in transport and in housing design, made the revolution possible. Millions of separate, free decisions on the part of families and firms then accumulated into mass movements of people, services and economic activities into the suburbs (see table 8.1).

That movement was also both a major separating-out of people and work, as well as a major political change. People sorted themselves out by race, by income, by education and ability, by enterprise and aspiration, by original nationality, by religion and by politics. There are exceptions, but the norm in city after city has been for white, middle-income ambitious and educated people for a time to form the majority in the suburbs. They are the so-called WASPs — white, Anglo-Saxon protestants. The majority of those left behind have tended to be black Americans, immigrants from Latin America, more recent immigrants from Asia, and the least-educated blue-collar workers becoming increasingly the long-term unemployed. More often than not this has resulted in a political difference between the Democrat Central City and the Republican suburbs and the rest of the state.

The political shift is often not as simple as this. Even when the same party is in power on both sides of the city limits, there is still a great reluctance for the wealthy suburbs to support the impoverished Central City. They usually express this along such lines as the prudent suburban communities having more sense than to throw good money after bad into the profligate, irresponsible centres. In a nutshell, the problems predominate in the Central Cities while most of the wealth is controlled in the suburbs and the state capitals. Increasingly, the suburban communities and economies are becoming aware that they do not need the old centres any more; but the Central Cities still need help from somewhere.

4

URBAN RENEWAL

A commonly observed sequence, when a new policy is introduced or a new trend identified, is for a few, far-sighted observers to give dire warnings of the eventual consequences. Everyone else then shouts them down, and when the prophesies prove to be only too accurate, the shouters demand to know why something wasn't done. The case of the spatial re-arrangement and political division of American urban areas presents a remarkable exception to that rule. In many cases the eventual problems were foreseen and understood, and many city authorities did take some action. The disappointment is that the action often did more damage than the processes it was meant to remedy; and in only one or two cities can such action be said to have been successful.

As early as 1943, during the Second World War, the authorities in Wichita, for example, reviewed the spatial changes in the urban area, then looked forward to what Wichita might be in 1970. They produced two maps of Wichita projected forward to 1970, one labelled 'This?' and the other 'Or This?' The second map shows a larger Wichita, although still very compact around the city centre, in the old, concentrated, concentric form. The first map shows what would happen if the centrifugal trends already identified by 1943 continued. There would be unplanned, uncontrollable growth, suburban sprawl, low-density areas, and the loss from the city of real estate and revenue. The city authorities of Wichita were alive to the problem and were already trying to take some action.

As outlined in Chapter Two, the really rapid suburbanisation involving large numbers of people did not get under way until after the war; but as early as the 1950s other city authorities were beginning to take remedial action. In theory there were two avenues open to them: one, to redraw the city limits to encompass the new growth; two, to try to keep all the new development within the city in the first place. In the United States the first option has very rarely worked. The few examples seen since 1945 have been only minor boundary changes. The whole legal basis of land ownership, from the platting surveys — the first marking out of federal land under the Ordinance of 1785 — and the land laws through states' rights, up to the Constitution has been too strong. Cities have tried to enlarge, and in most cases their efforts have been very successfully resisted.

The practical result has been that in the last half-century those cities which have tried to face the problems resulting from the loss of people and revenue beyond their administrative limits have opted for urban renewal. It must be emphasised what is, and is not, meant by the phrase urban renewal in the context of American cities. Too many British people readily jump to the wrong conclusion that urban renewal in America was like slum-clearance and re-housing in Britain. We do, in fact use the phrase now to mean that kind of thing. But the aims of urban renewal in the United States in the third quarter of this century were not social; they were entirely economic.

The aim of urban renewal in American cities was to keep, or more often to bring back, within the city limits, industries, businesses, services — in a word *commercial* enterprises — to preserve the tax base of the city. In some cases high-salaried upper middle-class residents were kept, or attracted back. But urban renewal definitely was not a philanthropic movement to re-house people, certainly not the poor. It involved major schemes of massive rebuilding of commercial properties of various kinds to get, and to keep, wealth production within the city. It must also be emphasised that not all the large American cities adopted schemes of urban renewal, and some started much earlier than others. Of these, two striking early examples are Pittsburgh and Boston.

As early as the 1950s, Pittsburgh, whose steelworks had helped to produce munitions for the war effort, was beginning to show many of the problems outlined in the last chapter, particularly air pollution. The downtown area was, and is, on the low triangular piece of land where the river Monongahela flows along one side to join the Allegheny flowing along the other, to become the Ohio river flowing westward towards the Mississippi. These rivers run between high, steep-sided hills so that they, and the downtown area of Pittsburgh, are at the bottom of a deep, fairly steep-sided trough. With the steelworks and the coke-ovens pumping out smoke, steam, gas, and poisonous sulphurous fumes, Pittsburgh had an acute problem of air pollution and was ranked as America's least desirable city in which to live. To their credit, the authorities at the same time were among the very first to bring in a clean air law and to introduce an urban renewal scheme for downtown.

On a rare clear day, the downtown area of Pittsburgh at the confluence of the Monongahela and Allegheny rivers was a desperate sight. Half a dozen assorted steel-truss bridges spanned the rivers on each side. Warehouses, a goods yard and railway lines covered the land at the point of the confluence and ran along the river banks. About half a mile back from the confluence a motley collection of 23- to 30-storey skyscrapers, encrusted in soot, just managed to scrape the smog laden skies because the latter were usually down near river level. Pittsburgh was the typical congested, worn out river-port site, hemmed in by heavy industry with particular problems of its own. But by means of an urban renewal scheme the city authorities set out to turn this mess into The Golden Triangle.

Urban renewal in Pittsburgh, judged by the particular local aims which were set, was a success. With the co-operation of the steel companies the air was cleaned up. Most commercial activity was kept in the centre and the Golden Triangle was completed. The real test is that in the long run Pittsburgh did not slide inevitably into bankruptcy like so many other cities. In those respects the urban renewal achieved its specific ends. Perhaps Pittsburgh had some special advantages. By the 1950s conditions in the city down in the trough had become so bad that the majority of people agreed that there was a crisis which had to be tackled. (This was not the case in Boston, as will be seen shortly.) The residents could see, breathe in, feel, taste and smell one of the most urgent items to be tackled; they continually had to wash it out of their hair and clothes. Moreover, Pittsburgh was relatively small and compact then, both in comparison to cities now, and to other cities at the time. Further, the renewal was largely confined to the small area of the triangle between the rivers.

However, as in all the other cities, there was a price to pay. That price was paid by the poorest people in Pittsburgh, just as it was in Boston and other cities which embraced urban renewal. The new skyscrapers, offices, hotels, stores, banks, sports halls and other landmarks of the Golden Triangle were built, quite properly in America, by private enterprise. But what was not so proper was the way the land was made available to the developers by the city authorities.

In the 1770s, nearly two hundred years earlier, when the new government was just beginning to survey the land into sections ready for sale to the new settlers, all land in the United States not already settled was declared Federal Domain. It didn't matter whether Indians were living on it or not, or whether Mexicans and Californians had deeds granted by Spain, the land west of the original thirteen colonies was claimed as federal property to be sold for government revenue. For those not familiar with land policy on the frontier, free land was not available until after the Homestead Act of 1862, when most of the fertile land had already been sold. For the purposes of urban renewal this concept of Federal Domain was revived under the title of Eminent Domain. Under this, city authorities were empowered by the federal government to appropriate city land which they considered necessary for redevelopment, and to give it to the private developers. The same attitude which had been shown to the Indians was shown to the black people, European immigrants and the white poor who formed the majority of the residents in the inner-city property in the areas marked for renewal. All the city authorities had to do before confiscation of the property and eviction of the people was merely to *show* that other accommodation was available elsewhere.

In Pittsburgh with its Golden Triangle scheme, relatively small numbers of people were evicted to make way for profitable commercial property, compared with other cities. Most of the area to be renewed was covered by industrial, wholesale, retail and financial functions. But there were old wooden houses on the hillsides which were destroyed, and small businesses on the fringe of the downtown area which were snuffed out. The poorest people, the small businesses, those with least power suffered most. Even in those early days, because land and property was confiscated under the trick of Eminent Domain, urban renewal was already being referred to as the Federal Bulldozer.

So, in Pittsburgh, the old, dilapidated wooden houses of steel workers living near to the factories were torn down and replaced by modern apartments to attract wealthier residents who could pay higher local taxes. In some cases the residential property, particularly terraced rows of brick houses in a few streets, was either sound enough or of sufficient historical interest to make it worth renovating. This process of stripping the structurally sound shell of a stone or brick building, renewing the woodwork, putting in electricity, new water and sewage systems, central heating, double-glazing and the like is usually called gentrification. Not only is the uprated property attractive to wealthier people, they are the only ones who can then afford it. The original residents really have no chance of returning. Jane Jacobs calls gentrification 'unslumming', but it is unslumming of the property, not the people. One repeats that this is not a process of re-housing the poor. The property may be 'unslummed' but the former residents definitely are not, and usually end up further from the city centre in the new slums created by the overcrowding as the stock of residential property within the city is reduced.

When the Golden Triangle was finished it looked good, and there were many more sunny days down in the valley on which to admire it, thanks to the smoke abatement. There are tall modern skyscrapers,

71

wide office buildings set back in plazas, a domed exhibition and conference centre, all free of soot. Motorways have replaced the railways, and while most of the old, untidy bridges are still there, and there is a motorway interchange near the confluence, the point of the triangle of land is now occupied by an attractive open park. Considering the site, the location and the original set of problems, Pittsburgh's urban renewal achieved a great deal.

One of the assumptions in Chapter One is that, once laid down, the major features of a large city can not be changed; the site, plan and major structures remain to influence later generations. Boston nearly proved this wrong. Aerial photographs taken in the late 1950s and early 1960s show large areas of the Shawmut peninsula cleared and levelled ready for development, literally the clean slate so many architects and town planners fantasise about. That the whole of downtown Boston was not subject to urban renewal was thanks to political and social pressures, not to any insurmountable technical problems for a city which had cut down the former hills on the peninsula and used the prodigious amount of material so obtained to fill in Back Bay in the nineteenth century.

In the 1950s Boston did not have the overwhelming problems in the centre which faced Pittsburgh. The historic colonial buildings, the Public Gardens and Boston Common gave it one of the most attractive centres in the country. But the suburbs were pulling strongly, especially after Route 128 was completed, and Scollay Square at the focus of downtown was an unsightly slum which would have embarrassed any city. But the authorities in Boston planned to renew much, much more than the few central eyesores. The city authorities had a grandiose plan to renew the whole of the Shawmut peninsula in four huge draconian stages. With the minimum of publicity, plans were drawn up for the West End, the North End, for downtown — to be renamed Government Centre — and for the South End. Only Beacon Hill, the Public Gardens, the Common and the exclusive residential area of Back Bay were to be preserved. The waterfront round Faneuil Hall was to be gentrified.

Probably most Bostonians would have applauded the renewal of Scollay Square. A picture of it in 1961 looked like Shude Hill in Manchester just after the war. The shabby, decaying brick buildings, shops and offices, none more than six storeys high, had been built piecemeal, without any plan, almost in disorder. Boston had few highrise buildings then, and none of distinction; certainly none with enough prestige to attract wealthy corporations.

The West End may have been nearly as seedy as Scollay Square, but very few of the inhabitants of the mixed area of businesses and homes, a typical transition zone, would have agreed to it being completely flattened. The largest group of residents in the West End was Jewish although, like most other immigrant communities in American cities, there were significant proportions of other nationalities and religions too. But as the West End scheme in Boston was one of the very first urban renewal schemes in America, they were taken very much by surprise and their community was destroyed. If the Shawmut peninsula is imagined as a clock face, then air photos of the time show a sector completely flattened from ten o'clock round to twelve o'clock. What makes the atrocity even worse on a monochrome photograph, is that the pie-slice of destruction stands out against the dark grey of the parts of the centre still standing and the black of the Charles river in stark deathly white.

Fine new high-rise buildings filled the West End of Boston in the 1960s. There arose hotels, stores, offices and a new major hospital. The authorities made much of the new facilities which had been provided, and they played down the increased revenue to the city. Most of all they tried to ignore what had happened to the Jewish and other residents of the old West End. This was in the days when urban renewal authorities did not have to compensate anyone for their loss, say of a business, nor re-house those made homeless. They merely had to show that somewhere other accommodation did exist. The result for Boston of the successful completion of the first stage of its urban renewal was the addition of a new northwestern quadrant to the downtown area. The result for the people was the destruction of a tightly-knit community. Soon afterwards a sample was taken of the new locations of the people evicted from the West End. Instead of a close community in a small sector of innermost Boston, the survey showed the people had completely dispersed in all directions. Some of them ended up as much as nine miles to the south, the distance between small market towns in England, others were dispersed in every direction, and nowhere was there any longer a single Jewish community as a specific replacement for the West End.

It may have been of little comfort to those displaced and dispersed people, but what happened to the West End in Boston had a profound effect on the subsequent urban renewal schemes in America. What happened to the West Enders alerted people in other cities to what very soon might happen to them. As Jane Jacobs defined it, a neighbourhood became a group of people big enough to fight City Hall. The next area in Boston on the list for renewal was the Italian community of the North End. The air photos of the time show a compact area of closely crowded houses and apartments between the original docks on the bay and the Charles river flowing round the northern end of the Shawmut peninsula. North End proved to be a neighbourhood big enough to fight City Hall. One would like very much to know what the leaders of the Italian community said to Boston's city fathers after the removal of the West End. Whatever they said, it worked. At the time of writing the North End is still there.

Boston's urban renewal shows much more clearly than Pittsburgh's that the major building projects were intended not just to renew the old CBD but to enlarge it and the whole downtown area into something wider, higher and grander. Boston's urban renewal schemes obviously were intended to take in the inner residential areas of the West, North and South ends of the peninsula and incorporate them into a much larger downtown. It can be argued that this was a continuation of the natural growth of the CBD into the transition zone; but that old process operated under free-market mechanisms, and many of the renewal plans transformed that slow, piecemeal growth into one massive instantaneous pounce.

Urban renewal went upwards as well as outwards. In several cities one can now buy postcards showing the downtown skyline before and after urban renewal. In Boston's case the change is most dramatic. Before: no skyscrapers worth a mention, but the graceful spires of the colonial churches standing elegantly above the low rooflines of the old city. After: a skyscraper skyline to rival New York or Dallas; and that is very much to the point. The image says, in effect, don't locate your new corporate HQ in New York or Dallas, locate here in splendid, modern downtown Boston.

South End did not escape the bulldozer as the Italian North End did, but the black ghetto in the south did not suffer as much as the Jewish quarter in the west had done. This was largely thanks to the adverse publicity which put so many inner city residents all over America on the alert, and even on the offensive. They organised, resisted, and fought back, preventing some of the destruction. The final two parts of Boston's urban renewal plans were less controversial, at least on social grounds if not architectural. Witnessing the unbelievable changes in the appearance of central Boston in less than thirty years, one can fully appreciate Prince Charles's concern for central London. To many people, Bostonians and others alike, Government Centre is an architectural success. Unlike the tall skyscrapers of the CBD, the administrative buildings which make Scollay Square a distant, tiny, unpleasant memory are massive rather than high. Moreover, they are set in and round such wide, attractive open spaces that they have become a tourist attraction as well as a working centre. City Hall, by the Japanese–American architect E.M.

Pei, may horrify some observers, but like the Beaubourg in Paris it is one of those complete contrasts with its surroundings which works very well and attracts many people just to be in interesting and pleasant surroundings.

The urban renewal transformed the old, small and unattractive business area of Boston in 1950 into a Central City as modern in its new buildings and as attractive in its historic preservations as any in America. Beacon Hill and Back Bay seem to have changed very little. The old docks of the waterfront on the eastern edge of Shawmut have been turned into the inevitable precinct of boutiques, restaurants and pavement entertainers. With the old store and meeting house of Faneuil Hall restored as the centrepiece, this works as well as dozens elsewhere in other renewed cities.

Unusual in Boston, however, is the emergence of a second, separate business district. Paris has the centre and La Défense, London has the City and Canary Wharf, New York has Downtown and Midtown. Boston now has the original CBD with tall new skyscrapers towering round Faneuil Hall, and it also has a linear cluster of tall skyscraper office buildings along the spine of the isthmus joining Shawmut to the mainland. Here is a score of major buildings and famous names, including the headquarters of the Prudential, and of the Christian Science movement. There is also yet another John Hancock building which, because all the glass cladding blew off in high winds when it was first erected, had to be boarded up for a time until the problem was solved, so getting its nickname of the Plywood Hilton. Anyone walking around central Boston now, when all the social upheaval is becoming forgotten, would probably judge the urban renewal a success. Some of the colonial buildings are overpowered by skyscrapers in narrow streets and the docks are fakes, but most of the centre is attractive, very busy, and apparently working. But judged on the essential criterion of whether all that upheaval and effort achieved the aim of maintaining the city's finances, then that urban renewal failed. In 1981 Boston, like New York in 1975, was on the edge of becoming bankrupt.

Urban renewal activity reached its peak in the 1960s. Many, but not all, of the largest American cities put schemes into operation, as did many small- and medium-sized towns where urban renewal was not vital in the sense of there being a need to attract business back into the town. Just as small cities with plenty of space had built a handful of small skyscrapers for speculation and prestige, so a number of smaller places launched elaborate renewal schemes — as far as one can judge mainly because that was the thing to be seen to be doing at the time. Places like New Haven Connecticut and Hartford with its Constitution Plaza are examples of this.

At the other end of the scale were Chicago and New York which, measured by the sums of money spent, and the numbers of structures renewed, had by far the most ambitious renewal schemes. But whereas one can see the results very clearly in the places mentioned above, it is very difficult to get an idea of how much was done in Chicago and New York just by looking about the streets. Some parts of Pittsburgh's renewal are on the valley sides, but the Golden Triangle presents the visible result in a compact area. One can easily walk round the renewed areas of Boston. When New Haven got its glass boxes, it lost only three or four short streets, however interesting they may have been. Hartford from a distance did look a mess huddling by the old bridge and Constitution Plaza looks much better, although the small area, accessible on foot before, now demands a car. But in the cases of Chicago and New York, however much was spent, those cities are so huge, and the various buildings and other structures are so scattered, that there is relatively little visual impact for two decades of great expense and effort.

This would not necessarily mean that the urban renewal in those two cities was a failure, providing it kept wealth-producing activities and people in the city and/or brought others back in. But there is little evidence that it did this. At most it may have delayed the crisis — in New York's case until summer 1975. In Chicago the situation was not as serious because the city receives financial help from Cook County and the state of Illinois. During the period of Chicago's urban renewal the Loop got many new buildings, including the Sears Tower, and skyscrapers were built both north and west of the river, enlarging the downtown area. But the fact is that the commercial buildings in downtown Chicago have been rebuilt several times without any special pressure from urban renewal schemes. Photographs from each decade show a series of ever-changing Chicago skylines. In contrast, apart from the crude gesture of the World Trade Center, one has to seek out the parts of Manhattan which have been renewed, like Times Square, and only at the Lincoln Centre is the result visually impressive.

Many people who find it hard to accept that urban renewal was the Federal Bulldozer, that it was purely financial and commercial in motivation and not a slum re-housing scheme, point to Chicago. Within that city's limits are several clusters of blocks of high-rise apartments with pretty names. These are cited as evidence that urban renewal in America was driven by social rather than commercial pressures. If one looks at photographs of inner-city neighbourhoods of Chicago in the 1940s, under the smog one sees narrow streets with power lines strung up on wooden poles, an oldish car or two parked here and there. The wooden two- and three-storey houses are dilapidated and subdivided into flats and single rooms, sometimes for a whole family. The evidence is the many staircases and flights of steps built on to the outsides of the original villas, which had filtered down to the blue-collar workers, to immigrants and to black people. The factories, warehouses and railway lines complete the picture of the slum.

Then visit, or look at pictures of Prairie Shores, Lincoln Park, Hyde Park near the university, Federal Street and Carl Sandburg 'Village'. The architecture and plan varies from one to the other, according to what the architect visualised for his prestige development, but the wide roads, service streets, underground car-parks, trees and parks present a most dramatic contrast with what existed there before. Were these double-glazed, centrally heated, air-conditioned, doorman-guarded service apartments intended for the immigrants and the black people *at the time they were built* under the urban renewal scheme? Some of the buildings are filtering down to those people now, as these 'villages' are in fact islands in the sea of slums in the inner city which were never renewed. But the intention, perhaps more of a hope, is clear: to get middle-income people back into an area close to the CBD where their local taxes would go to the city.

In most cities with urban renewal schemes, slums were demolished. The renewal concentrated on the downtown areas which had to be made new, higher, wider, more prestigious, attractive and, above all, accessible. As more and more of the executives lived in the suburbs, making the new downtown accessible meant, above all, making it accessible to the car. A few cities constructed underground railways or monorails, but the great majority cut motorways in and out of the centre. This was not done in any half-hearted fashion. Giving the suburbs access to downtown meant at least four lanes in each direction and service roads on each side of these urban motorways. With ten car lanes and the attendant hard shoulders, verges and fences these urban motorways cut giant swathes through the inner residential areas. The motorist getting into a ready-heated car in winter inside the suburban garage, driving downtown insulated from the slums and ghettos, driving into the named space in the basement parking lot then taking the express elevator to his or her skyscraper office never had to know how many houses, apartments and rooms had to be destroyed to enable such a daily journey to be made.

In total this may well have exceeded the destruction in the down-town area during its enlargement because few people lived there anyway. Now, every major city in the United States has its wide motorways slicing into the Central City. Moreover, most of those Central Cities are now completely surrounded by complexes of inner ring-roads, flyovers and interchanges and are effectively walled off from the outer residential areas for pedestrians. Nowadays the poorest people live on the other side of the inner ring of urban motorways rather than the other side of the tracks. Los Angeles is the extreme, with some 25% of its total surface covered by streets and freeways. Chicago is one of the most dramatic, where the inner ends of three expressways reach the Loop at one massive interchange with an inner ring-road. The total amount of space needed for these radial and ring-roads and their cloverleaf interchanges has resulted in the destruction of large proportions of the older, poorer, inner residential areas, while what has been built has not re-housed anyone. Rather, the massive motorways effectively seal off the slums from the eyes of business people and tourists alike in the city centre.

Philadelphia hid something else in a different way. As the railways leading into the city termini became obsolescent, and as more space was needed for prestigious office buildings, skyscrapers were built over the railway tracks in the 1960s. Many other cities have done the same thing since. The scheme which hid derelict lines and renewed and extended the CBD garnered some approval for Philadelphia, but another aspect of its urban renewal effort gained the city much notoriety. In *Scientific American* for September 1965, an issue devoted to cities, there are three maps of Philadelphia printed side by side. One shows where average family income was below $4,720. These were the poorest areas in the city, blocks immediately north, west and south of the CBD. The second map shows where black people exceeded 80% of the residential population. The third shows the areas marked out for urban renewal by destruction of the homes and the building of commercial property. Except in the small southern area, the three maps are identical.

In Philadelphia and in many other cities black people, and many white people too, believed that urban renewal schemes were an excuse to get the black people out of the inner-city areas. To the phrases Urban Renewal and the Federal Bulldozer was added the phrase Negro Removal. The motive and the effect need to be separated. The motive was to attract money back into the city. But as the renewal schemes involved expanding the downtown area outwards as well as upwards, the very poorest residents, including a high proportion of black people, were evicted because they were the ones who lived in the oldest, cheapest, innermost residential areas. The motive was money but the effect was, in fact, to remove a high proportion of black people from the zone immediately next to downtown.

In Britain, up to 1980 when policy changed, about 30% of all residential property was in the form of subsidised council housing, houses, bungalows and flats. In the United States the nearest equivalent, which is called public housing, has never amounted to much more than 2% of the total housing stock. This varies from city to city, well-known examples being the Pruitt-Igoe blocks in St Louis and the Knickerbocker Village and the Jacob Riis Houses on the Lower East Side of Manhattan. In the 1950s, in fact, Philadelphia built more than its fair proportion of public housing, but the rest of its record helps to emphasise that urban renewal was for industrial and commercial wealth-producing purposes. Of all Philadelphia's land cleared for urban renewal, 15% was used for public housing, 28% for houses for sale, 42% for industry, 12% for private institutions and commerce, and 3% for public institutions. As in Chicago the private housing was designed for the well-heeled upper middle class. As in Boston and Baltimore, historic parts of the city were gentrified in addition to the work mentioned above. Philadelphia is perhaps unusual in the amount of manufacturing the authorities wanted within the city limits.

In Philadelphia black people formed 67% of those evicted to clear the land for renewal. When they did find new accommodation entirely by their own efforts their average rents had increased from $41 to $71, which was a rise of between 14% and 20% of their average income. Only 14% of the people evicted managed to obtain public housing.

Over the years and up to 1976, the bicentenary of the Declaration of Independence, a number of photographs has been taken from almost the same point in Philadelphia. The oldest photo of this series must have been taken from one of the first high-rise buildings in the city centre. It is a picture looking westwards down over Independence Hall out across the inner-city end of the black ghetto. Just across the street behind Independence Hall start the low, old, brick houses, shops, schools, churches and workshops of a crowded residential high-density neighbourhood. A later picture, taken from almost the same spot, shows a neat little garden behind the Hall where one residential block has been cleared away between the Hall and the receding ghetto. A third, from a different viewpoint, and perhaps a low, oblique aerial photo, shows that two or three more residential blocks have been cleared away. By that time one of the blocks was being used for a car-park beyond the garden. By the time we queued one day in 1975 to see the Liberty Bell in the eighteenth-century brick building it was completely overshadowed by the skyscrapers of the CBD. Looking westward I could not see any residential property at all. When people queued in their thousands the following year to celebrate the anniversary they would have seen only gardens and car-parks where the ghetto used to be. Recent photographs show just how much of the black neighbourhood has gone. From such examples one can understand why black people believe that the real motive was their removal.

In 1970 the laws relating to urban renewal were modified. From that year onwards compensation had to be paid to residents evicted and businesses adversely affected. This was in response to the increasingly effective lobbying which had developed since the surprise had been sprung on the unsuspecting West End of Boston. However, the major thrust of urban renewal had largely run its course by 1970 and, in the precise sense that it is described here, urban renewal officially came to an end in 1975.

Judging by the fact that so many of the largest American cities came to the brink of bankruptcy in the late 1970s and during the 1980s, urban renewal was a failure in all but a handful of cases. But an added problem was that as more and more of the cities embarked on urban renewal schemes, many of which could have been predicted not to achieve financial renewal, other cities had to join in just in order to keep up with the competition to attract businesses. They had to run in order not to be left way behind. At least the efforts may have delayed the bankruptcies in some cases, but in others the massive expenditures may well have hastened the inevitable reckoning, a case of swings and roundabouts.

So, since 1975, the financial problems have remained, or have become worse; but urban renewal as the specific remedy has been abandoned. Piecemeal renewal of buildings and small areas has continued, of course, just as it did before 1950 and as it does in other countries. What happened in the quarter-century between 1950 and 1975 was that most of the big cities in the USA achieved brand new Central Business Districts full of higher, more modern skyscrapers — many of them white elephants. They appear to be CBDs grander than would have developed under a more normal course of events, but they still failed to prevent enough of the loss to the suburbs to continue as vital centres.

Since 1975 four other types of remedy have been recommended for Central City financial problems. One, not surprisingly, is for the cities to cut expenditure, to match what they spend to what they raise in revenue. This would simply continue the decline which started with suburbanisation, but to many informed observers this would be a perfectly acceptable outcome of a free-market system.

A second suggested remedy has been that of boundary re-organisation. In the extreme case this would be for the city limits to be redrawn outside the built-up-area, to include all the people and wealth-creating activities within one political unit, as Toronto did in Canada. In practice this has proved to be all but impossible.

Moreover, it has been argued that even if cities could widen their boundaries, there would be nothing to guarantee that the middle-income and the rich would necessarily vote to redistribute any more of the wealth to the poor or to support the obsolescent centres.

A third proposal was called Gilding the Ghetto. The details of what was proposed for the inner-city black ghettos, immigrant quarters and blue-collar areas would sound familiar to residents of inner-city areas in Britain: job training, cheap housing and anti-poverty programmes were urged. But it was never agreed who should pay for all these, it was never clear where the jobs would come from when the training was completed so, like all such hare-brained ideas, Gilding the Ghetto was quickly forgotten.

The fourth splendid idea was to open up the suburbs. The trouble here was that the suburbs had always been open anyway. The suburbs had always been open to those who could afford to live there, but most of those living in the Central City hadn't got the money. So, the implicit logic of this idea was that in order for people to move into the suburbs to make more money, they would have to stay in the city first to make enough money so they could afford to move into the suburbs to share in the prosperity there. So many of the Utopian ideas are impracticable and, on close scrutiny, show that the proponents have not thought through the implications and provided the necessary cash and organisation for the ideas to have even a faint chance of succeeding.

Silly as the fourth idea was, it emphasises a key point, that people can confuse the aims. Was the aim to help the city, or to help the people? If help is available for the city and the people in it, then the Central City remains solvent and viable. But if the help simply allows all the people to move into the suburbs, presumably the Central City ends up as a ghost town, like the old mining towns of the Rocky Mountains. In time, of course, following this idea to its logical conclusion, everyone would be in the suburbs, the very poor people would be there as well as all the others, and everyone and every business would again be within the same administrative unit. Then the same reservations would apply as in the case of boundary re-organisation. The people would be arguing still about redistribution of wealth to the distant thunder of World Trade Centers, Sears Towers, Bankamerica Buildings and assorted John Hancock Buildings crashing to the ground in the abandoned old city centres.

During the Johnson era the administration tried the Model Cities Program. The idea was to improve housing, education and health in the worst slums of the 150 largest cities of the USA. This formed part of LBJ's plans for his 'Great Society'. It and they failed partly because federal funds were diverted to the escalating Vietnam War, but mainly because there was no long-term private funding. Johnson, however, blamed the failure on the apathy of the black people.

When Richard Milhous Nixon reached the White House, policy on cities, as on so many other things, reversed completely. Nixon's idea was New Federalism, which was *1984*-type Newspeak for less government and less cash. Just as Nixon cut financial help to farmers, he cut it to the cities too. It was Nixon, too, who in effect ended federal help for urban renewal, although it came into effect the year after he resigned as the result of Watergate. Nixon also ended public housing, substituting instead housing subsidies for residents in Central Cities in cases where the rent amounted to more than 25% of income. This became known, from the part of the act in which it appeared, as Section Eight Housing.

Johnson was a Democrat, Nixon a Republican, so it was no surprise that Nixon reversed Johnson's policy and aggravated cities' financial distress. The greater surprise was that Jimmy Carter, a Democrat, continued Nixon's harsh policy unchanged, although under the spurious new name of Community Development. It is Carter's presidency in particular which emphasises that the majority of the American electorate, now living in suburban areas, had no great concern for the decaying, bankrupt Central Cities. Carter and the electorate saw no reason and no political imperative to help them out. Carter introduced UDAGS, Urban Development Action Grants. These were intended to help overcome obstacles in the way of private developers, but few American developers were interested in the central areas any more. Foreign developers continued to invest in places like New York, where skyscrapers were still being built on Manhattan until the mid 1980s. One has to presume that these British, European and particularly Japanese developers did not fully understand the decline at the time; or else did not care.

Carter was followed by twelve years of Republican rule during which the identical policies of New Federalism/Community Development were continued in a very low-key style. No president wants the extreme political embarrassment of a major city going bankrupt during his administration, as Gerald Ford faced with New York in 1975. Equally, no president wants to be seen diverting federal funds to cities with deceptively prosperous skylines when money is needed for so many other purposes. Moreover, none wants to appear to be giving way to moral blackmail, which is what many suburban voters believe threats of cities going bankrupt to be. As a result, a tightrope-balancing act has been practised for nearly two decades, giving cities just enough to stave off bankruptcy, but no more. The different names of the different schemes under different presidents are neither here nor there. Unfortunately the tightrope act has wobbled more often than it has held steady, and at the time of writing most Central Cities are still teetering on the edge of financial collapse. Urban renewal prolonged their lives for a time, but did not bring immortality.

5

SPECIAL CASES:
TORONTO; LOS ANGELES; NEW YORK

A. TORONTO — A DIFFERENT SOLUTION

This book is about the large cities in the United States of America, but several cities in Canada are very similar. Toronto in particular shows both similar characteristics and one solution to some of the problems already discussed, and as such is relevant to the theme. Toronto is smaller than the very large American cities, has developed in a slightly different economic, social and political environment, but the similarities outweigh the differences, which are no greater, say, than those between any two large cities within the United States.

Like the American cities being examined, with the exception of Los Angeles, Toronto started as a port, on the northern shore of Lake Ontario. While more slowly, and on a smaller scale than in the USA, Toronto developed as a concentrated city clustering around the docks and the commercial centre. It continued to develop as one of the main manufacturing centres of Canada, and as the retail, wholesale and business centre for the Lakes Peninsula of Ontario, a similar location and set of functions to Cleveland, Detroit and Chicago on the other side of the Great Lakes. With very little competition in that part of Canada, Toronto grew as a concentrated city, the focus of routes in the Lakes Peninsula, and its CBD the focus of all routes in the built-up-area. While most of the features of the concentrated city described in Chapter One developed, they tended to be on a modest scale and somewhat later than on the other side of the lakes. Nevertheless, immigrant peoples started to move into the inner city, Anglo-Canadians started to move to the suburbs, and the skyscrapers in the Yonge Street area got taller and taller.

By the 1960s there were large communities of Italians, Jews, Hungarians, Germans, Ukrainians, Poles, Chinese, Greeks, Portuguese, Indians, West Indians and French Canadians. With the more obvious British legacy, Royal Canadian Mounted Police in the streets and the distinctive Canadian accent, one could not entirely mistake where one is. However, the skyscrapers, the congestion, the adverts and the polyglot population, the variety of 'European' restaurants all contribute to the feel of a big American city. Hardly surprising, therefore, with its similar origin, similar type of location, the same types of factors producing the same type of growth and form, that Toronto developed the same set of problems seen in the American city. The congestion, traffic jams, pollution, inner-city decay, loss of industry and people to the suburbs and the lack of revenue were less publicised versions of those in New York. Similarly, there was the need for a plan for the whole built-up-area.

Toronto started in York County, and the suburbs grew northwards to join up with the towns of North York and much more extensively east and west into Scarborough, Etobicoke, and Mississauga. The net result, as in the States, was a declining central city, stretching over many administrative units, a need to coordinate certain activities over the whole of greater Toronto, plus a need for revenue in the original city. The point here is that, unlike in America, Toronto and the Provincial Government did something about it.

By the time things came to a head, greater Toronto spread over four counties:

- York
- Peel
- Halton
- Durham

and in addition to the Central City itself, covered ten other townships with their own separate administrations. These were:

- The City of Toronto
- Etobicoke
- North York
- Scarborough
- East York
- Leaside
- Forest Hill
- Swansea
- Mimico

- New Toronto
- Long Branch.

In 1954 Toronto started to do what has been advocated as one of the possible solutions for American urban problems: widening the administrative area to include the suburbs and the wealth-producing areas. In 1954 the Municipality was created and then in 1967, with the help of the Government of Ontario, Metropolitan Toronto came into being covering, in effect, the southern two-thirds of York County. The Metropolitan area joined Toronto, North York, East York, Scarborough and Etobicoke (which include the townships listed above) into one administrative unit, Metro Toronto, with revenue from the whole area and certain defined responsibilities throughout that area. These are:

- policing
- emergency services
- water supply
- sewage disposal
- housing
- welfare
- libraries
- parks
- planning
- transport.

This list is, of course, familiar. It pops up again and again when American urban sprawl is being analysed. The emergency services and the police needed to be coordinated, as in New York and other cities, in case inner-city problems got out of hand. Water supply, sewage and refuse disposal, together with a need for a rationalised transport system have been at the centre of American urban problems. The other five items on the list — planning, welfare, housing, libraries and parks — may be cosmetic, because the riots in Miami and Los Angeles have emphasised that little has been done in the States since the 1960s, but, to be fair, in Canada these may well be taken more seriously, just as has the boundary re-organisation itself. So it could be said that Toronto shows the way. Moving about the city in 1986 I certainly thought so then. But the creation of Metropolitan Toronto has not addressed all the problems and is not without its critics.

The Metro authority has worked with the Government of Ontario to create a coordinated transport system for the whole BUA. A subway system was initiated, with the first line along Yonge Street, in 1954. Since then expansion has been slow, with a total of six lines. The nomenclature of limited access roads is confusing; while Toronto calls its motorways Expressways, they are in fact free, like the Freeways in Los Angeles, but the network is spare. Queen Elizabeth Way, Don Valley Parkway and Gardiner Expressway were hailed as great advances in their time, but that time of motorway building is already over. In addition there are the modishly named GO-Trains, but this only means Government of Ontario suburban lines and they branch in only four directions to spread out into a spindly lattice in the suburbs.

The plans for a proposed Spadina motorway were successfully opposed and defeated by residents who would have been adversely affected. A subway line may be built instead. Surprisingly, especially considering the slow development of coordinated transport, Metro Toronto was considered too small an area for the planning of an effective network. Consequently, by the 1970s the Metropolitan Toronto Planning area was created. This is about three times the size of Metro Toronto, includes 20 municipal authorities in an area of 1,900 square kilometres, and is responsible for roads, buses, trams and subways but not, apparently, trains, GO or otherwise.

The final criticism is that however dramatic the creation of a single unit — Metropolitan Toronto — may have been, by the 1970s it was already too small. Just as the Bureau of the Census in the USA can lump together all the administrative units in one continuously built-up-area for purposes of gathering and presenting data, even if the units do not co-operate on the ground, the Canadian Census now recognises that greater Toronto spreads well beyond the Metro area. The BUA now includes:

In Peel County
● Streetsville
● Toronto Gore
● Mississauga
● Brampton
● Port Credit

In York County
● Vaughan
● Woodbridge
● Markham
● Richmond Hill
● Stouffville

In Durham County
- Pickering
- Ajax

In Halton County
- As yet unincorporated suburbs.

Many observers point to Toronto as the model for American cities. Toronto certainly made an effort along the right lines, faced the problem and widened its boundaries dramatically. Since the 1970s, however, the slow development of the single transport network and the continued spillage of the suburbs beyond the city's control serve to demonstrate how intractable the problems are. They show just how much political will and continued massive effort would be needed to solve the problems in the United States. More, they show that a continually changing situation needs a readily changeable organisation to be able to cope with new situations, both unforeseen and foreseen.

B. LOS ANGELES — A DIFFERENT ORIGIN

In a work which makes many general statements about the American city, Los Angeles must be singled out as the major exception. This is not just because it is different in many ways, but also because so many people believe it is the same kind of urban system as described in Chapters One and Two, and use it erroneously as an example of an extreme case of the others. Above all, there is one persistently repeated belief about Los Angeles which is completely wrong, and there are two often-repeated quotations which may turn out to be true. The first quotation surfaced in the 1920s and is attributed to far too many different people to mention. The quotation is: 'Los Angeles is six (sixteen, sixty, six hundred) suburbs in search of a city (or centre).' There is just enough in this for it to be worth repeating, but the quotation originated at the time when a new English translation had been made of Pirandello's *Six Characters in Search of an Author*, so it is neither an original idea, nor description of LA.

The second quotation has also been attributed to many people; I first heard it in the 1960s attributed to Adlai Stevenson, who was reputed to have looked at Los Angeles and said, 'I have seen the future, and it doesn't work.' Adlai and the thousand others who claim the quote may be right. But when one reads in books, magazines and learned journal articles that the dispersed pattern of Los Angeles, so many centres without one focal point, is the creation of the motor car, one is reading a gross inaccuracy, an incompetent lie which too many

88

people who should know better actually believe, and which can prevent proper understanding of a very complex city.

Today the built-up urban area usually meant when referring to Los Angeles stretches some 50 miles north–south and 90 miles east–west. Greater Los Angeles covers an area equal to that from Bedford to Leatherhead and from Oxford to Canterbury. The lowland in which the city started is smaller than this, some 50 by 30 miles, and the urban area has spilled over the mountains northwards and eastwards.

This coastal area was first visited by Europeans when Cabrillo explored northwards from Mexico in 1542. It was over two hundred years later before some tiny settlement was given the name of Los Angeles, or, more correctly, El Pueblo de la Reina de los Angeles — The Town of the Queen of the Angels. More precisely still, a mission was added in 1771 and Los Angeles legally became a pueblo, a town, in 1781. In 1836, over half a century before the invention of the motor car, Los Angeles was made the capital of the Two Californias — California as we know it and the peninsula Baja California. But this was late in the day for Mexico and by 1848 Mexico had been conquered and upper California and the City of the Queen of the Angels became part of the United States of America.

The little town, unlike all others which were to become multi-millionaire US cities, was not a port. It was, and the original centre still is, some fourteen miles from the beach at Santa Monica and twenty miles from the port at Long Beach. This completely separate port was annexed later, resulting in the narrow corridor running southwards from the original city limits of Los Angeles to the south coast. However, railways were much more important in the growth and success of the newly acquired town. With some inducements and sharp dealing, the transcontinental railways were persuaded to move their western terminal southwards to Los Angeles rather than some place further north in California. Both places would then have had different histories. In any event, the railways arrived at the small town in 1876 and 1885, a town still unknown and insignificant compared to Chicago, New York, London and Paris, which was building the Eiffel Tower in preparation for the celebrations of 1889.

As they had done across the High Plains and across the inter-mountain plateaux, the railway companies surveyed and marked out the land they owned on each side of their tracks. From the main termini, five branch lines spread out across the Los Angeles plain to San Bernardino, Anaheim, Wilmington, Santa Monica and into the northern San Fernando Valley. The railway land was marked out into counties, townships, farmsteads and individual house plots, and massive advertising campaigns back east extolled the virtues of this fertile land in the sunshine and warmth of the Southwest. At one stage the rival railway companies were in such bitter competition to get people on to their land that the rail fare from Chicago to Los Angeles was 'just one silver dollar!'

The main group of people to respond to this temptation were Mid-western farmers and people from the very small towns of the Midwest. Until the Second World War, Los Angeles was really an outpost of the Midwest, the place the Oakies and others automatically made for during the Great Depression of the 1930s. Those Mid-westerners went to the Los Angeles plain for two things: to farm, and to live in brand-new detached wooden houses. The railway companies, and their cronies the developers and the water company, laid out the land accordingly, expecting the future farm produce to supply massive amounts of freight to ship back east at a good profit, by rail.

Subsequently the plan of Los Angeles as we know it was determined by the actions of three power groups in the late nineteenth and early twentieth centuries. Fertile the soil may have been, hot and bright the summers before the invention of smog, but there was no water. Nowadays the Los Angeles river is a dry concrete chute looking like a motorway cutting and the other 'streams' of the area are streams of sand. The railway companies put in the transport, the developers started the orange groves and chicken farms, and the politicians brought in the water. By thus putting in the key infrastructure, the boosters not only started one of the most massive migrations and city growths in history, but also, by laying out the rails, water supply and detached house lots between citrus groves and small farms, they gave Los Angeles basically the same form which it still has today. The other transport systems to operate in the nineteenth century were the horse trams providing local services in Los Angeles, Pasadena, Long Beach, Santa Monica and Beverly Hills. By the end of the century the pattern on this Southern Californian plain was that of the five rail-ways radiating from Los Angeles, which was no larger than any other of the settlements, and then each of a dozen scattered tiny towns in turn having its own radial horse tram network.

The next major development came with the arrival of Henry E Huntington who in 1902 initiated the Pacific Electric Railway as a gridiron system, both to link up the dozen or so small centres on the plain, and to provide access to all the then-empty areas in between. Huntington's Pacific Electric Railway was a standard-gauge rail system which ran on its own right of way in what was still largely open countryside, and then on central reservations down the main streets in the scattered small towns. The Big Red Cars of the gridiron Pacific Electric joined up what are now too often erroneously referred to as suburbs, but which were then the incorporated towns of southern California. In this way it set the transport pattern for Los Angeles in the 1900s which was to be duplicated by the freeways and cars forty years later.

The horse trams arrived in 1873 and went in 1897. The Big Red Cars appeared in 1902 and the last one ran in 1961. As the Pacific Electric Railway prospered and began to join up the parts of what was to become greater Los Angeles, each of the small towns got its own local system of trams, the Yellow Cars of the Los Angeles Railway Company. A pattern of five radial railways with buds of radial horse tram systems was replaced by a very dense gridiron network of trains and many local Yellow Tram systems. Melvin Urofsky claimed, 'LA citizens never wanted a cosmopolitan city. They wanted a gigantic collection of villages.' At this point in time cars were still in their unreliable experimental stage, but the plain had a very good hierarchy of railed transport systems.

At its maximum extent the Pacific Electric Company had 1,100 miles of standard-gauge track running on private rights of way over the Los Angeles plain. One hundred and fifty routes extended from the San Fernando Valley to Balboa, and from Santa Monica to out beyond Pomona. As late as 1945 the system of Big Red Cars, often with three or five cars in trains, carried 103,000,000 passengers. In the early days a local trip was 5 cents, a thirty-minute ride 15 cents, one hour 50 cents, and passengers could ride 100 miles along the coast for one dollar. The Big Red Cars served fifty separate towns in the area which is now completely built up to form greater Los Angeles. While the two county administrative units of Los Angeles County and Orange County, both on the plain, are the best-known, the fifty-odd towns served by the Pacific Electric railway are located in eight counties which now comprise the continuously built-up-area commonly referred to as Los Angeles. From west to east these are:

Santa Barbara	San Diego
Ventura	San Bernardino
Los Angeles	Riverside
Orange	Imperial.

Most recently, Inyo and Mono Counties to the northeast have been added to make up an informal metropolitan region. As with other American cities, one has to distinguish between such things as town, county and sometimes state with the same name, between administrative areas legally joined together and those merely lumped together

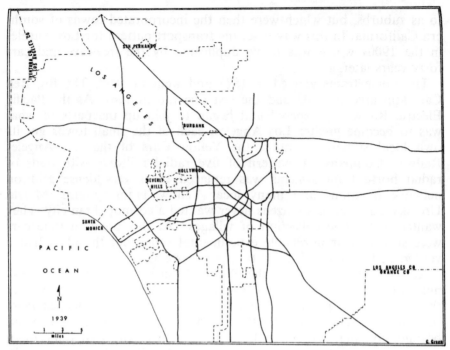

Fig 5.1a (above)

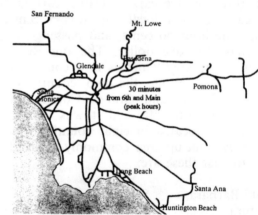

Fig 5.1b (right)

Figure 5.1 The Pattern of the Pacific Electric Railway compared with the Pattern of the Freeways in Los Angeles

5.1a 'The greatest electric railway system on earth' was the claim of the Pacific Electric, which in its heyday (1920s) covered 1,200 miles of track that laced the entire Los Angeles plain from shore to mountain.

Source: Editors of Sunset Books, *Los Angeles*, Lane Magazine & Book Co. Menlo Park, California, 1968, p. 42

5.1b Los Angeles Freeway Plan of 1939

Source: Warner, S.B. Jr., *The Urban Wilderness: The History of the American City*, Harper & Row, New York, 1972, p. 139.

92

for data purposes by the Census. Spreading over these are the Central City with its downtown and inner-city zones, then suburbia and exurbia beyond, the continuously built-up-area, and finally the daily urban system. In this respect, again Los Angeles is different from other large urban areas in America. The city has a boundary enclosing a tiny fraction of the whole BUA but normally Los Angeles functions administratively as a county, and much of the time it and the other counties work reasonably well together as if they were a metropolitan unit.

Even the city boundary of the relatively small Los Angeles enclosed other towns in the early days. These were:

Los Angeles
Venice
Van Nuys
Hollywood
San Pedro
Wilmington.

This last town is at the southern end of the narrow corridor linking LA to the sea and its come-lately harbour. Outside the city limits, but within the county of Los Angeles were:

Long Beach
Pasadena
Santa Monica
Beverly Hills.

Within Los Angeles County alone, 100 towns were laid out by the railway promoters after 1880 and of these 40 were actually successful, thrived, and became names of neighbourhoods in greater Los Angeles. A similar process, but with fewer towns, went on in the other counties.

For the convenience of the Bureau of the Census, from 1960 onwards cities in the area, *de facto* part of greater Los Angeles, were grouped into MSAs for the handling and presentation of data. These are:

Los Angeles–Long Beach
Ventura
Anaheim
San Bernardino.

But these names and combinations do not obscure the facts: first, that the whole area operates as one urban system much better than any other city in the United States — certainly much better than the first megalopolis, Boswash. And second, that greater Los Angeles started simultaneously from literally a hundred tiny town centres established by the railway boosters in the last quarter of the nineteenth century. Paradoxically, nowhere can it be seen more clearly that the Pacific Electric Railway, and not the automobile, created the form of Los Angeles than in the actual development of the freeways. In the 1930s an advisory board was established to consider the provision of urban motorways. That the town of Los Angeles was neither the focus, the CBD, nor the dominant centre in the region is evidenced by the fact that all the counties had members on the board. As Sam Bass Warner Jr. put it, membership, from the start, was 'multi-city and multi-county'.

By 1933 a plan had been prepared and three things became clear. First, that the motorways would cover the whole built-up area. Second, that they would not be focused on a single centre. Third, the motorways, or freeways as they became, would form a rough grid pattern over the whole region. This grid pattern is uncannily like the rail pattern for the Big Red Cars, which should be no surprise as the plan was for them to serve the same areas and the same people as the Cars had been doing. The pattern of freeways, the first opened in 1940, is so like the Pacific Electric Railway network started in 1902 that some writers on the subject have printed maps of railways and freeways side by side to emphasise the fact. New as Los Angeles may be, especially in contrast with old European cities, it is still not the product of the motor car. It has been much modified by provisions for the car, but its essential form was established by rail networks before the car became the dominant form of transport. Los Angeles was the city of the urban railway, seen in so many early silent movies shot out on the streets, sometimes just in the background, often with some of the Big Red Cars rushing down on some hapless Buster Keaton, Stan Laurel or Fatty Arbuckle stranded in a stalled car on the level-crossing.

Many of the ideas for the motorways in the 1930s were clear-headed and far-sighted. The gridiron pattern would minimise congestion at one focal point. Moreover, it would serve all of the down-towns in the plain and the valleys, providing the kind of transport system for the whole BUA which other MSAs only dream about. The motorways would be free, would have limited access, would have flyovers (no grade crossings) and would be capable of joining up with the federal Interstate system, which in the event had to be postponed until after the war.

Another far-sighted idea which did not come into being was to use the space over the freeways. The planners realised that a very large proportion of the land would be taken up by roads in contrast with the rail rights of way. Including streets and freeways, 25% of the surface of greater LA is now paved. They planned to have 'motorway buildings' over the freeways to use the space efficiently and profitably, much as Philadelphia built over its railways. Many of the motorway buildings would have been car-parks.

The Second World War slowed down the building of the early freeways and only the first, the Pasadena Freeway, was completed before the war and opened in 1940. With hindsight, one can say that with cheap mass-produced cars pouring out of Detroit, much more cheaply than out of British and European factories, and with half a dozen counties working together to provide free urban motorways, the writing was on the wall for public transport. But with cars not really beginning to take over Los Angeles until well into the 1950s, for two-thirds of its history to date Los Angeles was well served by its Big Red Cars and Yellow Trams. Both had gone by 1963 and Ray Bradbury, the fantasy author, said that it would take a Walt Disney to build and run again a Los Angeles public transport system which people would *want* to ride in. I don't think even Walt could have done it now.

There are several reasons why the small town of Los Angeles proper did not dominate the whole region with one old-fashioned downtown, did not become the industrial centre, and did not, until recently, build skyscrapers like the concentrated cities. In spite of the advantage of having the transcontinental rail termini, El Pueblo Grande did not have a port, and the various railways and tramways simultaneously gave many other towns on the plain almost equal advantage. People and manufacturing were as likely to locate in Santa Monica, Anaheim, and Long Beach as in Los Angeles. Moreover, there was never the kind of competition for space in the centre of Los Angeles which could result in a shortage of land, a shortage of premium sites, rising prices, and therefore an economic motive to build skyscrapers. The ban on buildings higher than 150 feet because of the danger of earthquakes was no practical restriction to development in such a low-density area with such good transport.

When the height restriction was lifted in 1957 there was no rush to build powered by long pent-up forces. In the last thirty years a cluster of skyscrapers has been built just north and east of the original centre of El Pueblo de la Reina de Los Angeles, but the forces are those of civic pride, desire for prestige, a need to build the kind of skyline which identifies San Francisco, Chicago and New York, a skyline which poor LA never had in the decades earlier this century when such a thing made economic sense. One sees the glass tubes and boxes of the new high-rise centre of Los Angeles frequently on the TV soaps transmitted all over the world, but few people realise or care that most of the buildings are speculative white elephants half-empty, or civic buildings like the library, theatre and opera house, although they look like commercial megastructures.

Anyone visiting Los Angeles for the first time in the 1990s might think that it originated and developed in exactly the same way as other huge American cities. The cluster of skyscrapers downtown, the inner-city slums and immigrant areas such as the Barrio and Watts, the many freeways and the low-density, widely sprawling 'suburbs' might well convince the uninformed that Los Angeles originated and developed like Chicago, but has just gone further with the process of suburbanisation and complete dependence on the car. If that were true, Adlai Stevenson would probably have been right.

But the history of the area reveals that what we see as a city now, began from over a hundred small points virtually simultaneously, and, paradoxically in the light of so many assertions that LA was created by the car, its form was created by the best system of public transport seen anywhere in America — or, at the time, perhaps in the world. It is the car which has not been able to cope with that. That an old-fashioned, concentrated-city-type skyscraper downtown has been created by non-economic forces in the last quarter of this century is a retrograde step. It creates congestion where none need have occurred. The suburbs may not have been in search of a centre, and no longer need a centre, but in order for Los Angeles to look as if it were like other cities, they recently got one.

By the mid 1990s the collapse of the USSR was resulting in massive job losses in Los Angeles' aerospace and missile industries. At the peak, 540,000 people were employed in these activities. 70,000 had gone and more were to follow in firms like Lockheed, McDonnell Douglas, Hughes, Rockwell and Northrop, and the fact became an issue in the 1993 mayoral election campaigns. At the same time, targets had been set to try to deal with both the city's car gridlock and the environmental pollution. These targets are:

- From 1998 40,000 extra zero-emission vehicles annually in LA to replace vehicles causing pollution.
- From 2000 AD 200,000 extra zero-emission vehicles annually.
- By 2020 6,000 zero-emission buses and 300 magnet-levitated trains or rail-cars.

As a result bodies such as the air quality authority, electricity generators, the government nuclear weapons laboratory, local government bodies, General Motors, IBM, Lockheed and Hughes have co-operated to form CALSTART, an organisation to carry out experiments, research and development into electric cars, electric buses, and something called an electric commuter vehicle. One idea, clearly, is for zero-emission vehicles to meet the future targets, running on the roads and freeways. But the major idea, one which is giving hope for massive employment in the future and exports to many other countries, is for a complete, integrated electric high-speed rail system for the whole of Southern California. To paraphrase the *Guardian*, 'That LA, a city [now] based on private cars, driven by worshippers of the individual entrepreneur, is now debating what amounts to an industrial policy of manufacturing mass transport, is itself a remarkable sign of changing times.' Perhaps CALSTART will produce big-red mag-lev zero-emission electric commuter vehicles. Henry E Huntington must be wearing a very big smile in his grave.

C. NEW YORK — A BIGGER PROBLEM

New York requires some extra consideration, not just because it was the first city in the 1970s to warn of impending bankruptcy, but also because of the special factors which combined with those affecting other cities to make New York a special case. This difference tempted many to blame New York, as if its difficulties were unique, and to close their eyes to similar difficulties in other cities where they were also systemic, though on a smaller scale and slightly later in coming to a head.

Put as simply as possible, a city has two major types of expenditure, and two normal ways of raising money. Much expenditure is regular and predictable: paying the wages and salaries of employees, civil servants, police, teachers, garbage collectors etc., and maintaining the infrastructure, roads, bridges, sewers, parks and the like. The other expenditure comes at irregular intervals for different amounts: to build a new bridge, airport or hospital; or to meet contingencies such as dealing with flood, hurricane or earthquake damage. The regular expenses are normally paid out of regular income: rates, poll tax, sales tax, local tax, whatever it may be called, and over the year the budget should balance. For special, unusual and one-off expenses, loans are usually raised, paying interest over a fixed term. When these large amounts are borrowed, most prudent city officials ensure that interest, capital repayments and also the normal annual regular expenses can be paid for out of income. In the past, cities, like national governments, were regarded as low-risk investments and could raise loans easily. But if interest, capital repayments and regular expenses can

97

not, in the event, be honoured, then the individual, the firm, or even the city may go bankrupt.

New York started to get into financial difficulties in exactly the same way as the other large American cities. The middle-income, local tax-paying middle class moved out of the city to the suburbs. Retail functions moved out, following their market, and both business rents and sales taxes were lost to the city. Then industry and commerce moved out, often because their taxes were increased to cover the falling revenue from other sources and so they were attracted by the lower costs and taxes in outlying areas. This would have been bad enough with the city still having to maintain the infrastructure of one of the world's largest and most advanced urban centres, but New York also accumulated extra expenses at the same time as it lost revenue. From the Second World War onwards black people, the rural poor, increasingly redundant during the 1950s and 1960s, plus the renewed waves of immigrants all moved into the cheap, vacated premises in the inner city. As retail, wholesale, industrial, commercial, administrative and domestic jobs moved out, a larger and larger proportion of these people became unemployed and a charge on the city.

The problem was aggravated by a process of circular and cumulative causation. As revenue decreased and the demands of an unemployed population increased, less was spent on the infrastructure; maintenance and renewal were postponed. The police force became ever more stretched as crime got out of hand, the streets, sewers, water supply, public transport, schools and hospitals ever more dilapidated. Even tourists usually preoccupied with the Empire State Building, the Statue of Liberty, Fifth Avenue and Radio City began to notice. But the residents noticed much more. More of the well-heeled left the city. Thus there was less city income, so the infrastructure decayed even more, so more local ratepayers who could do so got out, so the infrastructure continued to deteriorate, so more people and businesses left, so there was even less money... Then the New York authorities did a wonderful thing. They further raised local taxes on retail and manufacturing businesses, to get the infrastructure back into shape. They seemed surprised when the net result was that many of the remaining companies at last made for the hills.

However, New York's financial problems did come to a head earlier, and in a more dramatic fashion than those of any other city. In the spring of 1975 the Mayor had to announce that, if it did not receive immediate help, New York would go bankrupt in the middle of the year. There were many reasons for this historic first, among them: the fact that New York is one of the oldest American cities,

98

with an old infrastructure; that it is one of the largest cities; that it was among the first to see the start of the flight to the suburbs; that it had unique features and functions not found in other American cities; and also that the administration was alleged to be incompetent and possibly corrupt. It was this last characteristic which anaesthetised what otherwise would have been justified alarm that many other cities were in similar financial danger. The federal authorities and most people in America *wanted* New York to be both unique and entirely to blame through incompetence and maladministration, then the city would have to take the blame and get itself out of its own mess. Moreover, they would not have to face up to the prospect of other cities following suit.

There *are* unique features which make New York special to most Americans and to many foreigners. Although New York is not, of course, the capital of the United States, it has had many of the functions which one associates with a capital city which is also the metropolis, as is the case in London, Paris, Rome and Berlin. Many of these functions, both metropolitan and national, universities, art galleries, museums, libraries, archives, and other public institutions were attracted to New York rather than Washington in the first place, partly by the offer of free land and low taxes or tax-exempt status. Some would probably have established in the metropolis New York in any case, but that city was anxious to secure them in the nineteenth century when Boston and Philadelphia were still serious rivals for status.

As a result, not only is New York failing to raise revenue on some of its most valuable land in Manhattan but also, as a World City, a status achieved partly by being the home of world-famous and internationally important institutions, it has had the extra obligation of maintaining their setting, the infrastructure, the complete and whole urban environment required to be worthy of World City status. When New York was no longer financially capable of doing this in the 1960s things started on the downward spiral.

The city's administrative structure has been described as Byzantine. The more one learns of other organisations the more one suspects that this is just a description of the inevitable end-state of any very large human system. Nevertheless, the term certainly is appropriate in the case of New York. Moreover, Byzantine applies not just to the city administration but also to the thousand-odd separate authorities within what we too easily and incorrectly think of as the single entity of the city; and to the fact that it is in part administered by the state governments in Albany, NY, Harford, Conn., and Trenton, NJ. The duplication of services, the lack of coordination between departments, the sheer waste of money not only in the repetition of functions but also in the time-consuming and largely ineffectual interdepartmental negotiations gave New York a top-heavy, expensive, self-serving administration which by 1975 was frustrating its own purposes.

One might say New York had shot itself in the left foot in the nineteenth century by taking in the loss-making institutions. Then the city took aim at the right foot by becoming, in the twentieth century, the city with the best welfare service, and a reputation for that service, in the USA. The United States in this context is best compared with the whole of Europe rather than with just the UK. Until the years of Thatcherism, National Health provision and social security were reasonably uniform throughout the UK, giving most people no very strong reason to migrate to one particular place for advantageous treatment. In contrast, such services vary considerably from one European country to another, just as they vary enormously from one state to another in the United States of America.

Among the 50 states things like welfare are by no means provided on anything like a uniform basis (for example contrast the data for Massachusetts and Mississippi), but people *are* completely free to move from one state to any other. As a benevolent New York City, usually with a Democrat mayor provided good welfare schemes compared with most other cities for its residents, and as people all over the continent got to know about this, so the down-and-outs from Mississippi, Arkansas, West Virginia, North Carolina, Little Rock and Podunk moved to Manhattan, Queens, Brooklyn and the Bronx to take up even the worst residence to qualify for handouts.

In the 1970s New York had 50% of all the public housing in the United States. That isn't saying much by British standards, but it amounted to 250,000 low-rent flats. New York was also paying for one million people on welfare, for eighteen public hospitals, including the gigantic Belle Vue Hospital, for one million children in school and for 250,000 university places for teenagers from poor families. When one remembers that Oxford had only 8,000 undergraduates at that time, one may just be able to grasp the size of the costs. When one also includes other points from a long list, such as the fact that the city employees were described as 'an inefficient, highly paid, poorly supervised workforce', one gets a glimpse of the ramifications of the situation which had been allowed to deteriorate over decades. Dennis Smith, a New York fireman who described his life in *Report From Engine Company 82*, was just one of the tens of thousands who were paid very well for their work in the city. He explains why he and his fellow firemen, police, teachers and others lived in the suburbs, not in the city which paid them. They all received good salaries from New

York, retired after twenty years on half-pay, which meant they were still a charge on the city, and they spent most of that money, and paid all their taxes in fields other than that occupied by the dying cow they were milking.

This far New York has been referred to as if it were a machine, an organism; at best a group of anonymous people. Certainly in a city of such size and complexity a large number of people each carries a tiny bit of the responsibility. But a few key personalities were central in accelerating the decline and bringing the situation to international attention. In the early 1960s the Governor of New York State, Nelson Rockefeller, was known as a big spender. That almost says it all. Many large American cities were approaching bankruptcy and Rockefeller, unlike later governors from Carey to Cuomo, encouraged New York's spending and merely speeded up the race to reach the edge first. Perhaps such rich, famous and powerful people think they can operate outside the laws of economics, or, more likely expect that they will be retired before the chickens come home to roost. That expectation certainly seems to have been the case with John Lindsay, Mayor from 1966 to 1973, who was known as an appeaser. He allowed massive pay rises to the city's workforce which the city could not afford, basically to avoid trouble with the trade unions. It was Lindsay who extended the system of retiring on half-pay after 20 years in the police to most other groups of city employees. At least Lindsay tried to tackle some of New York's problems, those discussed in Chapter Three. He tried to clear the ghettos, to build hospitals and to improve the traffic flow: again, expensive measures for which there was insufficient income. In the early 1970s New York's average annual expenditure was $500,000,000 more than the annual income. The city had a welfare budget of $700,000,000 at the time when that of Chicago was $14,000,000. As pensions increased to take 10% of New York's expenditure, Lindsay attempted to increase the city's income. He raised property taxes. The result was that the great exodus of tax-paying businesses and residents accelerated rapidly. The city lost 1,000,000 taxpayers in 20 years.

If Rockefeller was a spender and Lindsay an appeaser, Abe Beame, City Treasurer under Lindsay and Mayor of New York from 1973 to 1977, was accused of being a crook. Well aware of the impending financial crisis, Beame tried to deal with it in two ways. First, he attempted to raise loans to pay regular expenses. This strategy always leads to disaster because if a person, a firm, or a city can not pay regular outgoings in the first place, they are even less able to repay both the money borrowed and the interest later. Many who had already lent money to New York were suspicious by 1973, (and it was

Figure 5.3 Headlines about New York's financial crisis in 1975.
Source: *The Guardian*, 1975

claimed) Beame hid the deficits and tried to maintain the confidence of lenders by claiming as Mayor and former Treasurer that New York was soon about to receive $2,000,000,000 owed to it, which in fact he knew was pure fiction. It is difficult to decide which is harder to believe, that a mayor of a World City could lie so blatantly, or that international banks could believe him so readily.

Secondly, Abe Beame used what he called 'roll-over financing'. This turned out to be the less-than brilliant method by which the city, already deeply in debt, borrowed more money — a second set of loans — to use to repay the interest on the first set of loans. Moreover, Beame had to arrange this second set of loans at higher rates of interest than the first set because, by 1974, New York was no longer rated a triple-A risk. Only the tip of this spiralling nightmare ride into chaos can be illustrated here, partly because the details soon become tedious and repetitive, mainly because some details are known only to Beame himself.

As a result of the mayor's scheme to pay higher interest on the second loans than on the first, for which they were used only to pay the interest, not the capital repayments, on the first loans, interest on loans became the largest single item in the whole of New York's expenditure. The weekly payroll of $200,000,000 amounted to half of the rest and, of this, 90% went on just four departments: police, fire service, education and cleansing. Welfare payments were getting out of hand as more bears came out of the woods to find the honey. Meanwhile, Beame kept talking of doing things to tide over the cash flow problems, as if they were unusual and temporary. But New York by then was bleeding to death with a perennial problem which some believed he was making much worse.

As New York started to hint that it needed financial help, critics seized on the welfare budget, claiming the city could balance its books if it cut what were seen as excessively generous services. But welfare payments were a red herring. No single factor like this ever explains a complex problem in real life. In 1975 New York was a city of 8,000,000 people and it was a complex of many inter-related factors which caused the problem. In addition to the welfare drain, New York's crisis derived from:

- a deteriorating infrastructure;
- the accumulation of national and international institutions;
- a too-complicated administration;
- short-term crisis measures which in five years lost a quarter of a million taxpayers, half a million jobs and $100,000,000 in annual revenue;

103

- excessive loan charges;
- an exceptionally expensive workforce which trebled in numbers under Lindsay and Beame.

So much has been written about New York's financial crisis in so many publications that a diary of events is provided here as a guide to the mass of detailed evidence to be found in the newspapers and journals of the time.

1971

Although New York had city taxes twice the average in amount for the United States, John Lindsay proposed to increase them. Income was 11 billion dollars, expenditure 12 billion. Lindsay planned:

- a payroll tax
- to tax commuters from the suburbs
- increased sales tax
- a $200 car-parking tax.

In the same year he was asking the state of New York for grants from Albany.

1972

A moratorium was declared on repairs to the city's infrastructure, including maintenance of the streets, bridges and subways. Treasurer Beame was working hard to play down the extent of the financial crisis.

1975

January
The deficit for January reached $800,000,000 and banks raised their interest rates to the city which was becoming a disaster rather than just a high risk.

Mayor Beame decided to sack 200 policemen, 150 firemen and to stop all building work on schools and hospitals.

March
In March New York borrowed $540,000,000 at what was, then, a record 8.7% for the city. All the alarm bells were ringing by then because this loan was used to pay normal running costs. Beame announced a further 10% cut in police personnel, firemen, teachers and garbage collectors.

104

May

In May 1975 the mayor formally announced that New York would go bankrupt in June. The stark reality was that in order to pay wages, keep the city running, pay interest charges and debt repayments, New York needed an extra $1,000,000,000 by the end of June.

Hugh Carey, the Republican governor of NY State, reluctantly agreed to lend Beame, the Democrat mayor of NY City, money to tide him over. There was no love lost between city and state and the majority of Americans saw no reason to bail out profligate New York.

June

The city offered an 8% discount to local tax-payers if they would pay in advance. After much semi-secret panic behind the scenes in New York, Albany and Washington DC, the Municipal Assistance Corporation was set up to raise funds for New York by issuing bonds. For New York, things were desperate. What it meant to the rest of America then may be gauged from the fact that the Municipal Assistance Corporation was at once dubbed Big Mac.

The MAC, controlled by a nine-man board in Albany, discovered that New York was some seven billion dollars in the red. Big Mac managed to renegotiate the short-term loans into long-term ones and local taxes were earmarked to repay the MAC bonds.

July

1 July 1975 saw in a new financial year. 19,000 city workers were sacked and Beame planned that another 21,000 would have to go including:

5,000 police
1,500 firemen
3,000 garbage workers
10,000 teachers, nurses and welfare staff.

For a city to contemplate firing nearly 40,000 people gives an indication both of the size of the World City and the seriousness of the problems it faced.

Not surprisingly, on 3 July the garbage workers went on strike. The smell was worse on Independence Day in the streets than that from the alleged corruption in the city's treasury. Also not surprisingly, the garbage workers were reinstated. Very surprising, however, was the fact that their pension fund lent the city $1,600,000.

105

On 21 July 1975 the MAC issued its first bonds. None were sold. Nobody would touch them with the longest barge-pole. At about the same time the banks refused to lend New York any more money. Beame had the nerve to blame the trade unions for his problems. There was increasing friction with the unions throughout the rest of 1975 and into the following years, with both sides going to court on occasion.

On 28 July the MAC offered its second issue of bonds. There were no takers. There were no suckers anxious to buy Brooklyn Bridge any more; not when it needed painting and was, anyway, falling down.

August

Beame, rather than the unions, was recognised as a major problem and the MAC insisted that the city should be administered by a three-man commission consisting of Beame, Carey and Levitt, rather than by Abe alone.

By this stage the leading politicians and bankers in the United States had faced up to the one inescapable fact. Much as they detested helping a failure in a republic in which if you are a success you demonstrate how great the system is, but if you fail, nobody, nobody at all, wants to know — it's your own fault not the system's — the politicians and bankers realised that if New York were allowed to go bankrupt banks could be ruined and nobody would dare to lend money to any other American city. They had to save the Big Apple to save themselves.

It was at this time, as the nine-man board worked to unravel the city's finances, that Beame's possible criminal actions as former Treasurer came to light. The rest of New York's eight million were at once too readily labelled as crooks, spendthrifts and panhandlers. There was no popular mandate to help the city.

September

September brought no relief. New York was unable to repay $866,000,000 due on the eleventh of the month and the Federal Reserve Board announced that there was no possibility that it would help out. 700 teachers were sacked and 60,000 others immediately went on strike. One has to admire that kind of support and solidarity. With the reductions in the numbers of teachers to save money, class sizes averaged 60 pupils in New York in 1975.

On 10 September the city received $800,000,000 from the state and $1,500,000,000 from the pension funds of city employees to stave off financial disaster. There is no way that I can explain the reasoning of police, firemen, teachers, garbage workers and nurses; I can only record the fact. They knew the city was bankrupt but they lent the city their own money so that the city could pay them their September salaries.

On 17 September the US Secretary of the Treasury, William Simon, repeated that there would be no federal aid for the city. After the announcement of the Federal Reserve Board to the same effect, with more and more politicians saying there could not possibly be any government help, everyone except the completely insane knew that a bail-out scheme was in active preparation. To a disinterested observer this was wonderful entertainment in 1975.

October
Finally even the inmates of padded cells knew that the city would be rescued when, on 10 October, President Ford announced that there would be no federal money for the city.

So, as expected, the Emergency Financial Control Board came into existence on 16 October 1975 to oversee New York's financial recovery. The board ordered that the city must balance its books by 1978. As no extra income could be expected, this meant simply cutting expenditure. Beame and the other mayors could have done this, but they would have lost votes, and possibly office, in the process. Now they had the Fed., Big Mac, the EFCB and Ford himself to blame. Beame celebrated by bringing in a package of economies:

- 8,000 more employees to be sacked, including 5,000 teachers
- a three-year wage freeze
- free places at City University to be abolished
- fire stations, hospitals, clinics and day-care centres to be closed.

The teachers' union applauded the sacking of 5,000 members by lending the city another tranche of $450,000,000 from its pension fund.

In the last week of October Governor Carey warned President Ford that the city of New York would, in spite of all that was being done, still go bankrupt in December 1975. The MAC had failed to sell any bonds and people like Carey were beginning to fear that a city as big and as world-famous as New York going bankrupt would be as disastrous for the country as the Wall Street Crash of 1929. They believed the destruction of confidence in financial institutions would be irreparable.

Gerald Ford — in spite of LBJ's damning indictment — may actually have managed to fart and chew gum at the same time for once in his life. He changed the federal bankruptcy laws in a way which shows he knew there could be terrible trouble. The new law stated that instead of the banks having first claim on any assets, the police and the fire service would have priority and their pay would be absolutely guaranteed. This was a splendid U-turn after so many had been fired to save cash. Clearly Ford was thinking of letting New York default, but was expecting and preparing for riots, shooting, burning and looting worse than anything seen in the black riots of the 1960s. On 29 October he said he would veto any legislation to help New York. Gerry Ford had no Big Brother to save *his* votes. As Truman said of the president's desk, 'the buck stops here'.

At the end of October Governor Carey announced that the New York State was by that time so involved that it might well go bankrupt too if the city defaulted.

November

Early in the month the city spent money on a national advertising campaign to try to gain America's sympathy for the idea of federal aid to just one city. Then on 16 November the city deliberately defaulted on payments due in order to try to force the federal hand. Immediately New York State imposed a three-year moratorium on repayments of $1,600,000,000. It renegotiated loans for a longer term at lower rates of interest. It was better for the big banks to get less, rather than nothing at all. It was reported that 200,000 small private investors had in fact lost the money they lent to New York. This was a much bigger shock then, in the days before BCCI and Maxwell, than it seems now. Another 8,000 jobs were slated to go, sales tax was to be increased yet again, and further reductions in maintenance of the infrastructure were planned.

Good as the reverse of his word, on 26 November President Ford approved a $2,600,000,000 federal loan for New York City after insisting he would veto any such move, and the unions rejoiced again by lending the city more money from their pension funds. Beady eyes must have been watching this folly with great interest all round the world. Carey pledged to help to find a further $4,000,000,000 to cover the gap until 1978 when the books had to balance. But one wonders what real incentive there was for Beame to balance the books when the President, the Governor and even the unions were so ready to solve his problems for him by providing billions and billions of dollars.

Still, there were some faces peering over Abe's shoulder by this time: Ford, Carey, the EFCB, Big Mac, the union reps, *Time*, *Newsweek*, the major papers, old Uncle Tom Cobley and all. A three-year plan was agreed:

- local tax increases of 25%
- a wage freeze
- more redundancies
- reduced city services
- no new capital works in the city
- a 50% surcharge on property tax
- increased sales tax
- cuts in welfare
- a moratorium on loan repayments
- banks and unions must buy MAC bonds.

As a result, tax-payers, wage-earners, civil engineers, property owners, shoppers, lenders and even down-and-outs had yet more incentive than before to consider very seriously the delights and attractions of the suburbs, Florida, Texas, California, even New Jersey and Cleveland. Midnight Cowboy took the Greyhound out of the Big Apple and headed for Miami. When people are free to move, welfare payments may pull them in, but huge tax increases and cuts in services definitely push people out and away.

1976

September
In spite of Gerald Ford's guarantees that the police would continue to be paid, come what may, provided that when the time came they kept a mob of eight million enraged residents under control, in September 1976 3,000 police were sacked. The rest held a demonstration against the sackings and the inevitable increase in workload for those still employed.

October
On 10 October 1976 a kind of perfection was achieved when the police who had been guaranteed jobs to quell riots, themselves rioted because they had been sacked. They rioted outside Madison Square Garden, and some were arrested by their colleagues still in work.

November
The New York State Court of Appeals told the city that the three-year moratorium was illegal; bonds were due on the dates originally pledged.

On 26 November:

- 2,500 firemen
- 3,000 garbage workers
- 6,000 additional police
- 6,000 nurses
- 20,000 teachers

and other city workers to a grand total of 40,000 were sacked to save money. In this diary the numbers of people sacked now add up to tens of thousands more than were ever employed at one time by the city; but that is correct in this wonderful morality story. Many of the workers sacked immediately got their jobs back after each round of sackings. Either they went to court, as indicated earlier, or their colleagues threatened disastrous strikes, or they reminded the authorities of the lever they held in the loans from their pension funds. So the same thousands of people appear in the statistics again and again. One begins to think that some of the mass sackings, at least, were merely cosmetic actions to provide newspaper headlines and make it look as if the city was really trying to put its house in order. The year ended with more hospitals, libraries and museums closed, and with transport fares raised.

1977

As accountants studied New York's books, even more expenses and borrowings never mentioned by Mayor Beame came to light. The new President, Jimmy Carter, also refused to help. This was another classic example of Newspeak. Many politicians equivocate as a matter of habit, but in America the big change came with Lyndon Johnson. During his presidency emerged the phrase 'the credibility gap', meaning the difference between what the president says and the truth. So, in Newspeak, 'absolutely no help for New York', means 'expect help within a fortnight'. Carter, in fact, worked out the rescue plan, a consignment to continuous coma, which is still in effect.

March

By March 1977 the city was desperate for short-term loans, but the banks would not lend the mere $500,000 needed until a Budget Review Board had been set up. This suggests that the banks had precious little confidence in Carter, Carey, EFCB, MAC and the rest. As each layer of supervision was added, another had to be put on top to try to force it to get on and do something effective.

November
Ed Koch was elected mayor, replacing Beame. Notably, Koch fought a very hard battle to be elected. That is, he *wanted* to be Mayor in the middle of this disaster. Again I do not pretend to understand this death wish and merely record the fact. Big Mac failed to sell yet another bond issue in spite of the diktat which had naively ordered that in the land of free enterprise, banks and unions must buy the bonds. Where was the sanction?

1978

Perhaps in 1975, the year 1978 seemed a long way in the future, and apparently offered time to balance the budget. For New York the years 1975–78 passed in about three months and 1978 arrived with no budget balanced, Beame's plan not working, all Uncle Tom Cobley's feeble friends proving ineffective, and the city pleading for more money. The police added to the general joy by demanding a pay rise of 30%. Ed Koch gave them 8%, while asking Congress for another $2,500,000,000 loan.

March
In this month Jimmy Carter launched his Urban Programme. Some believed he was applying it to all cities just to avoid the political flak from appearing to help New York alone. But many other cities were in the same sort of financial trouble, and enough people in Carter's administration had the sense to see it. Briefly, Carter's Urban Programme aimed to make some money available to all big cities in the following ways:

- four and a half billion dollars made available for grants and loans;
- a National Development Bank to arrange low-interest loans for depressed areas;
- federal grants to those States which do most to help their cities.

This programme, and later modifications, is sometimes referred to as New Federalism. It wasn't much, but it did three important things. First, it acknowledged that New York was not the only big city in severe financial difficulties. Second, it accepted that the Federal Government has some responsibility to help the situation, if only because so many voters are affected. Third, it tried to push the effective action down to state and city level, where local action could be tailored to local needs. Carter said that simply guaranteeing bonds for New York was like trying to cure an addict by guaranteeing an endless supply of dope.

September

Six months later Ed Koch announced his plan for New York's recovery, seven points which combined administrative and economic arrangements:

- incentives for manufacturers to return to the city;
- administrative help for them, and for new firms locating in the city;
- a ten-year start-up tax deferment;
- the removal of tax on stock and machinery;
- low-interest loans;
- a public relations campaign;
- the appointment of an ombudsman to help with red tape.

It is interesting to note that in the following year, Michael Heseltine used a very similar plan for London's Dockland.

1980

To some people in 1980, New York's future looked better. The number of industrial jobs within the city boundary had increased since 1975 and new buildings were going up in Manhattan. However, this was deceptive. The industry had been lured in by massive subsidies which the city could not sustain. Moreover, the investment in new property was being made by Japanese, Dutch and British firms who, surprisingly, were not fully aware of the depth of New York's financial problems. Meanwhile, American firms were busy building in Connecticut.

The real situation was that while Manhattan looked better, brighter and busier than five years before, the inner-city areas were devastated. Drug abuse and drug-related crime and gang warfare had been added to the growing list of urban problems in Long Island and the Bronx. New York in 1980 had a deficit of $2,650,000,000. It was becoming apparent that Ed Koch was working very hard to give the city centre every attraction and incentive for the middle class. At the same time he was refusing any responsibility for, or expenditure on, even the city's own poor, the people who had voted him into office, let alone those from other parts of the country. As the rich got richer and the poor society literally collapsed, Koch left Washington to pick up those pieces.

Time magazine took stock of these moves in 1980 and again in 1985. In 1980 it reported that New York transport workers had received a 20% pay rise, that there was a marked deterioration in the inner city, and that the budget still was not balanced, although short-term debts had been paid off. The surprise was that the magazine praised the success of Urban Renewal in New York. As Urban Renewal came to an end officially in 1975 and certainly had not been a success in New York then, this comment may be hard to understand. The problem arises because Carter's Urban Programme is often referred to by other names, particularly under later administrations. New Federalism was the official label under Reagan, but Urban Renewal is commonly, and carelessly, also used. In the *Time* article it refers not to the rebuilding of the 1960s, but to the meagre financial aid since 1975.

1985

The 1980 and 1985 *Time* reports say roughly the same thing in almost the same words. By 1985 New York's condition was the same as in 1980 with the budget not balanced, the inner city still in decline, Koch becoming known as the Procrastinator, and Reagan reducing the funds available under New Federalism schemes.

1989

By 1989 New York, like most major cities, had been hit by the worst recession since 1930. The new black Mayor, David Dinkins, was responsible for a city with a budget of $27,000,000,000 and a deficit of $5,000,000,000, twice the shortfall ten years earlier. Multinational firms were leaving the World City, some retrenching, some going to the suburbs, some to the Sunbelt; but others were going to New York's rivals — London, Frankfurt, Singapore and Hong Kong. New York's income was falling rapidly. In 1989 alone the revenues from corporation tax declined 18%, mortgage tax 25%, property tax 30% and local income tax 8%.

1990

Much attention was diverted from New York's financial problems in the 1990s by the increasing racial strife in the inner city. Dinkins's partial responsibility in this is described in Chapter Nine. A few facts will show how the situation continues to deteriorate. In 1990 $108,000,000 was spent subsidising companies which moved into the city; in 1991 $203,000,000. Wall Street companies, who should be able to read the financial future better than others meanwhile were decamping to Connecticut as fast as they could go. Since 1980 New York has taken on 50,000 extra municipal workers, swelling the total

Table 5.1 New York Selected Data 1990

Revenue from government sources, in dollars
New York	12,334,000,000
Washington	1,306,000,000
Baltimore	802,000,000
Chicago	752,000,000
Boston	746,000,000

A. Central city population		B. Metro area pop.	C. A as % of B.
New York	7,323,000	18,087,000	40
Los Angeles	3,485,000	14,532,000	24
Chicago	2,748,000	8,066,000	34
San Francisco	724,000	6,253,000	11
Philadelphia	1,586,000	5,899,000	27

Debt outstanding, in dollars
New York	26,005,000,000
Los Angeles	6,278,000,000
Chicago	4,298,000,000
Jacksonville	4,297,000,000
San Antonio	4,035,000,000

City employees per 10,000 of the population
Washington	776
New York	537
Buffalo	397
Baltimore	387
Boston	361

Class 'A' office space in the CBD. In thousand square feet
New York	251,537
Washington	92,500
Anaheim-Santa Ana	52,359
Chicago	47,147
Boston	35,000

Source: Statistical Abstract of the US 1992

to 300,000 on the payroll. Many believe this is how Koch and Dinkins had to repay the more powerful of those who voted them into office, as in the old days of the city machine.

Meanwhile, many observers in America were urging that the poor people in the USA are a national, federal responsibility, rather than a local, urban one. They suggested that just as the rural poor in the

Depression had been made a national responsibility, so in the 1990s the urban poor should be helped at national level. Rural poor, immigrants and the poorest black people collect in the inner cities as there is nowhere else to seek cheap accommodation and help, even if the work is no longer located there. But they have become an impossible burden on individual Central Cities.

Some geographers, true to the American ethic, have urged that nothing should be done by an interfering central government. They believe that market forces should, and will, deal with the situation. According to such geographers as Neil Smith, as city-centre and inner-city land and property become cheaper and cheaper with the decline, people, businesses and manufacturing will relocate. Smith believes they will move back into the cities to take advantage of the huge potential gains. This is a very narrow view, looking only at costs of land and property. It does not seem to take into account such things as the very poor transport of these inner sites, nor does it seem to quantify the costs of crime and riots in the inner cities. Perhaps people and corporations will move back in eventually. But how long will it take, and where will the poor move to as the land and rents rise in price beyond their very slender means?

In addition to those problems discussed previously, in the 1990s New York's list of problems is increasing:

- Slums, especially in the Bronx, are now described as merely piles of rubble.
- A quarter of the people are below the official poverty line.
- 100,000 or more are homeless.
- There are 500,000 known drug addicts, probably more.
- Four out of five children are born out of wedlock.
- An unknown, but rapidly increasing, proportion of the population has Aids and tuberculosis.
- Less than half the inner city children complete their schooling.
- Child abuse, gang warfare and racial riots threaten to get out of control.

But the visitor will not see any of this if he or she stays south of Central Park and away from areas like the Lower East Side on Manhattan. There are still dangers even there, on the subways in particular, plus the signs of encroaching poverty, garbage smelling on the streets, broken pavements, the world's best traffic jams, panhandlers everywhere, and the chance of getting shot.

At the time of writing the situation has not been resolved, although hopes have been raised after so many years by President Bill Clinton's election promise to look at the problems of the poor in America. Under a variety of labels since Jimmy Carter's time the cities have been receiving some federal help. But this is not a systemic solution. The amount of money is very finely calculated — just enough to keep the cities solvent and to postpone the danger of uncontrollable riots, but not enough to anger Congress and the voters, which would stir up the political strife about supplying free drugs to addicts. Moreover, just as America took so long to get over the national trauma of defeat by North Vietnam, there is the danger that if the whole electorate were forced to see clearly just how many big cities have to be subsidised, it might call into question one of the basic beliefs of the American system.

No politician can afford to let a major American city really go bankrupt. But very few American politicians, not even Democrats, believe it is the purpose of government to run economies, city, state, or national. At the moment it looks as if the heart-dead cities will stay on the creaking life-support machines for ever because no-one will turn them off. Killing the Central Cities by leaving them completely to market forces, the Central Cities which suburbanites still think they belong to even if they rarely go there, would be like switching off the ventilator on a great-grandparent one never sees any more. No-one will apply, say, the Canadian cure, but the patients have insufficient inner resources of their own to recover.

6

IMMIGRANTS IN THE CITIES

This chapter will examine the location, movement, relocation and sometimes dispersal of immigrants within the American city, as part of the wider study of social conditions in the following chapters. First, one or two points need to be clarified and working definitions established.

There are many immigrants in the United States now, that is, people who now reside in the US but were born in other countries. However, in geographical and sociological studies of immigrants, the word often refers to two or three generations, so that it is the grandparents or even great-grandparents of native-born Americans who, strictly speaking, were the immigrants. In the widest sense, of course, all white, black, Hispanic and Asian Americans are immigrants, having arrived on the continent in the last four hundred years. American Indians are then the native people. Thirty years ago, one group of people was simply called negro. Later, those same people called themselves black, pointing out that black is beautiful. Now the term is Afro-Caribbeans. Most black people in America are descendants of people who lived on the continent long before the US gained its independence; they are second in occupation only to the Indians. (I shall refer to Indians, black people, whites, Hispanics, Asians and other immigrants by those simple names, and the context will show that there is no disrespect.)

In the discussion which follows, for very practical purposes, distinction will need to be made between 'immigrants' and 'Americans'. The further one goes back into the nineteenth century, the more likely the immigrants were to be of European origin, and the more likely that the native-born white Americans were to be of British origin. They were white, so-called Anglo-Saxon, and predominantly Protestant: WASPs. However, as one traces succeeding generations the convenient term Americans, to refer to the host society, will be balanced against the term immigrants for the recent arrivals, covering two or three generations. As time went on, the Americans counted among their numbers more and more people of German, Irish, Italian, Polish, Russian and other origins — Catholics, Jews and others as well as Protestants. Gradually they changed from being immigrants to becoming Americans in the working definitions to be used here. As they, in their turn, sided with the WASPs to oppose newcomers just off the ships, it makes this usage a bit more logical.

Finally, the quotation on the base of the Statue of Liberty, 'Give me your tired, your poor, your huddled masses yearning to breathe free...' has become loaded with assumptions. Most immigrants *were* poor by the time they arrived in America. But they had not necessarily been poor when they left home. Our view may be coloured by the tales of the Irish famines, and by television documentaries which make everything a calamity. But even people with some money originally were poor by the time they reached America. The journey across Europe, often also across England — eastern European Jews travelled Hamburg, Hull, Liverpool, New York — and then the cost of the ocean voyage left them with no money to spare on the quayside, and determined to be careful with what they had left until they became established. However, these 'poor' people were not necessarily unintelligent, uneducated, or lazy, as was so often assumed by the residents of the American cities with whom they came first, and most closely, in contact, and who resented the competition from these new arrivals.

Some of the European immigrants from the mid-nineteenth century onwards were well educated. Many more, unschooled as they may have been, were very able, and the vast majority had to work very hard to survive on arrival in America. An important point is that the respective perceptions of 'immigrants' and 'Americans' were different. The people leaving Europe, leaving families, homes, everything they knew, risking everything in a land they knew very little about, considered themselves adventurous, strong, determined, open-minded — ready to risk all and make a go of things. The fact that many of those watching the immigrants coming down the gangways in American ports saw them as the dregs of Europe led to far too much misunderstanding and trouble. In the literature, those troubles are often stressed. Some will be outlined here. But the vital point to stress here at the beginning is that, in the long run, for the vast majority of those European migrants, immigration into the United States of America has been a story of success.

Whatever their many different reasons for leaving Europe, most migrants to the USA in the nineteenth century had very similar

118

reasons for choosing America rather than any other destination. They were looking for religious and political freedom and, above all, economic opportunity. They perceived America, rightly or wrongly, as a place where they could be themselves, and where they could prosper. Their history in the United States demonstrates this very clearly. One of the types of problem they immediately faced was that the Americans already there, whether second- or seventeenth-generation native-born, expected the new immigrants to become Americans, to Americanise, as soon as possible. But the newcomers did not always see it this way themselves.

There was more agreement on economic matters, but not complete harmony. The immigrants wanted to get rich themselves, while those already there wanted to get richer by exploiting the foreigners just off the boat. Most immigrants committed themselves to the new country, but a proportion intended to work in America for a time, send money home or save it up, and then retire to, say, Italy later as wealthy people in their own town or village. That particular type of dream turned out to be the one least likely to succeed.

While immigration has been an almost continuous process to the United States (see table 8.5), slowing down in wartime and during the Depression, distinct waves have been identified by many observers. Until the 1840s movement was predominantly from Britain, establishing the English language, the British systems of government and law, British economic ideas, social customs, attitudes and prejudices. In the middle of the nineteenth century the largest identifiable groups were from Germany, Scandinavia and Ireland. While significant numbers of immigrants came from all parts of Europe throughout the century, such as the Portuguese to Boston and the Welsh to Cleveland, in the 1870s and the 1880s the largest numbers were from Italy, Sicily and Greece. Into the turn of the century and up to the First World War the largest numbers of immigrants arriving in the United States were from Poland and Russia.

The terminology used in the many books and articles on immigration appears to be most inconsistent. Some of the newcomers are called Blacks, some are called Greeks, others are called Jews. But this, in fact, reflects very accurately how the newcomers were labelled at the time they arrived in America. The ordinary Americans already there labelled the migrants by their most obvious characteristics, or by the features which were most different from WASP, most foreign or alarming. Xenophobia has always been part of the nation of immigrants. Thus some were labelled by the colour of their skin, some by their country of origin, some by their language, and many by their religion. The massive waves of people arriving in the first two decades of the twentieth century are usually referred to as Jews, not as Poles or Russians, the countries from which they came.

The vast majority of migrants to the USA, then, up to the time of the First World War, moved from Europe. If one uses a globe instead of a flat Mercator world map, one will see that sailing from Hamburg, Le Havre, Naples and Liverpool, the migrants approached the United States from the north-east, not, as a flat map erroneously suggests, from due east. Thus the immigrants reached the northeast of the United States first. It was thus that the northeastern cities of the new country became the destination for this and several other good reasons: they were the first ports of call; the growing industries and markets offered work; the South, further away, did not attract because of its history of segregation. The Midwest was accessible via the Great Lakes and via the railways later, and European migrants got as far as Denver and Seattle, but the overwhelming majority located in the industrial cities of the northeastern quarter of the country first.

Whether they arrived at a particular city by ship in the early days, or by train later, by using those types of transport in the nineteenth century the European immigrants first set foot in the very centre of the concentrated city. The quays and the railroad stations were hard by, if not actually inside the CBD, the downtown area and the encircling ring of manufacturing areas where, together, all the work was to be found. Not surprisingly therefore, in city after city, Philadelphia, Pittsburgh, Chicago, Cleveland and the rest, the immigrants sought accommodation as near to the city centre as possible. There were many reasons for this type of residential location. The immediate concern, the minute an immigrant disembarked or stepped from the train, was to find somewhere to live, and then somewhere to work. The sooner a few dollars started coming in the better, and in the meantime the new arrivals, dependent on their savings, needed the cheapest accommodation available. This they found in the innermost residential ring of the concentrated, concentric city. The location suited everyone just fine. It was the oldest, least desirable residential property in the built-up-area. It was cheap. Much as the 'Know-Nothing' — the American party, which aimed to limit the political influence of immigrants but, when questioned, claimed to 'know nothing' of this — and other anti-immigrant groups made a fuss, the landlords were often happy to get rents from rooms, houses split into flats, and tenement buildings which other people were leaving as they prospered and the city expanded.

Such accommodation was acceptable to the Scandinavians, Irish, Italians, Poles, Russians or whichever group was moving in — for a time. They did not intend to stay in that property in that location for very long. The rent was the lowest they could get, and another feature which made the property the least desirable to better-off Americans was the fact that it was located next to the factories. Until the Second World War much of the unskilled and semi-skilled labour was hired at the factory gates or in the markets on a daily basis, just as illegal immigrants are hired now. The closer one lived to the factory gates, the better chance one had of being chosen for a day's work early each morning. This kind of residential location was not the achievement of the American Dream that the immigrants were seeking, but the location and the system worked well enough for each successive wave of immigrants at least to make a start in America and in the city.

Although one group of Europeans tended to predominate in each decade, people were arriving in each big American city from several European countries at the same time. They all tended, for the same compelling reasons outlined above, first to take up residence in the inner residential rings of the city; but they rarely mixed together in these zones. Very quickly, distinct immigrant quarters appeared, often given obvious names like Little Italy and Chinatown, sometimes getting names harder to explain, but all very quickly identified and labelled by those on the outside. The labels were crude indications of the national or ethnic make-up of the quarters. For example, Little Italy may well have had only 40% of its residents from Italy. All the crude labels really indicated was the origin of the largest single identifiable or highly visible group in the neighbourhood.

Just as the European immigrants of the nineteenth and early twentieth century had good reasons to locate in the inner city, each group had good reasons to cluster together. For example, take the first Italian men to arrive in a given city. Their particular first lodging within the innermost residential ring may well have been a matter of pure chance; but from then on the development of the Italian community was the result of identifiable forces with very little left to chance. Those men sent letters home, to the back streets of Naples or to a village in Calabria, containing money, advice, and instructions for family and friends who were to follow.

Thus the relatives and friends, women and children as well as more men, migrated to join the very first to go to America. Then other men and other families from the same Neapolitan street or the same farming village joined them too. After the first, most adventurous souls had braved all the unknowns, the ones who followed had some information, some advice, above all an address to make for in America. So the new arrivals not only went to the same city as people they knew or had heard of, they actually tended to cluster close to the first arrivals in the same city streets. Ethnic neighbourhoods began to form and in this way the people derived the benefits of clustering. These benefits included help to find accommodation, help to find work, help with the customs of a different host society, the new ways of doing things in the New World. Thus, although the clustering often alienated the native Americans, and delayed integration, there were sensible, practical reasons for Swedes, Irish, Germans, Italians, Greeks, Letts, Serbs, Poles and Russians each to group together in the same city neighbourhood with their own kind.

Other advantages, less urgent, then accrued. The community could set up its own church, perhaps not vital if they were Protestants, more necessary if they were Catholic or Orthodox. They established their own schools. Immigrant people soon realised that schools provided by the city were there not so much to educate foreign children as to 'Americanise' them. The details of a full day for some immigrant children can be daunting. They all attended grade school as required by law; then many spent nearly as much time each day in the community school as required by their parents; then some of these had to lend a hand later with the family business.

Their own churches, schools, political clubs and social clubs had vital functions for the immigrants. They supported the newcomers in an alien society, they helped to preserve the language, history, literature and other cultural elements of the homeland left behind, and passed this on to later generations. They helped the immigrants to adjust without too much culture-shock. Very often, the help given by neighbours, the church and the political clubs became formalised, became more of a system. Newcomers in some communities became dependant on the old hands who had developed power through these institutions. In some cities new immigrants became dependant for homes, for jobs, for promotion and for political power on the organisations which eventually, particularly in cities like Boston, Cleveland, Cincinnati and Chicago, became part of the city machine.

In the early days the development of ethnic neighbourhoods and the functions of schools, churches and clubs in promoting them became counter-productive. The difference in appearance, language and religion between the newcomers and the native-born, the more the ethnic neighbourhood had cohesion, then the greater the reaction and resentment from Americans. Some immigrant communities exaggerated their differences from their hosts and did much to perpetuate them as long as possible; others played them down and did their best to Americanise. But the development of the immigrant quarters in easily identified locations in the inner city did much to foster and focus the opposition to immigrants trying to make their way in America.

122

As time went on, the inner residential zones in most large cities where European immigrants located were subdivided into ethnic neighbourhoods, distinctive immigrant areas. Chicago is a well-documented example of this. Immigrants clustered in a semi-circle of neighbourhoods round the north, west and south sides of the Loop, cheek by jowl with the concentration of work. There were some native-born Americans in the zone too, particularly the rich people in Streeterville, Tower Town and the inner end of the Gold Coast, all just north of the mouth of the Chicago river. Diametrically opposite them were the black people of the inner end of the city's southern black belt. Working anti-clockwise, immediately west of Tower Town was Little Europe where a mixture of Eastern Europeans, Russian Jews, Scandinavians and Germans first settled. Round further west was Little Sicily, housing Italians from the mainland as well as the island. Across the north fork of the river first settled people from what is now Poland, but which at the time was part of Russia. People from that part of Europe were labelled variously as Poles, Russians or Jews. A separate, second Italian community was established on the west side of the Loop. (Much later a second black community was added here. The southern belt is too often referred to as the only black neighbourhood in the centre of Chicago, i.e. as *the* black belt.)

On the west side, too, were Floptown, the Slave Market and some identifiable features of the Underworld. Floptown was the most dilapidated area where the poorest migrants could find the very cheapest, least desirable accommodation while they looked for work from those with jobs to offer in the Slave Market. Here, of course, were the greatest opportunities for rackets, exploitation, bribery, crime and corruption. (WP Bryan actually marks 'the Underworld' on one of his 1930s maps of Chicago.)

Round to the southwest of the Loop was an area called the Delta in which Greek people formed the largest single national-religious-language group. There is also a reference to Bohemians here, immigrants from that area of Europe which for a time was part of the short-lived Czechoslovakia. Poles and Lithuanians formed the best-known neighbourhoods along the south fork of the river, the Lithuanians locating south of the timber yards and next to the stockyards which were a feature of south Chicago in the nineteenth century. Upton Sinclair describes vividly the life of some Lithuanians working in the meat-packing factories in his book *The Jungle*.

Finally, round almost to the southern black belt, are two names at opposite ends of the semantic spectrum. Chinatown meant what it said then, the place where Chinese immigrants lived. Chinatown in places like New York now means a place to draw in tourists. But in the nineteenth century the word ghetto meant what it had meant since it was used to refer to a part of Venice — the Jewish quarter. It is not clear when the word changed its meaning in America to refer to an area where black people live. But in Chicago, then, it referred to the Jewish, mainly Eastern European, community.

In some cities not only were the immigrant quarters identified by this localisation of particular groups of people near the CBD, but also quite often a particular group was identified with a particular type of work, in the first generation at least. This connection should not be pushed too far but, for example, one can understand how, say, so many of the small community of Lithuanians found work in the stockyards and meat-canning factories next to which they lived in Chicago. Similarly, in virtually one-industry towns, as with steel in Pittsburgh, the European immigrants became identified with that dominant type of work. In the largest cities, with the widest variety of types of work available, immigrants either found work in the area nearest home, found accommodation near to the work which suited them best, or often set up in some kind of business for themselves. With so many millions of immigrants arriving from all over Europe by 1910, many of them were educated, trained, experienced, intelligent and ambitious. Many of those who took unskilled jobs in the nearest industry which they could reach quickest in the morning saw that as a temporary expedient until they could get some money together, find a better job, and start to climb up the socio-economic ladder. Along with everyone else in America, they wanted to get up that ladder so that they could, like the WASPs before them, one day slide down the snake into the suburbs.

Central Boston is a city where the connection between immigrants and types of work has been studied in detail. The Irish found work in the docks and later in the railway yards. The Italians predominated in the wholesale trade, import and export, and particularly in the fresh food markets. Many immigrants found an opportunity importing or retailing food and other goods from the home country, in demand among the immigrants but not yet produced in America. In Boston Jewish people tended to find work in the financial district or set up their own businesses manufacturing clothes.

There are horror stories, and horrifying pictures, of immigrant experiences and of immigrant quarters from the nineteenth century. With so many people from such diverse backgrounds arriving in their millions in the raw new cities not designed or organised to receive them, it would be surprising indeed if there were not. However, for every tragic story there must have been a hundred happy endings, because the fact is that the vast majority of immigrants *did* succeed, whatever slum they first lived in, whatever menial job they first took. Like *Robinson Crusoe* and *The Swiss Family Robinson*, it is the story of trial, danger and trouble which persists in the popular imagination, though for most European immigrants the American story is one of eventual success.

So, there were sweat shops. There are early photographs as well as harrowing descriptions of unscrupulous employers exploiting the innocents just off the boat. But, equally, some of those photographs and some of those stories are of one extended family: granny, mother, father, aunts, uncles, children, nieces and nephews all crowded into one walk-up cold-water apartment in a tenement, slaving away eighteen hours a day at the family business — determined to make it on their own. In this sense the immigrant areas became what the city centre had been not many decades before — a confused mixture of residences and industrial and commercial enterprises, very often in the same building and sometimes in the same apartment.

Photographs taken towards the end of the nineteenth century in the immigrant quarters of Boston, New York and Chicago show similar scenes. The streets were lined with five- and six-storey tenement blocks, usually with a mass of iron balconies and fire escapes clinging to the sides. The streets were crammed with people. There is a quaint explanation somewhere, written by an unreconstructed WASP, that this was because the people came from countries like Italy where they liked to sit out in the streets. A more thorough examination of the photos and a little knowledge of the situation at the time will show areas so packed with people at such incredibly high residential densities that they are practically bursting out of the buildings. In most cities villas were divided into flats, and apartments subdivided into rooms to try to provide accommodation for the incoming millions. In Chicago thousands of extra buildings were thrown up in the gaps between existing structures and then in the back yards to try to cope. All this was private enterprise restrained with varying degrees of success by city authorities. The Dumbell Buildings, referring to the shape of the ground plan, were designed by the city authorities to try to get light and air into the overcrowded quarters, but these were still put up by private speculators complying more or less with those regulations.

Even in the photos of the better streets one sees beds and tables on the balconies where use was made of every square inch. Bedding and linen was hung out to dry and air on the sunny days when the pictures were taken on the slow photographic plates. There were canvas sun-blinds and awnings over the shop fronts, canvas covered stalls and vendors' carts clogging the pavements and roadways. In the pictures there are barrels and boxes all over the place. People were moving in and moving out; the main feature in each picture is the mass of people. Look carefully and you will see that they are not idly sitting out for a siesta, or posing for the camera. The people are working, or moving about looking for accommodation and work. One wonders how even Swedes, let alone Italians, could have sat outside in a New York or Chicago winter. These are busy, animated, above all, optimistic scenes of very high-density areas.

Photographers like Jacob Riis captured the other end of the spectrum. Riis sought out the worst slums in Boston and New York and too often his pictures show the women and children inside huddled in squalor while the men apparently lounge about in the narrow streets and passages, lethargic, dispirited. Some pose under the dripping washing, indifferent to that and to the photographer. The probability is that they had failed to get a day's work that morning and had nothing to do until the following dawn when they would line up at the factory gate again. Such images echo scenes taken in Manchester, Nottingham and Leeds. But the similarity in the superficial visual content can be most misleading. By the time people in Britain had arrived in slums like that, they had fallen all the way down the social scale. In America, in the greatest possible contrast, they had just arrived and were getting ready to climb up.

In the early 1960s Charles Stokes published his model of slums, based on his work in large Latin American cities. The model is the more convincing when used to help in the analysis of British and US cities in that it was developed independently of them. Stokes first divides slums into Escalator and Non-escalator types. In the Escalator slum there is the possibility for the residents to get up and out. In the Non-escalator slum some absolute barrier prevents the upward movement on the socio-economic ladder, as the Apartheid laws did in the South African townships for so long. Stokes then divides each of these two into Slums of Hope and Slums of Despair. These are where the majority of the people, young and active, at least believe they can get out by their own efforts, and so eventually move to a better residential area. Slums of Despair are those where such hopes and beliefs never existed, or have died.

People whose education has concentrated on British history are perhaps too familiar with the concept of slums of despair. When they see Jacob Riis's pictures, or a modern barrio, they too easily equate it with British slums of the industrial revolution. In Britain the slums of our big industrial cities, time and again, were places where people ended up when the system had failed them. British slums tended to be non-escalator slums of despair. In the United States for over a hundred and fifty years the immigrant slums, where people from other countries first found lodgings in the big cities, have proved to be stepping stones to better things. In the literature phrases like 'springboard to the economy' emphasise that the slums were places from which newcomers entered the economy, not where tired natives dropped out of it. Dreadful as some of the immigrant quarters were, they served their purpose, and immigrant slums in the USA in the vast majority of cases proved to be escalator slums of hope.

Thus there is a third element to be added to the characteristics of immigrant geography. First we had location in the inner ring; second, clustering into ethnic neighbourhoods, and now third, the almost universal feature of movement outwards towards the suburbs. In the abstract sense this was upward movement as immigrant people got better jobs and succeeded economically. It was also upward movement as increased income bestowed higher social status. Some people who do not know it very well refer to America glibly as a classless society. In reality it is as class-conscious and class-ridden as any other, but one where class depends entirely on wealth. Old wealth is better than new, but money is status. Socio-economic status means exactly that in America.

In the physical sense the spatial movement of the immigrants was, and still is, outwards; it is directly away from the CBD, and making a beeline for the suburbs. By this one means the suburbs at the time — whether they were the streetcar suburbs of the last century or the Chevy and Subaru suburbs of this. The cases where an immigrant community has not moved out can be counted on the fingers of one hand — the Italians of the North End of Boston and the Chinese of San Francisco come to mind. But in city after city, as the European immigrants got better jobs, learned the language, got used to the system — indeed, often using it better than the WASPs — or prospered in their own businesses, they moved into better housing.

Because of the concentric nature of the cities in the nineteenth century, with very little replacement of property, simply newer and newer residential rings being added further and further outward, moving into better housing normally necessitated moving further from the CBD. This movement of the immigrants partly depended on what the WASPs were doing. Some observers describe the immigrants as forcing the previous residents out as the once all-WASP areas gained more and more foreign-born people. Examples of residents moving as a neighbourhood loses its tone are common all over the world, and support this type of explanation. But when one remembers that new houses were being built on the edge of the city all the time, and that native-born Americans aspired to get as far from the CBD as the transport at any given time would allow, then at least an equal part of the explanation must be that many earlier residents of property into which immigrants moved were moving outwards themselves of their own volition, for other reasons anyway. Resistance to the European immigrants slowed down their outward movement rather than stopped or diverted it. Moreover, resistance to any one immigrant group came as much from other immigrant groups as from Americans. As each successive wave started to become established in the USA during the nineteenth century, it tended to resist the next new wave, particularly if the new people came from a different European country with a different language and a different religion. The newcomers were perceived as a threat to jobs, as competition for housing, and generally as undesirables who would upset the newly acquired apple-cart.

Some years after he described the immigrant areas in Chicago, Burgess published a map showing their movement outwards from their early locations next to the Loop. His map, in its idiosyncratic labels, reveals not only the directions the different groups took, but also attitudes towards them. As a sociologist, Burgess can be assumed to have had some empathy with the peoples he studied, so presumably the labels on his map give a flavour of what reactionary Americans felt towards the newcomers. The movement of Germans and Scandinavians away from the Loop is labelled Northward Migration. One presumes that people from northwestern Europe were considered OK. Across the north branch of the river, however, the Polish outward movement is labelled the Northwest March — a bit threatening. West-northwestward the Italian outward movement is labelled a Trend — a bit slippery those customers. As one goes anti-clockwise round the compass, outward movements of Jews, Czechs, Poles, Lithuanians, Letts and Irish are variously labelled Extension, Expansion, Movement and Settlement, a different slant for each nationality and religion. Although not strictly with reference to foreign migrants, but certainly in the context of immigrants into that particular city, the extreme bias is revealed when the movement of people southward in the black belt is labelled Negro Southward Invasion. Germans migrated but black people invaded.

In the same way as those in Chicago, groups of people of foreign origin, including the first and second generations born in America but still subject to strong ethnic influence in the family and the community, moved outwards from the centres of other cities, Seattle, San Francisco, Denver, Detroit, Cleveland, Philadelphia, Baltimore and Boston. In each case they were replaced by a new wave of arrivals, often from a different country. In Boston the Irish moved out

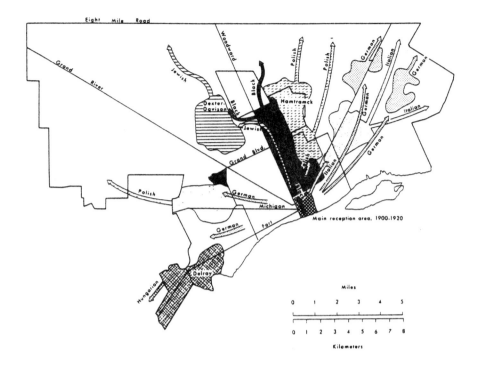

Figure 6.1 'Old Immigrant' Areas in the Concentrated City, Detroit 1950
Note the original locations around the CBD and the gradual movements out towards
the suburbs from 1900 onwards.
Source: Sinclair, R. & Thompson, B., *Detroit*, Ballinger Division, HarperCollins, 1977, p. 11

of the Shawmut peninsula between 1840 and 1875 to be replaced by
Italians and Russian Jews. They in turn began to move out by 1910 to
be replaced by Chinese, and by black people from the South. In the
process, as it got older, the same residential property filtered down
from white-collar WASPs to blue-collar WASPs, from them to Irish
and Germans; from western Europeans it then usually filtered down
to Italians and Greeks as they arrived in the country later; then to
eastern Europeans, predominantly Jewish and, as they in their turn
started to move out during the First World War, the ageing property
finally filtered down to black people.

As immigrant people and their descendants moved further and
further out from their original locations in the innermost residential
zone, the similarities in spatial behaviour faded. Some groups moved
much more quickly than others. Some moved much further than
others. Some Americanised quickly, others very slowly. Some
groups are still, now, resisting complete loss of their identities many

129

generations after their ancestors' arrival in America. Above all, some groups are remarkable for the way they have kept together, forming tight-knit communities way out in the suburbs while, in contrast, other groups have completely dispersed and disappeared.

It is much less easy to generalise about which European groups kept together and which dispersed than it is to explain their original location in the city. One can note only tendencies. Immigrants of the earliest waves — English, Irish and Germans — tended to disperse as they moved towards the suburbs. The later waves of Polish, Italian and Jewish immigrants tended to keep together, although there are many exceptions. Much depended on the conditions in particular cities and the predilections of the different immigrant groups. In Seattle, Japanese and Chinese who had arrived on the west coast by the turn of the century showed a similar pattern of behaviour. At first both nationalities clustered in tight communities near Seattle's CBD in the area known as the International District. These Japanese and Chinese neighbourhoods were most exclusive and distinctive at the time of the First World War. By 1970 the descendants of both groups had dispersed evenly throughout eastern Seattle.

The three main factors operating to determine clustering or dispersal seem to have been: time; ability to Americanise; and the strength of community ties. Three studies of small communities illustrate this well. Dutch immigrants arrived in Kalamazoo in the 1870s and in that small town, unusually, grouped into two communities some distance from the centre to north and south. As late as 1945 those two neighbourhoods still persisted and it was only when the fourth generation began to mix with other Americans as a result of the greater mobility and educational opportunities after the war that people of Dutch origin dispersed throughout Kalamazoo's residential population as a whole.

In the Globeville district of Denver, again from the 1870s onward, four groups of European immigrants were brought in to provide labour for the Globe smelter works. They formed tightly-knit Polish, Slovenian-Croatian, Serbian-Russian and Volga-Deutsch neighbourhoods. These last were Germans who had first tried Russia, then moved to the USA. As late as 1950 the families were living in the same streets in which they first located in the industrial area and the communities did not start to disperse until an urban motorway was built through Globeville, physically breaking up the neighbourhood. In other cities urban renewal schemes had the same effect of dispersing tightly-knit communities.

A microcosm of immigrant spatial behaviour is provided by Emrys Jones's study of Utica in upstate New York. In the early 1860s communities of Welsh and German immigrants were established close to the city centre of Utica, with the canal, railway and the factories nearby. Over the century he studied to 1965, Jones traced their movement further and further away from the CBD. As the Welsh and Germans moved out of the old property, the next wave of immigrants — this time Poles and Italians — moved in. The children and grandchildren of the original Welsh and German people moved further and further west into the suburbs. But there was a complete contrast between the two groups. Those of Welsh origin largely kept together as a clustered community while the Germans dispersed all over the built-up-area. One can imagine the successful, prosperous Welsh community in the outer suburbs, supporting the chapel, keeping the language alive, listening to their choirs, organising trips to Wales, celebrating St David's Day and, if not actually having a team in the land of baseball and something they *call* football, at least watching satellite relays from Cardiff Arms Park.

Many of the people of German ancestry could be traced in 1965 only by names in the phone book — often Anglicised, as so often happened at the port of entry when poorly educated immigration officers had to write down names in 30-odd languages and three alphabets. Individual families may be as enthusiastic for their German heritage as the Welsh for theirs, but the important point here is that they have not located together in one area, and they do not show any differences from the 'American' society at large.

Every decade Chicago publishes dot-distribution maps for each of the ethnic minorities which together make up the residential population of the city. Among those originally from Europe, as late as 1970 one could still identify clear Polish, Italian, Russian and Czech communities within Chicago. These did not account for all the people descended from immigrants from those countries, but large clusters of them did persist. The maps show only the distributions within the city limits and by now there may well be distinct neighbourhoods beyond the city limits, out in the suburbs, as with Utica. The later sets of Chicago maps also show distinct Mexican, Puerto Rican and Black communities, and these will be discussed in detail in later chapters. Distributions are also shown for people of German, Irish, Norwegian, Swedish, English, Scottish, Austrian and other origins. The more obvious features in these cases are blank spaces on the maps rather than clusters of dots. But once one has ascertained that the blank areas are the Loop, the southern and western ghettos, and the Mexican and Puerto Rican (or Hispanic) communities, then one can say that in the rest of the residential areas, people of Irish, German, British and Scandinavian origin are completely dispersed throughout the white population at large. For all practical purposes these former groups have Americanised.

Simple dispersion, of course, is not *ipso facto* Americanisation. This full absorption into the mainstream of the host society has been a process in time as well as space. Moreover, it has depended on a balance between the desire, or not, of the immigrants to lose their former national identity, and in turn their acceptability to the host society. To put it bluntly, whites have been welcomed more readily than blacks, Protestants more readily than Jews, English-speaking people more readily than those speaking Spanish. There are long, fine gradations and distinctions between these sets of extremes, but no amount of Newspeak can erase the historical fact of different degrees of prejudice.

Immigrants are not able to change the colour of their skin. They are able to change their language but, like their religion, they have often been very reluctant to do so. The white immigrant who was prepared to dress like the Americans around him or her, to speak the local version of English, to adopt the attitudes as well as the lifestyle of the hosts was the most likely to be accepted and absorbed; in short, to become an American — that is, of course, if he or she wanted to be accepted on those terms. Many of the Germans and Irish clearly did. In the process, of course, as so many Europeans became Americans, that which was 'American' changed; it was a two-way process. So the ability to become part of the American community which itself constantly changed as it absorbed millions and millions of Europeans, more or less willing to Americanise, depended on things like skin colour, language, religion, the strength of home ties, the degree of active participation in local politics, saleable skills, length of time in America and adaptability. Over a period of time absorption depended ultimately on the desire to be absorbed, and on the willingness of each generation of new Americans to accept the next wave of foreigners. For example, Jewish people tended to want to keep themselves separate for religious reasons, while Japanese have historically found it hard to learn the language and so merge.

A feature of European immigration to America was that, in the long run, most of the new arrivals expected to become part of the American society, and most of those people already there accepted the process to a greater or lesser extent. There were rites of passage. One was expected to step on to the lowest rung of the ladder and to climb up it only as those already above themselves moved up and made room. It was a matter of status. There was a clear pecking order: those who had arrived most recently got pecked most. Perhaps most important of all was the code that there was no overtaking on the climb up the ladder. But the process worked, and the concept of the melting pot appeared to be a reality.

In 1964 Andreas Feininger published a book of photographs taken in New York. There are countless books of photographs of New York and this is one of the few which stand out. Kate Simon, who wrote the text, labelled the last of the sixteen sections People. Between colour shots of night clubs, markets, clothes shops, a cemetery and the beach at Coney Island, are six superb monochrome studies. There are two old men sitting outside a shop with its signs in Greek. An old man stands at the door of a small shop whose window is full of prayer shawls and seven-branch candelabra. A man operating a sewing machine in a shop window is almost hidden by signs advertising weavers, weaving and stotting, darners, weaving while you wait; the rest of the lettering is in Hebrew. A strong young man with a heavy load on his shoulder is carrying produce out of a warehouse full of sacks, boxes and barrels; the sign says Italian American Grocer. A young man sits at a folding table. He has a cigarette in a holder, a leather cap, an oriental face; he is selling papers printed in Chinese.

Finally an old Chinese man, thin and wrinkled, with his trousers hitched up high, stands by his shop looking down a Manhattan street. His tiny shop is crammed with a large variety of strange vegetables. The sign tells New Yorkers that no. 49 is the Jack Lee Produce Co. The pictures and the date are significant. The people of European origin left in the middle of the city by that time tend to be old. There are Chinese, but no Vietnamese; a few Asians, but not many. The date of the book is 1964; one year before the revolutionary Immigration Act.

7

BLACK PEOPLE IN THE GHETTOS

Black people are considered at this point between the two chapters on immigrant peoples for several reasons. The first is that they began to arrive in the city in significant numbers between the major migrations of Europeans and the newer waves of Hispanic and Asian peoples. Secondly, the distribution of black people and their present locations have special, if not unique, features. Thirdly, while black people have become migrants to the city in this century, they have been in America longer than most WASPs, and in that sense are old-established Americans. There have been small numbers of black people in most American cities since the cities were founded. While they did remain a small proportion of the total population in any one city, black people seem to have attracted no special comment and did not live in any particular type of location. In relation to their total history, the ghettos of Boston, New York and Philadelphia are relatively recent phenomena in those cities. So the geography of black people in the American city shares some characteristics with that of both the old and the new immigrants.

Until the time of the First World War most black people, whose ancestors had been in America since the seventeenth and eighteenth centuries, were located in the southeastern quarter of the United States. They were concentrated, even as late as 1910, in what had been the slave-owning states. Most were slaves until 1863. But even after Abraham Lincoln abolished slavery, and even after his edict came into force in the South after the Civil War, black people continued to live much as they had done as slaves for the next fifty or sixty years.

With the end of slavery, landowners in the South no longer had labour. But, by the same token, black people no longer had work. In much of the South a system was developed called sharecropping by which the landowner provided the land, the seed and the mules, and the black people provided the labour in return for a small share of the crops. Black families moved out of the barrack-like slave quarters and, for obvious reasons, preferred to live in their own cottages on the land. These dwellings were often very simple sheds, but they had never housed slaves. Soon black people began to move to the southern towns in small numbers, and Atlanta, New Orleans and Houston developed black neighbourhoods in the nineteenth century. In the smaller towns the black population had to live on the edge, often on the other side of the newly arrived railway tracks which ran past the old towns. The railway line came to symbolise the line between any sets of white and black urban territories — we still have the phrase 'the other side of the tracks', denoting the part of town with the lowest social status. But until the time of the First World War blacks in the United States were predominantly farmers, rural, and confined to the South, that is from Virginia to East Texas.

The history of the Jim Crow laws, how rights were gradually taken away from black people in the South, is not relevant to the theme here, but some of the results in the towns and cities of the South proved to be pointers to what would happen in cities all over the country later. Black people were forced to live apart from whites in the black quarter, the black belt or 'niggertown'. As their votes were taken away, or as they were intimidated from registering to vote, much more immediate, practical, everyday problems confronted them. They could get only the worst, the lowest-paid jobs in the Southern towns and cities, and their children got the worst schools. If there happened to be public transport, black people had to use separate vehicles or sit segregated at the back, and stand if a white wanted to sit down. They were not allowed in many small shops but had to wait at a window or side door. In department stores and cafes black people were not allowed to mix with whites.

There are plenty of photographs taken before the 1960s of the offices of doctors, dentists and lawyers, boarding houses, hotels, cinemas, theatres and the like which have signs proclaiming either 'no coloureds' or, more simply, 'white'. In short, segregation of black people and demotion to status of second-class citizens started much earlier in the South than in other parts of America, and was much more overt and blatant. The activities of the Ku Klux Klan, burning crosses and lynching black people in the South, have received more publicity and dramatisation, but the day-to-day suppression, discrimination and exclusion affected every single black man, woman, boy and girl. They were uniquely segregated and rejected.

Black people began to move out of the south-eastern quarter of the United States in large numbers during the First World War. A

135

coincidence provided the pull factor to add to the push factors of low living standards and racial discrimination in the South. As the war in Europe, which the USA did not join until 1917, made more and more demands on American industry, that very war at the same time cut off the supply of cheap labour of European immigrants. Blacks were able to move north and find work in the factories of the north east, the part of the country which was known then as the manufacturing belt. Not only did the native-born black people replace immigrants as the cheapest element of the labour supply, they also located in exactly the same types of residential areas in the big industrial cities as the European migrants had done, and for exactly the same reasons. They needed work, and had to compete at the factory gates with one another. So again it was an advantage to live as near as possible to the factory, the store and the city centre where the jobs were concentrated. Unlike the immigrants who often arrived with some savings, most of the black people arrived in the city with nothing. Therefore the cheapest accommodation was vital. This meant taking the accommodation which absolutely no-one else wanted, usually the oldest property in the middle of the city. In most cases this is the only way in which black people in tens or hundreds of thousands could ever have established themselves so quickly in the northern white cities.

Accommodation nobody else wanted usually meant that which had already filtered down from middle-class whites, through blue-collar white owners plus two or three generations of immigrants. It meant accommodation nearest the noisiest and dirtiest factories, slaughterhouses, sewage works and the like. It meant accommodation in the most crowded and congested and dilapidated inner residential rings. By 1924 Burgess showed the so-called Black Belt of Chicago as one of the ethnic quarters ringing the Loop. In the same way Baltimore, Philadelphia, Newark, New York, Boston, Pittsburgh, Cleveland, Detroit, St Louis, Milwaukee and other cities in the north east had their black ghettos founded. Too many writers glibly use the phrase 'Northward migration' to describe the movement of blacks out of the South. Eventually black people located in every big city in the USA including Seattle and San Diego, but the phrase is accurate enough until the 1920s.

One exception to the rule of the ghettos starting, like the immigrant areas, in the innermost residential ring, paradoxically, is one of the best known. Harlem was some ten miles from Manhattan's downtown of the time, hardly the inner residential ring. But the location of the large influx of black people into New York in the early years of this century does illustrate another point already made: that blacks got only that accommodation which nobody else wanted. Harlem was built on the edge of the BUA at the time by speculative white developers in the 1900s. They built substantial stone houses on the edge of the city to attract wealthy whites to the quiet, suburban area of northern Manhattan. But at that date white people considered Harlem much too far from the centre of things, badly served by public transport, and very few bought property there. So most of the new property remained empty. As blacks began to arrive in New York in large numbers from the South a black local entrepreneur bought up as much of the unwanted property in Harlem as he could, and sold or rented it to black people. In this way they were in that instance able to move into *new* property, because Harlem might well have been on the other side of the moon as far as whites were concerned.

The decades between the two World Wars witnessed a marked slow-down in black migration, particularly in the depth of the Depression, though not a complete halt. The Second World War not only accelerated the movement again, but increased the numbers way beyond those involved during the First. Equally importantly, the Second World War drew black people north west, west and south west as far as Seattle, San Francisco, Los Angeles and San Diego. From the 1940s onwards it is imprecise to refer to black people migrating northward. By then they were moving out of the south eastern quarter of the country, the old South of the Confederacy, in every direction to every other part of the Union. Thus, by 1945, a social revolution was nearly complete. In 1865 the vast majority of black people were living in rural areas, working in agriculture and largely confined to the old South. By 1965 most were employed in industry and menial services, were represented in every city of any size from the Atlantic to the Pacific, and they were overwhelmingly urban.

After the war the momentum of the movement out of the South was sustained. It became possible to foresee a time when that reservoir would be drained. But it would not be correct to think of black Americans becoming distributed evenly all over the country. Precisely, by the 1950s, they were to be found very tightly contained in the inner-city ghettos in the big industrial cities. The pattern of distribution was one of highly localised, high-density nuclei. Being in the same socio-economic position, and the same geographical locations as the earlier waves of migrants to those cities, black Americans fairly expected to climb up the same socio-economic ladder and then themselves start to progress out towards the suburbs.

But the experience of those black Americans in the oldest big city ghettos, in Chicago's black belt, New York's Harlem and the others, suggested, ominously, that this was not going to happen. Two characteristics of the black ghetto developed which were not the same as the earlier or the contemporary immigrant quarters. First, black ghettos became 80%, 90%, even 95% populated by black people. In contrast to an Irish or Polish area where the dominant group might well have been less than half the total population, black areas soon became populated virtually entirely by black people. Secondly, although it is true that groups of European migrants to the city then moved out towards the suburbs at different speeds, the black ghettos grew outwards definitely the most slowly, encountering the greatest resistance of all.

With this slow expansion, the continued migration from the South, and the very high birth rates within the black population, residential densities in the ghettos increased to record levels and produced severe overcrowding. By the late 1940s black ghettos with, by then, very old property which had decayed as it filtered down again and again, with virtually no mixture of racial groups, with minimum contact with other neighbourhoods, and with increasing overcrowding, were very different kinds of places from European quarters. The black ghetto became something unique in each big American city. The literature on the problems of black people in the ghettos is massive, but the more one wades through it, the clearer it becomes that the many and varied difficulties — in the extreme the sheer desperation of some ghetto residents — derive from the poverty of the vast majority of them, in turn starkly the result of racial prejudice and discrimination.

The racial prejudice operated directly; if there were more applicants than jobs, the black people were the ones not taken on. Until quite recent federal legislation, even when black people were employed in the cities they were paid less than whites doing the same work. Complainants found themselves out of work again. This happened in every city, and surprisingly frequently in the literature there are allusions to a massive white conspiracy. It is hard to believe that a cotton-gin owner in Texas, a car muffler producer in Michigan, a sawmill operator in Seattle and a fast-food joint franchise owner in Jersey are all in on this fantastic conspiracy. But having witnessed Asians fighting West Indians in Salford, having observed overt racial prejudice in North Africa and Asiatic USSR, I know xenophobia and racial conflict occur spontaneously between all groups of the human race. No conspiracy is necessary; we think of it all by ourselves.

However, on top of the economic discrimination white people in northern and southern cities did react to the black communities differently. In northern cities whites as a whole took very little interest in the black people arriving in the inner city. What happened to the

138

latter was, above all, the result of indifference and neglect. In the southern cities, in contrast, the whites moved much more actively and openly to keep blacks in the ghetto, out of white areas, in their place. In the north, after the war, they were not wanted, not helped, and as far as possible, by those who did not have to come into contact with them, completely ignored.

Not surprisingly then, with the more open and active discrimination, and with the guidance of the brave men of the Southern Christian Leadership Conference, the Civil Rights movement began and predominated in the cities of the South. While racial discrimination and low economic status were the heart of the matter, the movement addressed specific and immediate manifestations:

- housing segregation
- segregation in buses, trains, waiting rooms and toilets
- segregation in restaurants, cinemas, hotels, and at lunch counters in stores
- separate schools and (only a few) separate colleges
- denial of voting rights
- exclusion from juries in the South.

As much of the history of the Civil Rights movement is outside the scope of this work, only the relevant key events will be mentioned. But they do nonetheless need to be mentioned, to emphasise that of all the peoples who have in the past, and still are establishing residential communities in American cities, only black people have had to resort to such drastic action as the Civil Rights movement, and then the riots of the 1960s in order to secure their rightful place in urban life.

KEY EVENTS

1. In 1954 in Topeka, Kansas, in the test case of Brown versus the Board of Education, the Supreme Court ruled that segregation in schools was unconstitutional.
2. Starting in 1955, led by Rosa Parks in Montgomery, Alabama, blacks boycotted the buses of the company which forced them to stand if whites wanted to sit down. In 1956 the Supreme Court ruled in favour of the black people.
3. In 1957 black people started to enter their children in whites-only schools and colleges in Arkansas, Mississippi and Virginia. The National Guard and eventually the 101st Airborne Division had to be called out to protect black youngsters from vicious white

139

attacks. In this brutal campaign the black people did not win until 1962.

4. Beginning in 1960 and organised by Dr Martin Luther King Junior, black people started peaceful sit-ins at lunch counters in department stores in southern cities. This later was extended to a complete boycott of all white businesses and shops in the downtown areas. There was a well-publicised march from the ghetto to the city centre in Nashville. King was arrested in Atlanta and put in gaol. The blacks persisted, and eventually lunch counters were opened to all.

5. 1961 saw the Freedom Rides when white supporters joined black people to ride on long-distance buses from Washington to New Orleans. The buses were firebombed in Birmingham, Alabama, and the riders were beaten up. There were riots when the damaged buses reached Montgomery, a place which has a particularly bad record in the history of civil rights. The black riders, but not the whites, were gaoled for 60 days in Jackson, Mississippi, another city which in theory existed under the same Constitution as all others in the Union. After all the TV publicity Attorney General Robert Kennedy intervened to ban segregation on all interstate transport.

6. In 1963, the year in which George Wallace, Governor of Alabama, declared that he believed in 'segregation for ever', national TV news networks showed to Americans all over the continent the police turning water cannon on black children, breaking up peaceful, non-violent demonstrations, and savagely clubbing black men lining up at city halls to register to vote. As with the terrible pictures it sent back from Vietnam, news coverage stirred the consciences of Americans all over the country. White people in northern cities could not ignore their TV screens the way they kept away from, and ignored, the ghettos. The publicity forced the federal government to act. John Kennedy introduced his Civil Rights Bill at last. But it was not until 6 August 1965 that Lyndon Johnson got the Voting Rights Bill through Congress and into effect.

In 1963, 1964 and 1965 black people continued to demonstrate. In March 1963 a quarter of a million marched to the Lincoln Memorial in Washington to hear King give his 'Let Freedom Ring' speech. But by then his ideas of non-violent action led by the SCLC were being forced into the background by the younger, more aggressive men of the so-called Student Non-violent Coordinating Committee (SNICK).

7. In March 1965 blacks led by Andrew Brown planned to march from Selma to Montgomery in peaceful protest against the killing

of Jimmy Lee Jackson by the police during violence after black people were again prevented from registering to vote. The marchers were beaten back by mounted police at the Edmund Pettus Bridge and once more police brutality was seen on national television.

Lyndon Johnson had to call out the National Guard again and he forced George Wallace to let the march take place. Johnson had signed the Civil Rights Act in 1964 and, less well known, had added the 24th Amendment to the Constitution, and thus removed the connection between the right to vote and the American poll tax, which had been the greatest burden and disincentive to register to vote for the poorer black people.

Johnson's administration witnessed the enactment of the Civil Rights legislation which Kennedy had belatedly initiated. The effect was felt much more directly in the southern cities than in those in the north and west. In the same summer that the Voting Rights Bill passed Congress — 1965 — black people rioted in Watts in Los Angeles, and more violent organisations began to take the lead from the SCLC. These included the Black Muslims, the Student Coordinating Committee led by Stokely Carmichael, the Black Panthers dominated by Eldridge Cleaver, and the Organisation for Afro-American Unity formed by Malcolm X. Most cities in the South have made steady, if very slow progress since the 1960s, although Miami and Houston still have severe ghetto problems. In 1963 James Baldwin published his personal essay on what it was like to be black in America, *The Fire Next Time*, and for the next decade attention was concentrated on black people in the big cities outside the South.

Once the black ghettos had been established in the inner residential rings of northern and western cities, the immediate concerns were low pay, unemployment, bad housing, declining services, increasing overcrowding, and confinement. As shown in the last chapter, many ethnic groups in similar urban locations developed distinctive neighbourhoods as the result of social cohesion, a desire to keep together, help each other, or preserve their national culture. It was a matter of choice and came from within the area. Whether or not black Americans wanted similar things is beside the point because the overwhelming evidence from every city studied is that the black people were kept together and confined by the external pressures on the ghetto. People living in blocks next to the ghetto, whether poor blue-collar WASPs or recent immigrants, actively resisted the growth of the ghetto. They resisted the spread of black people into the surrounding areas. Blacks certainly wanted to move out, to move towards the better conditions further from the city centre, as everyone else had either done or was still doing. Whether they would have dispersed in the process, like the Irish and Germans, or kept together like Italians and Poles, we will never know, The fact is that the majority of them were confined to the ghetto as much by this external resistance as by any choice of their own.

Richard Morrill's classic study of the Seattle ghetto has proved, sadly, representative of all the big-city black ghettos. Morrill studied the very slow growth of the ghetto north eastward from the centre of Seattle over the two decades from 1940 to 1960. While Seattle's ghetto was not as long and narrow then as some better-known examples (Chicago's southern black belt, New York's Harlem Bedford-Stuyvesant, Los Angeles' Watts), clearly aiming purposefully away from the centre towards the suburbs, its characteristics are very similar to those such as Milwaukee and Miami. Morrill found that black ghettos grew in a series of spurts, separated by long periods when there was no spatial increase. A cyclic development could be discerned. In the initial phase pressure built up in the ghetto as more and more black people arrived and more babies were born. During that long period increasing numbers of young black people wanted to set up their own homes, and more of the small proportion of successful people wanted to obtain better housing further from the city centre. For black people at the time the best most could hope for was to look in the next city block outwards, the next one-eighth of a mile. In that next block outwards, and in the blocks on either side, for a long time both native-born whites and European immigrants did everything they could to keep blacks out.

The most direct resistance was the refusal of people living in the next block to sell or to rent property to black people. Behind them were estate agents (realtors), who themselves were boycotted if they showed black people round white-owned property. A black family could ask to see an apartment, to be told that it had been let only five minutes ago. Next day white people would be being shown round the apartment which was still on the market, for whites.

Further behind these front-line defenders were the American equivalent of building societies, the Savings and Loan companies. They, before the disastrous de-regulation under Ronald Reagan, were in general naturally reluctant to extend mortgages to anyone who might not be able to keep up the repayments, and in particular were reluctant to lend money on old, dilapidated property in poor inner-city areas. People in run-down areas were the greatest risk, and the black people were the poorest of all in the worst property. It had been only government guarantees via the Veterans' Administration that had encouraged Savings and Loans to extend mortgages to so many

142

returning ex-servicemen after World War Two, and which in turn had enabled the suburbs to grow. As the black people were the poorest section of society, with the least job security, and as the areas next to the ghetto were among the oldest property, there was an understandable problem about mortgages, especially as government guarantees did not apply. Savings and Loan companies had maps of the city showing the areas where they would not lend money on property. These became known as the Red Line areas. If a black person went to a Savings and Loan wanting money for property in a red-lined area, at once there were two insurmountable counts against him.

Since federal legislation to outlaw this crude kind of discrimination has come into force, more subtle methods have been used to make it as difficult as possible for black people to move into a non-black area. In the suburbs, for example, keeping property values as high as possible is an obvious and legal method, as are such zoning laws as no more than one residential property per three acres. Keeping the price up keeps out all undesirables without any mention of colour of skin.

Morrill found, as was the case in most cities before 1914, that when black people comprised less than 10% of the population in a block, white people were indifferent to their presence. As the percentage rose beyond 10% and approached 20%, tensions rose. He found that if, one way or another, black people could move in small numbers into a block over a period of time until they comprised over 25% of the total population, then the former residents moved out as fast as they could. Suddenly the extreme resistance collapsed. Black people could then move into the next block relatively easily as property values dropped. After the period of very slow growth, suddenly another block had been gained. Then, of course, resistance was at its peak in the next white block outwards, and the cycle of stop and go, stop and go is repeated over and over again.

In the study of Chicago ghettos and those in other cities similar processes were observed and a terminology was developed. After black people had moved into a new block, students recognised Early Consolidation. Then, in that block, plain Consolidation followed as more blocks were added further out and the block in question was no longer the frontier. Late Consolidation, then Piling Up followed as the block became 90 or 95% black, by migration and by natural increase, and as pressure grew for further spatial advance. But the two terms used to describe the beginning of each forward surge are most revealing. Sociologists, geographers and other students of the ghetto used the terms Penetration and Invasion; prejudice seemed to have crept into supposedly academic studies.

143

In the quarter-century after the Second World War conditions in the black ghettos were different in both degree and kind from conditions in the areas of other migrants to the city and from the condition of black people in the South. Only after the black urban riots of the 1960s were the conditions and problems brought to the attention of the American public at large, particularly the white suburban population. This was the result of the work of the National Advisory Commission on Civil Disorders, the Kerner Commission. Set up to look into the causes of the violent urban riots in the black ghettos in the sixties, Kerner identified twelve distinct problems, grievances and special conditions of black people, the most often-quoted of which, in the order of importance given to them by black people themselves, are:

- police harassment
- unemployment and underemployment
- inadequate housing
- inadequate education
- racial discrimination
- inadequate public services.

A more thorough analysis would tempt one to put racial discrimination separately, the other items being the media through which discrimination was and is operated. In turn, unemployment and low pay when work has been obtained result in the bad housing, slum conditions, poor education, and a new generation unprepared for skilled employment: a vicious circle of circular and cumulative causation.

The inadequate public services need dividing more specifically into two categories. First, poor urban infrastructure, the decaying street lighting and power supplies, collapsing water and sewerage works and lack of garbage collection services all of which help to turn ghettos into slums. Second, into lack of welfare and social services which become essential once people have been blocked into poverty, but which would be nothing like as great a burden on the city finances if discrimination had not operated to produce the poverty in the first place. Prevention may or may not be better than cure, but it is cheaper.

Time and again, in cities throughout the USA, black people put police harassment at the top of their list of grievances. The police and fire services are the two which the city does *not* underfund for the ghetto, unlike education and the rest of the infrastructure. When New York was about to go bankrupt in 1975, Gerald Ford made no extra money available for teachers or garbage collectors, but he guaranteed that the police and the fire department would continue to be paid. Those two bodies were, and are, essential to keep the lid on the ghettos and to deal with riots when, not surprisingly, they do erupt.

With so few whites living in the ghetto, 5–10% at most, and with poor black people having minimum movement outside the ghetto, then on a day-to-day basis the police — black officers included — are the only white people many blacks frequently came into contact with. While I can find no evidence of any national conspiracy against black people, as has often been alleged — it being simply a matter of them sinking or swimming by their own efforts — it is still easy to understand that black people, largely confined to the ghetto and coming into contact with more policemen and women than with any other single group of white people, saw the police as their oppressors and gaolers. Employers and city officials may have been the prime cause of the poverty and the slum conditions, but the police got the immediate blame.

The small numbers of non-black people living in the ghetto is a fact which can be verified by reference to the census. The assertion above that black people in the 1950s and 1960s had little experience of the city outside the ghetto may be much harder to accept for some. Two kinds of evidence support the contention that this in fact was the case. First, the evidence of Chapters One and Two above. As manufacturing, retailing, wholesaling, transport facilities and all kinds of tertiary service jobs have moved into the suburbs, they have moved further and further from the inner, poorer ends of the ghettos. Several studies in different cities have shown that as the jobs got further and further away, unemployed black people were not even able to search for, and hopefully find, work which was becoming scattered over a larger and larger area every decade; over hundreds of square miles of very low-density suburbs with virtually no public transport, where to look for a job even a desperately poor person just had to have a car.

The average distance of the total supply of jobs is still moving further from the inner end of the inner-city ghetto, so that work is becoming harder to find and harder to hold for the least advantaged black people. Those who both make the effort, and are lucky, have to do so in the face of a system which works against them. Often they have to make the longest journeys to the lowest-paid jobs, either by expensive car or by an inadequate transport system which is a relic from the days of commuting *in* to the centre, rather than organised for reverse or cross-commuting. Thus the black people have limited experience of the suburbs where most of the action has moved.

Secondly, evidence comes from a completely different and independent quarter: educational research. One of the tools which social scientists use to measure people's experience and knowledge of their surroundings is the mental map. This is not a test of map-reading or of cartographic skills, but a means by which we can find out what people perceive and know of the space around them. For example, those questioned are asked to draw sketch maps of the parts of their own town which they know and use, their own country, to see what they do and do not know, or consider important to them. In other tests people are asked to show where they would like to live, or to work, and they can do this only for places that they know something about and aspire to. The quality of the draughtsmanship is not important. In this way one can get some idea of people's knowledge of areas and awareness of the spaces in which they live and move.

A mental map which amuses me greatly as a northerner is one reproduced by Gould and White in their book *Mental Maps*. It has the caption 'how Londoners see the North'. The mental maps of the Londoners, of course, show a great deal of London and the area to Dover and Brighton. There is an arrow pointing vaguely towards Land's End, Wales is a tiny lump in the west, the Arctic Circle is drawn along Hadrian's Wall, the M1 goes up the middle of England, railways end at Manchester and icebergs float around Scotland, which is shown as a bifurcated peninsula. Thus the maps reveal knowledge, lack of knowledge, and misapprehension.

In the same way, Gould and White have revealing maps of Philadelphia and Los Angeles. In Los Angeles black and white people with as similar backgrounds as possible (and this *is* a weakness) were asked to draw their mental maps of the city. Those drawn by the white citizens are very detailed. There are mistakes, of course, because the task was posed without advanced notice; so, for example, the San Fernando Valley is shown larger than the Pacific Ocean. But in the whites' maps everything is there in more or less correct relative position: Malibu, Pasadena, Long Beach, the airport, the Civic Centre, the Music Centre, hundreds of details with one very surprising omission — Disneyland is missing. What those maps show is that the white people have either been to, or at least know about, all the main features of the city.

The maps drawn by the black citizens are disturbing. The total number of features can almost be counted on the fingers of two hands. Moreover, the few details are mainly the details of the Watts ghetto. The Pacific Pond is there, but the beaches are not marked, as in the maps of the whites, and there is no San Fernando Valley which is beyond the knowledge of the black citizens of similar age. Santa

146

Monica, West LA, Beverly Hills, Hollywood and Pasadena account for five fingers, and even these may be distorted because of their connection with the film industry — they are possibly the result of knowledge from secondary sources. But where the maps of the whites show beaches, parks, arts centres and freeways, all that the maps of the black people have left to show are about ten east–west streets in the ghetto and about a dozen streets and boulevards running north–south through Watts. As Morrill said of the Seattle ghetto, 'It is difficult to be a minority as a group, but more difficult still to be a minority alone.' So many black people suppressed 'the desire to escape the ghetto and move freely in the larger society'. Black people then tended to stay together for safety, and this further limited their knowledge of the city outside the ghetto.

Elsewhere a map of Los Angeles (Figure 7.1) illustrates other features referred to by the Kerner Commission. Five features were mapped by means of hatching and by dots:

- median income below $5000
- blacks more than 75% of the population
- maximum population density
- school drop-out rates
- maximum crime rates for LA.

Some white areas like Long Beach have low incomes — one of the five features mapped. Areas round Santa Monica have high population densities, but none of the other features. School drop-out rates are high in much of the inner-city area, including the Barrio, and high rates of crime cover much of southern Los Angeles. But one community alone has all five characteristics, all five types of shading are overprinted on each other, making the Watts ghetto stand out starkly on the map. Other areas have their problems, but black ghettos, particularly the inner ends of the black ghettos, had the accumulation of all the problems.

In the forty-year period from the mid-1920s to 1965, when European immigration had passed its peak and Asian immigration was just getting into its stride, the proportion of black people in the American city greatly increased. Spanish-speaking people, labelled Hispanics, often became the second largest group of newcomers to the city, but the proportion of black people increased so much that by the 1980 census they were not a minority group in ten or a dozen Central Cities. The Bureau of the Census shows that in 1980 and 1990 the percentage of black people in Central Cities was:

147

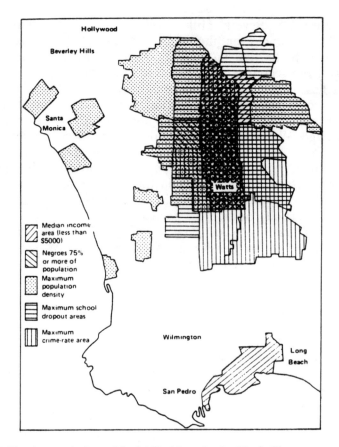

Figure 7.1 The Accumulation of Social Problems in the Black Ghetto
Other parts of Los Angeles, shown here, had some of the problems, but in the 1960s,
the decade of the black riots, Watts had them all.
Source: Smith, D.M., *The Geography of Social Well-being in the United States*, McGraw-Hill,
New York, 1973, p. 47

	1980	1990
Washington DC	70	66
Atlanta	66	67
Detroit	63	76
Newark	58	58
Birmingham	55	63
New Orleans	55	62
Baltimore	54	59
Richmond	51	55
Oakland	46	44

	1980	1990
St Louis	45	47
Cleveland	44	47
Flint	41	48
Chicago	40	39
Montgomery	40	42
Philadelphia	38	40

By 1990 another six cities had joined the list of those whose populations were over 50% black:

	1990
Gary	81
Jacksonville	56
Memphis	55
Inglewood (Cal)	52
Macon	52
Savannah	51

As the earlier immigrants to the city were successful in moving out, more and more blacks were left behind. The ghettos became very large, in some cases taking up half or two-thirds of the area of the Central City. In many others there are now several separate large communities of black people within the city limits. It may be too early to say definitely yet, but there are signs that as middle-class black people managed at last to move out to the suburbs, these peaks may have been passed.

As time has passed, a proportion of the black people have received good education, have achieved reasonable careers, and have managed to move out towards the suburbs. Middle-class black people have had to make much greater efforts, and much greater sacrifices, than most migrants to the city. It was the black middle class which persisted with the long, hard-fought Civil Rights movement, and it was the black middle class which led the urban riots of the 1960s, which were different in cause from those of the 1990s. The Kerner Commission found, one suspects to its surprise, that middle-class black people often featured among those who rioted in the 1960s. The explanations given are the frustration felt in the sixties after their expectations had been raised in the preceding decades, and the grievance that such a high proportion of black men was being sent to Vietnam (more than their fair proportion being put in front line units and, consequently, many more being killed and maimed). The book by Masotti and

Corsi, *Shoot-Out in Cleveland*, in spite of its title and the names of its authors, is not an account of Mafia gang warfare but a superb description of the causes, the course, and the aftermath of the black riot in Cleveland in 1968, plus a review of the Kerner Commission findings.

But a major problem for the blue-collar and unemployed black people left to form the majorities in the cities listed above is that their middle-class leaders have gone. With the striving up the socio-economic ladder, the striving outward along the suburban trail against odds greater than those which faced any other group before, black people became sorted out spatially, first within the ghetto, and then between the inner-city ghetto and the suburbs. The middle class moved out and the poor were left behind. As usual, there are more studies of, and information on, the southern black belt in Chicago than for any other ghetto, but smaller studies from Boston, New York and Los Angeles confirm the trend. In the very large ghettos black society is very different at the outer end from that at the inner end. Some of the ghettos are enormous in numbers of people and in area. The southern ghetto in Chicago is some twelve miles in length, and can resemble an industrial city at one end and a dormitory village at the other.

At the inner end of such ghettos, where the least successful black people have been left behind, one finds the highest proportions of:

- poverty
- school drop-outs
- illiterate people
- blue-collar workers
- unemployed people
- single people
- single-parent families (usually a female head)
- desertions
- juvenile delinquency
- crime
- gang warfare
- Aids
- drug abuse
- prostitution
- poor health
- infant mortality
- malnutrition
- tuberculosis
- rat and roach infestation.

Many of these conditions, of course, are similar to those features of urban blight mentioned in connection with earlier European immigrants, although the proportions of the population and the total numbers of people affected tend to be much higher. While there was often precious little sympathy from American society at large for the plight of the newcomers, there is virtually none now for those left behind in the inner-city ends of the black ghettos. Again, cause and effect in social affairs are perceived differently in America. In Europe we tend to think of lack of jobs, schools, hospitals, training centres, clinics, libraries, parks, particularly the lack of money in a given neighbourhood or social group as causes of and contributors to bad social conditions. In America, even from white, liberal-minded people including some of my acquaintances, too often the argument, the cause and effect, is reversed — no wonder those people have no schools and hospitals, they won't get out and work for them. The suggestion is often that they would rather be streetwalkers, drug pushers and muggers than do a day's work; the bland assumption in this being that a day's work is there for the doing. Most people only turn to those things as the very last resort. What has to be admitted, although disputed by some observers, is that as the conditions persist and worsen each decade, now all the factors are so completely inter-related that people may well perpetuate the slum conditions as much as the conditions handicap the people. In such a context one must be very precise with one's terminology. Some use the word slums to refer to the physical structure. Others use the phrase social blight to refer to the people. The two are not necessarily the same thing.

The characteristics in the list of elements of social blight given above, measured per thousand of the population, are paralleled in the appearance of the inner ends of the ghettos. Not only are the houses and apartment blocks old, they are old-fashioned; they lack modern fittings, are close together, subdivided, badly maintained and depressing. For example, the inner end of the eastern ghetto in Washington, surprisingly close to the White House and the monuments of the beautiful city centre was like this in the 1980s. The substantial old stone houses clearly had been built for much wealthier inhabitants. During the filtering-down process they had acquired the outside stairs subdividing them into flats, the cheap air conditioners stuck in the windows and chain-link fences to protect them from random vandalism. The general appearance of depression and poverty was made worse by the very old cars lining the streets, by the damage done to the trees, verges and street lamps, by the sight of sheets of plywood and cardboard at many windows, and by smoke-blackened walls above the windows of rooms where squatters had started fires.

151

Another set of features in the older, inner ends of the ghettos are the kinds of businesses and institutions. Several observers have been surprised by the number of hairdressers and beauty parlours, although many were simple, sometimes shabby places. One eminent geographer, some time ago, explained at length in an article in a learned journal that that was because black people take such a pride in their appearance. The article did not quite ring true for the inner end of the ghetto. Those beauty parlours are like the dozens of hairdressers in side-streets in desperate little towns in depressed areas in Britain: they are where people without any capital or training are trying hard to make a living. Get a chair, a comb, a pair of scissors, a sheet and an aerosol and you are in business. You can open a beauty salon in your kitchen. The trouble is, both here and in the ghetto, so can everyone else. There are more such salons on some streets than there are people to provide the trade.

By the time one has seen the sign 'Loan Ranger' on the nineteenth pawn shop, the pun has worn too thin. Cheap food stores, nearly-new clothes shops, junk furniture showrooms, liquor stores, endless second-hand hardware shops cum money-lenders make up the rest of the local retail mix, interspersed with one kind of feature very rarely seen in Britain. This is the store-front church or the store-front school. Black people who have no capital to set up decent businesses in rented shops certainly can not raise enough money to build their own churches or specialist clinics and schools. Hence former shops on the street are taken over, the large windows covered over cheaply in one way or another, and the once retail land-use is converted to a Southern Baptist Church, a Black Muslim Mosque, a welfare clinic or a 'Street Academy', perhaps to help local youth learn to read and write.

Ten or twelve miles away, the growing outer end of the black ghetto, often close to, or beyond, the city boundary now, has markedly different characteristics. Here are the black communities which have the highest proportions of people who have completed school, and the highest proportions of college graduates. These are the black people who, as a result of a combination of intelligence, drive, education, very hard work and more than the average amount of luck, have obtained relatively well-paid and reasonably permanent jobs. A much higher proportion of them are white-collar workers and self-employed. Most of them are home-owners. They tend to be second-, third-, fourth-generation city-born. Perhaps most hopefully for the future, these outer ends of the ghettos are the areas with the highest proportions of married couples with small families; that is, with stable social conditions. Many of the problems of black ghettos still apply — that must be emphasised. These are still relatively deprived areas in relation to the WASP communities around them, but the rates of unemployment, crime, drug abuse and gang warfare are as nothing compared to the other end of the ghetto. Seeing the southern, outer end of the continuation of the Watts ghetto in Los Angeles, it is hard to believe that the neat, new, brightly-painted wooden bungalows, set in wide gardens and on wide streets with neat grass verges, trees and undamaged street lights are part of the ghetto. What, then, precisely makes this a part of the Los Angeles ghetto?

The answer is that in those suburban blocks 95% of the inhabitants are black; that white people do not want to live there and they do not want even successful black people to move into their neighbourhoods. When the black people have achieved everything else — education, good jobs, stable families and a middle-class lifestyle — there is still the fact that too often they remain segregated simply because of the colour of their skin. That part of the outer end of the ghetto is an attractive place to live, but for the residents it still has a stigma because it is still a kind of open prison from which they can not entirely escape.

Many American cities, even those with less than half the population within the city boundary black, have black mayors now. The successful mayors live in the new neighbourhoods with attractive houses, proper churches, clinics, supermarkets and schools; but the populations of those areas are made up predominantly of black people. Some years ago the *Sunday Times* had a large supplement on successful black people. Four images persist from the illustrations. First, a highly optimistic picture of a white girl and a black boy sitting at the same school desk. Second, very well-dressed men and women, leaders of the black community, standing on the steps of the new church. Third, Mayor Coleman Young of Detroit in a march mourning the death of a policeman. Fourth, and most telling of all, is a close-up in a barber's shop. The black barber is cutting the hair of a black boy. Through a mirror we can see a black man waiting, and a crucifix on the wall. Many barbers provide *Playboy* for the waiting gentry, but seldom Bibles. On the wall is a sign 'no profanity please'. Behind the boy, dressed up, is his father who has taken him to have his hair cut. This is not just middle-class aspiration, this is, *par excellence*, modern, New Man. But however mainstream American those people in that shop that day, at the church and in the march, every single one was black. However far they may have moved out, very few black people have dispersed and merged with the rest of the urban population at large.

8

ASIANS IN THE METROPOLITAN AREA

At the time when the vast majority of immigrants to the USA came from Europe they travelled by sea, got off the ship or the subsequent train in the city centre, and found work and accommodation in the inner rings of the concentrated city. Although suburbanisation was well under way by the end of the mass movement of blacks out of the South, in a similar way the black people arrived at the rail terminus or the bus station, found homes vacated by successful immigrants, and found work in the Central City. But the Hispanics and Asians, particularly the latter who have arrived in America in very large numbers since 1965, arrive on the edge of the urban area by air, move from the airport by car, and now perceive that possibilities for work are scattered all over the built-up-area and are no longer all concentrated near the traditional immigrant areas downtown.

The US Government has kept complete records of immigration only since 1820. The immigration depot at Castle Garden, New York, was not opened until 1855, and Ellis Island, now a museum, was not in operation until 1892. Contrary to popular belief, specific groups of people had always been excluded from the United States until 1965. In 1882 the Chinese Exclusion Act came into force when their labour was no longer required on the west coast. The Immigration Act of 1917 took this further by applying a ban to all people of Asian origin.

The bias to Britain and Europe was strengthened by the National Origins Act of 1924 which granted foreign countries quotas in proportion to the numbers of their people already in the USA. Thus Britain had the largest quota, often not fully taken up, northern and western Europe were favoured, and the number of entrants fell dramatically the further one moved from that fortunate, small part of the world. Until the late 1940s then, immigration policy was very selective and, after the peak decades from 1890 to 1930 when millions entered the country each year, numbers were carefully controlled.

154

Table 8.1 City Populations 1990

Metropolitan area	× 1000	Central City × 1000	Central city as % of Metrop
New York–NJ–CT	18,087	7,323	40
Los Angeles	14,532	3,485	24
Chicago–Gary	8,066	2,784	34
San Francisco–Oak–SJ	6,253	724	11
Philadelphia–Trenton	5,899	1,586	27
Detroit–Ann Arbor	4,665	1,028	22
Boston–Salem	4,177	574	14
Washington–DC–MD–VA	3,924	607	15
Dallas–Ft Worth	3,885	1,007	26
Houston–Galv–Braz	3,711	1,631	44
Miami–Ft Laud	3,193	359	11
Atlanta	2,834	394	14
Cleveland–Akron	2,760	506	18
Seattle–Tacoma	2,559	516	20
San Diego	2,498	1,111	44
Minneapolis–St Paul	2,464	368	15
St Louis	2,444	397	16
Baltimore	2,382	736	31
Pittsburgh–Beaver V.	2,243	370	16
Phoenix	2,122	983	46
Tampa–St P–Clearw.	2,068	280	14
Denver–Boulder	1,848	468	25
Cincinnati–Hamilton	1,744	364	21
Milwaukee–Racine	1,607	628	39
Kansas City MO–KS	1,566	585	37

Source: Statistical Abstract of the US 1992

Hints of a changing attitude came in 1948, when the Displaced Persons Act allowed refugees to enter the country in addition to the quotas, followed by the McCarron-Walter Act of 1952 by which a small number of Asians was to be allowed to enter once again. But the period 1953–55 then witnessed Operation Wetback during which about two million Mexicans were deported. The immigration records failed to account for an enormous, but unknown, number of Mexicans who had come across the uncontrolled border between Mexico

155

Table 8.2 Immigrants, by Country of Birth: 1961 to 1990

(In thousands.)

Country of Birth	1961–70, total	1971–80, total	1981–89 total	1990
All countries	3,321.7	4,493.3	5,801.6	1,536.5
Europe[1]	1,238.6	801.3	593.2	112.4
Czechoslovakia	21.4	10.2	10.1	1.4
France	34.3	17.8	20.3	2.8
Germany	200.0	66.0	562.6	7.5
Greece	90.2	93.7	26.4	2.7
Hungary	17.3	11.6	8.1	1.7
Ireland	42.4	14.1	22.5	10.3
Italy	206.7	130.1	29.6	3.3
Netherlands	27.8	10.7	10.5	1.4
Poland	73.3	43.6	76.9	20.5
Portugal	79.3	104.5	36.0	4.0
Romania	14.9	17.5	34.3	4.6
Soviet Union	15.7	43.2	58.5	25.5
Spain	30.5	30.0	13.9	1.9
Sweden	16.7	6.3	9.0	1.2
Switzerland	16.3	6.6	6.2	0.87
United Kingdom	230.5	123.5	126.2	15.9
Yugoslavia	46.2	42.1	16.4	2.8
Asia[1]	445.3	1,633.8	2,478.8	338.6
Afghanistan	0.4	2.0	23.4	3.2
Cambodia	1.2	8.4	111.4	5.2
China: Mainland	[2]96.7	[2]202.5	[2]341.8	31.8
Taiwan	([2])	([2])	([2])	15.2
Hong Kong	25.6	47.5	53.6	9.4
India	31.2	176.8	231.2	30.7
Iran	10.4	46.2	129.8	25.0
Iraq	6.4	23.4	17.8	1.8
Israel	12.9	26.6	31.6	4.7
Japan	38.5	47.9	37.5	5.7
Jordan	14.0	29.6	28.2	4.4
Korea	35.8	272.0	306.5	32.3
Laos	0.1	22.6	135.2	10.4
Lebanon	7.5	33.8	36.0	5.6
Pakistan	4.9	31.2	51.6	9.7
Philippines	101.5	360.2	431.5	63.8
Syria	4.8	13.3	17.6	3.0
Thailand	5.0	44.1	55.5	8.9
Turkey	6.8	18.6	18.4	2.5
Vietnam	4.6	179.7	352.6	48.8

Table 8.2 *Continued*

Country of Birth	1961–70, total	1971–80, total	1981–89 total	1990
North America[1]	1,351.1	1,645.0	2,167.4	957.8
Canada	288.7	114.8	102.4	16.8
Mexico	443.3	637.2	974.2	679.1
Caribbean[1]	519.5	759.8	777.3	115.4
Barbados	9.4	20.9	15.7	1.7
Cuba	256.8	276.8	148.6	10.6
Dominican Republic	94.1	148.0	209.6	42.2
Haiti	37.5	58.7	119.9	20.3
Jamaica	71.0	142.0	188.8	25.0
Trinidad and Tobago	24.6	61.8	32.8	6.7
Central America[1]	97.7	132.4	312.5	146.2
Costa Rica	17.4	12.1	12.7	2.8
El Salvador	15.0	34.4	134.4	80.2
Guatemala	15.4	25.6	55.6	32.3
Honduras	15.5	17.2	37.5	12.0
Nicaragua	10.1	13.0	32.5	11.6
Panama	18.4	22.7	25.6	3.4
South America[1]	228.3	284.4	370.1	85.8
Argentina	42.1	25.1	20.3	5.4
Brazil	20.5	13.7	19.5	4.2
Chile	11.5	17.6	19.4	4.0
Colombia	70.3	77.6	100.2	24.2
Ecuador	37.0	50.2	43.5	12.5
Guyana	7.1	47.5	84.0	11.4
Peru	18.6	29.1	48.7	15.7
Venezuela	8.5	7.1	14.8	3.1
Africa[1]	39.3	91.5	156.4	35.9
Egypt	17.2	25.5	27.3	4.1
Nigeria	1.5	8.8	26.5	8.8
South Africa	4.5	11.5	13.7	2.0
Australia	9.9	14.3	12.1	1.8
Other countries[3]	9.2	23.0	23.5	4.5

[1]Includes countries not shown separately. [2]Data for Taiwan included with China: Mainland. [3]Includes New Zealand and unknown countries.

Table 8.3 Immigrants by Country of Birth 1990

Metropolitan area of intended residence[3]	Total[1]	Mexico	El Salvador	Phillippines	Vietnam[2]	Dominican Republic	Guatemala	Korea	China: Mainland	India
Total[3]	1,536,483	679,068	80,173	63,756	48,662	42,195	32,303	32,301	31,815	30,667
Los Angeles–Long Beach, CA PMSA	374,773	231,267	42,172	11,644	4,745	86	18,446	6,059	3,525	1,440
New York, NY PMSA	164,330	6,436	2,853	4,750	1,155	25,430	1,895	3,586	9,030	3,530
Chicago, IL PMSA	73,107	41,848	631	2,655	742	70	1,839	1,238	802	3,024
Anaheim–Santa Ana. CA PMSA	65,367	44,414	2,026	1,407	4,950	13	1,060	1,219	459	667
Houston, TX PMSA	58,208	34,973	9,285	677	2,014	48	988	263	473	854
Miami–Hialeah, FL PMSA	37,677	1,273	706	292	56	1,342	650	64	157	139
San Diego, CA MSA	37,208	25,540	226	3,539	1,575	13	190	205	278	114
Riverside–San Bernardino, CA PMSA	35,616	27,159	998	1,224	505	2	581	373	136	269
Washington, DC-MD-VA MSA	32,705	1,058	4,956	1,228	277	620	1,940	802	1,465	248
San Francisco, CA PMSA	29,144	7,060	2,871	3,574	1,459	6	686	358	3,782	523
Dallas, TX PMSA	28,533	19,391	1,595	270	1,015	15	377	391	248	816
San Jose, CA PMSA	26,250	10,766	654	2,440	3,881	14	148	516	963	769
Oakland, CA PMSA	20,894	6,884	643	2,678	1,040	5	157	401	1,506	
Boston–Lawrence–Salem–Lowell–Brockton, MA NECMA	20,776	215	698	246	1,435	2,093	494	241	1,115	501
Newark, NJ PMSA	16,089	127	521	883	197	538	235	195	226	813
Nassau–Suffolk, NY PMSA	14,823	262	2,643	424	94	829	365	389	394	807
Phoenix, AZ MSA	14,714	10,726	206	211	692	5	198	146	176	130
El Paso, TX MSA	14,476	14,009	25	33	5	1	15	59	18	20
Bergen–Passaic, NJ PMSA	13,144	665	275	724	15	1,480	85	727	161	790
Philadelphia, PA-NJ PMSA	11,440	382	64	577	1,228	126	37	909	439	931
Fresno, CA MSA	11,193	8,066	175	156	74	–	55	28	75	280
McAllen–Edinburg–Mission, TX MSA	9,937	9,719	29	10	–	2	27	7	2	1
Jersey City, NJ PMSA	9,921	155	636	889	61	1,153	173	160	156	612
Fort Lauderdale–Hollywood–Pompeno Beach, FL PMSA	9,906	349	112	127	87	111	67	58	92	145
Fort Worth–Arlington, TX PMSA	9,736	6,805	182	82	635	5	56	82	68	200
Oxnard–Ventura, CA PMSA	9,508	7,251	195	548	80	3	124	103	54	93
Sacramento, CA MSA	8,933	3,378	137	602	604	4	43	222	307	172

Table 8.3 *Continued*

Metropolitan area of intended residence	Total[1]	Mexico	El Salvador	Phillippines	Vietnam[2]	Dominican Republic	Guatemala	Korea	China: Mainland	India
San Antonio, TX MSA	8,668	7,304	103	139	99	13	95	104	47	43
Atlanta, GA MSA	8,079	1,363	180	150	923	31	52	430	132	319
Seattle, WA PMSA	7,335	573	61	1,025	1,083	2	26	542	403	153
Bakersfield, CA MSA	7,246	6,094	194	344	10	–	63	39	17	83
Detroit, MI PMSA	7,199	309	14	398	146	12	10	280	172	552
Honolulu, HI MSA	6,706	44	6	3,051	537	–	–	678	511	16
Salinas–Seaside–Monterey, CA MSA	6,695	5,570	119	292	66	1	13	106	33	24
Middlesex–Somerset–Hunterdon, NJ PMSA	6,414	177	68	433	46	636	51	205	222	1,093
San Juan, PR PMSA	6,181	41	22	11	1	5,171	7	4	55	5
Brownsville–Harlingen, TX MSA	6,175	5,883	75	38	–	–	22	1	6	1
Visalia–Tulare–Porterville, CA MSA	5,925	2,846	62	175	3	–	20	11	10	56
Denver, CO PMSA	5,509	2,967	36	148	364	3	32	202	110	77
Santa Barbara–Santa Maria–Lompoc, CA MSA	5,489	4,483	43	178	28	1	127	49	24	27
Stockton, CA MSA	5,463	2,886	33	490	292	–	16	16	64	87
Minneapolis–St Paul, MN-WI MSA	5,439	193	15	156	559	6	15	246	106	145
Austin, TX MSA	5,044	3,496	183	37	195	1	27	70	60	53
West Palm Beach–Boca Raton–Delray Beach, FL MSA	5,012	599	67	75	40	42	58	25	36	86
Las Vegas, NV MSA	4,986	2,607	250	413	132	7	67	148	105	33
Tampa–St Petersburg–Clearwater, FL MSA	4,721	913	36	168	418	37	35	88	40	91
Brideport–Stamford–Norwalk–Danbury, CT NECMA	4,507	111	62	77	146	123	92	44	69	207
Portland, OR PMSA	4,493	1,071	39	147	654	1	33	283	190	50
Santa Cruz, CA MSA	4,396	3,963	31	69	15	3	7	8	44	11
Tucson, AZ MSA	4,232	3,338	34	50	159	–	19	36	41	23
Modesto, CA MSA	4,062	2,869	36	62	34	2	22	26	20	98
Baltimore, MD MSA	3,732	99	38	223	108	21	13	544	122	221
Merced, CA MSA	3,696	2,755	37	47	1	–	8	9	10	118

Table 8.3 *Continued*

Metropolitan area of intended residence	Total[1]	Mexico	El Salvador	Phillippines	Vietnam[2]	Dominican Republic	Guatemala	Korea Mainland	China:	India
Hartford–New Britain–Middletown–Bristol, CT NECMA	3,673	35	17	55	223	47	11	68	68	151
Lake County, IL PMSA	3,587	2,429	98	157	4	–	45	94	24	126
Providence–Pawtucket–Woonsocket, RI NECMA	3,566	75	35	88	33	539	259	36	73	45
Vallejo–Fairfield–Napa, CA PMSA	3,510	1,758	99	983	61	1	22	45	24	80
Orlando, FL MSA	3,445	318	49	134	259	92	22	69	30	99
Aurora–Elgin, IL PMSA	3,085	2,601	15	37	15	4	17	25	4	51
Albuquerque, NM MSA	2,878	2,264	27	35	154	1	34	38	27	35
Oklahoma City, OK MSA	2,741	1,391	5	55	364	1	39	78	31	51
Laredo, TX MSA	2,557	2,498	11	1	–	–	19	1	–	5

–Represents zero. [1]Includes other countries, not shown separately. [2]Data for immigrants admitted under the legalization program are not available separately for Vietnam and thus not included in this column. [3]Includes other metropolitan areas, not shown separately

Table 8.4 Largest Metropolitan Area Ethnic Population = Population Size.

Metropolitan area[1]	Total population (1,000)	Percent of total metropolitan population			
		Black	American Indian, Eskimo, Aleut.	Asian and Pacific Islander	Hispanic origin[2]
New York–Northern New Jersey–Long Island, NY-NJ-CT CMSA	18,087	18.2	0.3	4.8	15.4
Los Angeles–Anaheim–Riverside, CA CMSA	14,532	8.5	0.6	9.2	32.9
Chicago–Gary Lake County, IL-IN-WI CMSA	8,066	19.2	0.2	3.2	11.1
San Francisco–Oakland–San Jose, CA CMSA	6,253	8.6	0.7	14.6	15.5
Philadelphia–Wilmington–Trenton, PA-NJ-DE-MD CMSA	5,899	18.7	0.2	2.1	3.8
Detroit–Ann Arbor, MI CMSA	4,665	20.9	0.4	1.5	1.9
Boston–Lawrence–Salem, MA-NH CMSA	4,172	5.7	0.2	2.9	4.6
Washington, DC-MD-VA MSA	3,924	26.6	0.3	5.2	5.7
Dallas–Fort Worth, TX CMSA	3,885	14.3	0.5	2.5	13.4
Houston–Galveston–Brazoria, TX CMSA	3,711	17.9	0.3	3.6	20.8
Miami–Fort Lauderdale, FL CMSA	3,193	18.5	0.2	1.4	33.3
Atlanta, GA MSA	2,834	26.0	0.2	1.8	2.0
Cleveland–Akron–Lorain, OH CMSA	2,760	16.0	0.2	1.0	1.9
Seattle–Tacoma, WA CMSA	2,559	4.8	1.3	6.4	3.0
San Diego, CA MSA	2,498	6.4	0.8	7.9	20.4
Minneapolis–St Paul, MN-WI MSA	2,464	3.6	1.0	2.6	1.5
St Louis, MO-IL MSA	2,444	17.3	0.2	1.0	1.1
Baltimore, MD MSA	2,382	25.9	0.3	1.8	1.3
Pittsburgh–Beaver Valley, PA CMSA	2,243	8.0	0.1	0.7	0.6
Phoenix, AZ MSA	2,122	3.5	1.8	1.7	16.3
Tampa–St Petersburg–Clearwater, FL MSA	2,068	9.0	0.3	1.1	6.7
Denver–Boulder, CO CMSA	1,848	5.3	0.8	2.3	12.2
Cincinnati–Hamilton, OH-KY-IN CMSA	1,744	11.7	0.1	0.8	0.5
Milwaukee–Racine, WI CMSA	1,607	13.3	0.5	1.2	3.8
Kansas City, MO-KS MSA	1,566	12.8	0.5	1.1	2.9
Sacramento, CA MSA	1,481	6.9	1.1	7.7	11.6
Portland–Vancouver, OR-WA CMSA	1,478	2.8	0.9	3.5	3.4
Norfolk–Virginia Beach–Newport News, VA MSA	1,396	28.5	0.3	2.5	2.3
Columbus, OH MSA	1,377	12.0	0.2	1.5	0.8
San Antonio, TX MSA	1,302	6.8	0.4	1.2	47.6
Indianapolis, IN MSA	1,250	13.8	0.2	0.8	0.9
New Orleans, LA MSA	1,239	34.7	0.3	1.7	4.3
Buffalo–Niagara Falls, NY CMSA	1,189	10.3	0.6	0.9	2.0
Charlotte–Gastonia–Rock Hill, NC-SC MSA	1,162	19.9	0.4	1.0	0.9
Providence–Pawtucket–Fall River, RI-MA CMSA	1,142	3.3	0.3	1.8	4.2
Hartford–New Britain–Middletown, CT CMSA	1,086	8.7	0.2	1.5	7.0
Orlando, FL MSA	1,073	12.4	0.3	1.9	9.0
Salt Lake City–Ogden, UT MSA	1,072	1.0	0.8	2.4	5.8
Rochester, NY MSA	1,002	9.4	0.3	1.4	3.1
Nashville, TN MSA	985	15.5	0.2	1.0	0.8
Memphis, TN-AR-MS MSA	982	40.6	0.2	0.8	0.8
Oklahoma City, OK MSA	959	10.5	4.8	1.9	3.6
Louisville, KY-IN MSA	953	13.1	0.2	0.6	0.6
Dayton-Springfield, OH MSA	951	13.3	0.2	1.0	0.8

161

Table 8.4 *continued.*

Metropolitan area[1]	Total population (1,000)	Black	Percent of total metropolitan population		
			American Indian, Eskimo, Aleut.	Asian and Pacific Islander	Hispanic origin[2]
Greensboro–Winston-Salem–High Point, NC MSA	942	19.3	0.3	0.7	0.8
Birmingham, AL MSA	908	27.1	0.2	0.4	0.4
Jacksonville, FL MSA	907	20.0	0.3	1.7	2.5
Albany–Schenectady–Troy, NY MSA	874	4.7	0.2	1.2	1.8
Richmond–Petersburg, VA MSA	866	29.3	0.3	1.4	1.1
West Palm Beach–Boca Raton–Delary Beach, FL MSA	864	12.5	0.1	1.0	7.7
Honolulu, HI MSA	836	3.1	0.4	63.0	6.8
Austin, TX MSA	782	9.2	0.4	2.4	20.5
La Vegas, NV MSA	741	9.5	0.9	3.5	11.2
Raleigh–Durham, NC MSA	735	24.9	0.3	1.9	1.2
Scranton–Wilkes-Barre, PA MSA	734	1.0	0.1	0.5	0.8
Tulsa, OK MSA	709	8.2	6.8	0.9	2.1
Grand Rapids, MI MSA	688	6.0	0.5	1.1	3.3
Allentown–Bethlehem, PA-NJ MSA	687	2.0	0.1	1.1	4.2
Fresno, CA MSA	667	5.0	1.1	8.6	35.5
Tucson, AZ MSA	667	3.1	3.0	1.8	24.5
Syracuse, NY MSA	660	5.9	0.6	1.2	1.4
Greenville–Spartanburg, SC MSA	641	17.4	0.1	0.7	0.8
Omaha, NE-IA MSA	618	8.3	0.5	1.0	2.6
Toledo, OH MSA	614	11.4	0.2	1.0	3.3
Knoxville, TN MSA	605	6.0	0.2	0.8	0.5
El Paso, TX MSA	592	3.7	0.4	1.1	69.6
Hamsburg–Lebanon–Carlisle, PA MSA	588	6.7	0.1	1.1	1.7
Bakersfield, CA MSA	543	5.5	1.3	3.0	28.0
New Haven–Meriden, CT MSA	530	12.1	0.2	1.6	6.2
Springfield, MA MSA	530	6.6	0.2	1.0	9.0
Baton Rouge, LA MSA	528	29.6	0.2	1.1	1.4
Little Rock–North Rock, AR MSA	513	19.9	0.4	0.7	0.8
Charleston, SC MSA	507	30.2	0.3	1.2	1.5
Youngstown–Warren, OH MSA	493	11.1	0.2	0.4	1.5
Wichita, KS MSA	485	7.8	1.1	1.9	4.1

[1]Metropolitan areas are shown in rank order of total population of consolidated metropolitan statistical areas (CMSA) and metropolitan statistical areas (MSA). [2]Persons of Hispanic origin may be of any race.

and the United States. In addition to the legal quota, poor Mexicans simply walked across into southern California, Arizona, New Mexico and Texas. The offensive term of wetback referred to the fact that many illegal immigrants were believed to swim across the Rio Grande at night and dry in the morning sun as they walked north.

After that history, the Immigration Act of 1965 was a revolutionary landmark opening a new era in American's attitude to its immigrants,

Table 8.5 US Population, Immigration and Urbanisation

Year	Pop. × 1,000	Immigration for decade	%	Tot. pop. classed as urban × 1,000	%
1820	9,618	8,385	0.09	693	7.2
1830	12,901	143,439	1.1	1,127	8.7
1840	17,120	599,125	3.5	1,854	10.8
1850	23,261	1,713,151	7.4	3,544	15.2
1860	31,513	2,598,214	8.2	6,217	19.7
1870	39,905	2,314,824	5.8	9,902	24.8
1880	50,262	2,812,191	5.6	14,130	28.1
1890	63,056	5,247,603	8.3	22,106	35.0
1900	76,094	3,647,564	4.7	30,160	39.6
1910	92,407	8,796,000	9.5	41,999	45.4
1920	106,466	5,735,811	5.4	54,158	50.9
1930	123,188	4,107,209	3.3	68,955	55.9
1940	132,122	528,431	0.4	74,424	56.3
1950	151,683	864,087	0.5	96,468	63.6
1960	180,000	1,428,000	0.8	126,000	70.0
1970	204,000	3,332,000	1.6	150,000	73.5
1980	227,000	4,493,000	1.9	167,000	73.6
1990	249,000	7,338,000	3.0	187,000	75.2

Sources: Historical Statistics of the US, Colonial Times to 1970 Statistical Abstract of the US 1982 and 1992

and changing dramatically what was to happen in the cities. The 1965 Act, at least in theory, permits people from any country in the world to enter the United States of America providing they satisfy certain basic requirements. While no country is specifically excluded, a maximum of 20,000 people will be admitted from each country each year in order that they can be absorbed in an orderly manner. A maximum of 410,000 each year, including up to 140,000 refugees, will be admitted as permanent residents. From a given country, preference will be given to educated and skilled people, and to the relatives of those who have already entered America.

In 1986 the Immigration and Control Act, known as the Simpson Rodino Act, extended an amnesty to all people who had entered the USA illegally and who could show that they had been there for five years. This applied, of course, mainly to Mexicans, and the practical problem remains of trying to prevent more than the permitted 20,000 legal Mexican immigrants crossing a very long unguarded border. The method being tried at the moment is the imposition of severe fines on anyone found to be employing illegal immigrants — thus making farmers, clothing factory owners, gas station operators and the like into police cum immigration officials.

Table 8.5 shows the low point of immigration this century during the Depression and the Second World War. While total immigrants had passed 4.5 million by the 1990s, and while this represents less than 2% of the total population compared to 9.5% of the total population in the first decade of the century, the new immigrants are having a dramatic impact on the city out of all proportion to their numbers. Crudely, this impact can be summarised as the immigrants changing the city rather than the city changing them; that is, the newcomers adapting America rather than the other way round.

For many decades Mexican immigrants, especially the illegal ones, worked as very cheap seasonal labour on farms. Now Mexicans, Puerto Ricans, Cubans and other peoples from Latin America are making their marks in urban areas. These immigrants are usually labelled Hispanics, the first time a major immigrant group has been labelled by its language rather than by nationality, race or religion. This is significant. Earlier groups of immigrants certainly kept their European languages alive by means of schools, libraries, clubs and, above all, their own newspapers, but they used English to operate in the American society and gradually adopted the language of mainstream America. British people, including colleagues of mine, who have worked in such places as New York, Miami and Houston have experienced a relatively new situation. Some are convinced, for example, that Spanish has become a second official language in New York, and many people now acknowledge that Spanish is essential in Miami and Houston. Local radio and TV stations operating entirely in Spanish have replaced the older media. Moreover, they seem to have a more pervasive effect, to the extent now that the younger generation of Mexicans, Cubans, and other Latin Americans no longer make the same effort to learn English. Many complain of minority discrimination if their children have to learn English in the state schools.

This being the case, the label Hispanic will stick, will stick for a long time, and will become increasingly appropriate. In some respects the Hispanic people show characteristics of earlier waves of immigrants blended with features which are new. For example, Puerto Ricans moved into property on Manhattan and first took the kinds of jobs vacated by the Italians and the Jews; but they arrived from Puerto Rico by subsidised air flights. They forced their way on to the bottom rung of the ladder in New York and started to work their way up and out in a recognised and almost traditional way. In fact their conflicts with groups such as the Italians have been immortalised in *West Side Story*, though the musical would have been a more convincing piece of supporting evidence if the lyrics had been written and sung in Spanish.

Houston has large Hispanic communities, in this case mainly Mexicans from across the border. They were established in Houston early this century and in spite of the attention given to New York and Miami, are probably the oldest Hispanic neighbourhoods of any size in an American city. The first areas in Houston followed the traditional pattern, in the form of blue-collar communities located close to the city centre. But, again, the Hispanic communities in Houston now reveal new characteristics. The blue-collar Hispanic suburbs which have grown up in the urban area since 1970 have not been formed by people moving out of the centre. Rosenberg, Baytown, Pasadena, South Houston, Freeport City, Jacinto City and Galena Park have been populated by Spanish-speaking people from outside Houston. In this respect they are much more like Asian communities, more characteristic of the so-called New Immigrants than the Old Immigrants.

Most dramatic, however, is the case of Miami. While there are large Hispanic communities now in Chicago north and west of the Loop, and in Los Angeles immediately southeast of downtown in the Barrio, and Los Angelinos are convinced that the city is becoming Mexican, a much stronger case can be made out that Miami is becoming Cuban (see table 8.4). Just as, with some justification, Boston once claimed to be the largest Irish city, and New York the largest Jewish city on earth, Miami claims with equal justification to be the largest Cuban city. In Miami the claim is not based on just the numbers of Cubans and other Spanish-speaking peoples, but on their economic and political positions, on their power and wider influence both inside and outside America. In Los Angeles, Chicago, New York, Houston and other American cities, for all their modern features such as arrival by car or air, their TV stations and the predominance of their language, Hispanics are still largely on the lower rungs of the socio-economic ladder, and are over-represented in the older, poorer, inner parts of the cities.

While immigrants from Mexico, Puerto Rico and other Latin American countries tend to be the poor who can not find work at home, most of the Cubans in Florida are political exiles who fled Castro's Cuba. Amongst them are people from all walks of life, all levels of education and ability, and a complete range of social and economic backgrounds. Perhaps the only skewing of the characteristics is away from left-wing politics and towards the Republican Party and private enterprise. The net result is that either by moving surprisingly quickly up the socio-economic ladder in Miami, or by stepping on to the ladder two-thirds of the way up, ex-Cubans now dominate the social, economic and political life of the city. Moreover, they live all over the Metro area. Cuban politicians have held the office both of Mayor of Miami and Governor of Florida. Miami is now the *de facto* financial centre of a large part of Latin America, much as Angelinos hope and believe Los Angeles will come to be the city which dominates the Pacific Rim.

This rapid success and semi-takeover of a city in two generations may have been a breathtaking surprise to disinterested observers, but it has been a very nasty shock to poor people who were living in American cities long before this new wave of Hispanics arrived. None have been more shocked and angered than the black people. The last chapter indicated that blacks had expected to follow the old immigrants up and out into the suburbs. Their realisation that this was not to be so straightforward was a major factor behind the Civil Rights movement in the South in the 1950s and an even stronger element in the black riots in cities all over America in the 1960s. But with the arrival of the new immigrants, black people now feel their anomalous position even more keenly as they watch the newcomers get jobs, start their own businesses, move into better homes and achieve economic and political power — prizes still largely denied to black people. In a word, Hispanics and Asians are leapfrogging over the majority of blacks in the Central Cities; and the poorer blacks, in particular, are showing their resentment.

But black people in the inner-city ghettos are not the only group to resent the arrival and the success of the Hispanics. Many of the well-established groups of the old immigrant waves from Europe have been infuriated by the invasion too because things have been made so much easier for the new immigrants since 1965. As in the nineteenth century, the newcomers are resisted because it is believed that they take jobs away, particularly during recession, by working for very low wages. They are resented because they look different, have a different culture, have their own variation of Catholicism, and don't speak the language. Most of those criticisms were repeated again and again in the nineteenth century as wave of immigrants followed wave from Europe, but the fact that they themselves were treated that way does not soften the present Americans' treatment of the latest arrivals.

But new elements have crept into the list of features causing resentment of the Hispanics. Not only do Mexicans walk and motor over the border into America; they walk and motor back again. When things are bad, some of them go home. When a woman is about to have a baby, if she can, she goes back to Mexico so the baby will be born a Mexican. The Mexicans persist in speaking Spanish. In all these ways they demonstrate that they, at least a noticeable proportion of them, are not committing themselves to America. Another element, at least one given much more emphasis recently, and an accusation directed especially towards immigrants from South America, is that they bring in drugs and establish trade routes for drugs. As with all perceived threats, it does not matter whether the accusation is true or not. What matters is that enough Americans *believe* it to be true, and then act on that belief. The WASPs in the suburbs, except in Miami, may be sufficiently far from Hispanics at the moment not to be too involved. But with the arrivals of peoples from Asia in large numbers since 1965 there is a growing ill-feeling and conflict between three major groups — black people, Hispanics and Asians — in the inner parts of the Central Cities.

Although Asia covers an enormous part of the earth's surface compared to Europe, peoples from Asia are grouped together, as often as not, in the current literature in a way that Europeans seldom were. More to the point, most Asians are regarded as the same by the people who have lived in the city longer. While Sicilians were differentiated from mainland Italians, Arabs, Hindus, Thais and Chinese are, for the moment, seen together with other peoples from the continent and islands simply as Asians. Europeans from Ireland, Poland, Portugal and Greece had very different languages, but they were broadly of one race, shared the same family of religions, and came from a common culture. Yet the conflicts between them and the native-born Americans, and between each other, was often fierce in the nineteenth and early twentieth centuries. No surprise, then, that the very different peoples from Asia, of wholly different races, religions, language groups, cultures and economies are the catalyst for so much social unrest in the cities at the end of this century.

In order of the numbers of people entering the US since 1965, Asians have come from the Philippines, Korea, China, India and Thailand. In smaller numbers they have arrived from Japan, Vietnam, Cambodia, Taiwan, Hong Kong and the Arab countries of the Middle East. In the decade to 1980 37% of all immigrants to the United States were Asian; in the decade to 1990 39%. Nowadays they arrive by air and are more likely to land at west coast airports, Seattle, San Francisco, Los Angeles and San Diego, before some of them fly on to Houston, Denver, Chicago, New York and Boston. After crossing the Pacific that is little more than a short extra hop. While over half the Asian immigrants have tended to stay in the western states, the rest fly on to cities all over the country (see tables 8.3 and 8.4).

167

Obviously enough, the city airport is in or beyond the suburbs — as different a point of entry to the city as one could get from the quayside in the middle of the nineteenth-century concentrated city. From the airport the Asians move by car, taxi, bus, or the rare rapid transit to a very wide variety of locations everywhere in the built-up-area. For most of them the days of finding cheap accommodation in the inner-city slums have gone.

People from Asia arriving in the United States since 1965 have shown the widest range of social and economic positions in their countries of origin. *Time* magazine described some of them as 'the most highly skilled immigrants ever', including amongst their numbers academics and professional people. At the other end of the spectrum are poor Third World farmers who could just manage to borrow the fare to travel to America, or who came as refugees. As a result, Asian peoples have the widest variety of first locations within any given urban area. Some move straight to exclusive suburbs, some start in the Central City slums. But those Asians finding their first residence in the slums are no more typical of the whole group than are those going to Santa Barbara. At the moment the spread of locations throughout the built-up-area can be explained either by neo-regional geographical studies of specific communities, or by dividing the BUA into numbered squares and then getting a random number generator to assign locations to different Asian immigrant groups. For the moment it comes to the same thing.

Once, for whatever specific, local, particular reason a few Koreans, Chinese, Arabs or Pakistanis have found a home in any part of the city, then a similar process to that seen in the nineteenth century does operate and similar people follow them to that location and begin to build up a community in the neighbourhood. The point on which each focuses seems to be much more a matter of chance than in the past. As in earlier decades, like groups with like. Asian people from the same country, with the same religion, same language, similar background and socio-economic position group together. By clustering together people from a particular Asian country help one another settle in to the new, strange Western urban environment, to find homes near their own kind, to find jobs or start their own businesses; in short, the kinds of things which were done by Europeans earlier. But the emphasis is changing. Now language and religion, so very different from one Asian group to another, are much more important factors. The native-born people around them may lump them all together as Asians because they can not tell one Asian language from another and may not know a Buddhist is different from a Sikh, but most of the Asian newcomers are more acutely

168

aware of their differences from each other than of their difference from the hosts. And they appear at present to be striving to maintain those differences.

The Asian communities are developing a trait seen earlier in European communities to the extreme. Some are not just resisting becoming 'Americans', they are resisting any mixing with each other. The situation in some cities is more than the inevitable clash between hosts and immigrants; it is a multi-dimensional clash between WASPs, blacks, Jews, Muslims, Hindus, Hispanics, Pakistanis, Filipinos, Vietnamese, Koreans, Cambodians and others. Some of these groups hate each other more than they resist Americanisation. Middle-class, white-collar Asian immigrants, finding their first location in the American city well out in the suburbs, establish 'National Neighborhoods', to use the phrase coined by *Time*, where one might have expected multinational co-operation between professional middle-class people — class overriding nationality.

The surprise of finding so many immigrants moving straight to the suburbs after 1965, instead of starting in the escalator slums of hope, paying their dues, and working up the hard way like every other good American used to do, has caused many ordinary native Americans to look very hard at the Asians and, inevitably, to contrast them with earlier waves of immigrants. By comparison with those earlier waves, many of the Asians show the following characteristics:

- many are well-educated
- most have very high expectations
- they often move into waiting jobs, e.g. in professions
- others start sophisticated businesses
- many can afford to live in desirable suburbs
- they quickly overtake black people in socio-economic terms
- they are beginning to overtake many Hispanic people and are climbing the socio-economic ladder faster than any other group
- so far, they show little inclination to Americanise
- they show stronger loyalty to their home countries and put pressure on the US Government to help those parts of Asia
- they are now being perceived as overt racists
- Asians are introducing into American society, *en masse*, new religions and philosophies such as:

Islam	Hinduism
Shinto	Buddhism
Sikhism	Asian forms of Catholicism.

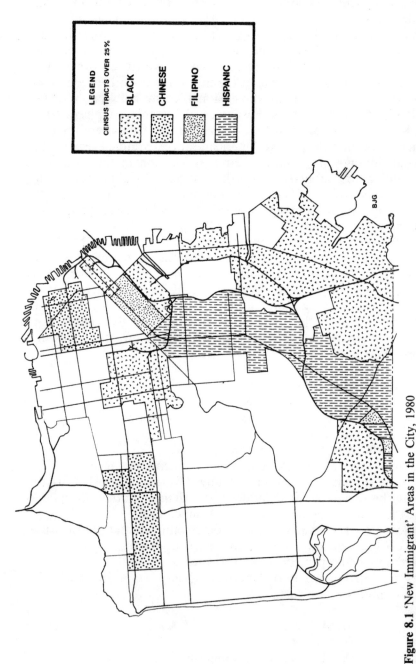

Figure 8.1 'New Immigrant' Areas in the City, 1980
By 1980 new immigrants from Asia and Latin America were replacing those from Europe, while the black ghettos, as here in San Francisco, persisted.
Source: Godfrey, B.J., *Neighborhoods in Transition: The Making of San Francisco's Ethnic & Non-Conformist Communities*, University of California Press, Berkeley, California, 1988, p. 126

170

There are, of course, poor Asians too, but a smaller proportion manage to reach America, and mainly as refugees. But even these poor Asians share the last five or six characteristics in the list with their countrymen in the suburbs. The poorer Asian immigrants do still tend to start in the inner-city slums where they are competing bitterly with the Hispanics and blacks to move off the first rung of the ladder.

For the majority of Asian immigrants in the last quarter of a century, however, the characteristics in the list apply, and some of those blunt statements need to be expanded. The first seven underline that what is being witnessed in American cities is the opposite end of the brain drains from many parts of the world, including the United Kingdom. When there are insufficient openings in industry, business and the professions we raise the alarm about our brain drain to try to get our economy to grow again. An even worse situation exists in many Asian countries where the expansion in higher education has not been balanced by the expansion of modern industry and commerce, so that the lack of jobs for educated people is even worse than in the UK. In countries like Pakistan there is an even stronger outcry when the young graduates, who were naively expected to be the engine drivers of a developed economy, emigrate to the USA, where their skills will at once secure them a lifestyle they could never hope for at home. While the old immigrants often were characterised as Irish navvies, Italian fishermen, Jewish tailors or Polack meat-packers, the new immigrants are more likely to be Korean entrepreneurs, Japanese financiers, Indian doctors, Filipino nurses, Vietnamese restaurateurs and Chinese engineers. The brain drain is most noticeable in the country of origin; the concomitant social and economic consequences in the destinations — in this context the American cities — are only now beginning to be appreciated.

The last three points in the list above indicate some of these consequences. A number of things were possibly subconsciously assumed by those Americans concerned with reforming immigration in 1965: that immigrants are immigrants are immigrants; that the economy would go on expanding; and that America would be America forever — i.e. exactly what it was in the 1960s. So the assumption was that any immigrants would fit into an unchanging urban society just as all had done before. But the arrival of so many people caught up in the brain drain has caused social tensions, if not so obvious economic problems. For the less able immigrants the position has been that they have been arriving in the cities in a quarter of a century when the American economy has been static, if not in actual decline. Since 1965 Japan has risen to dominate the world economy, and there is now talk of the major economic activity and trade passing to those emerging nations surrounding the Pacific Rim. Meanwhile Europe has united economically and developed a single market to the point where it is no longer dependent on American factories and farms.

As the final point in the list indicates, now that the waves of migrants are coming across the Pacific rather than the Atlantic, they are not white people steeped in Judaeo-Christian religion, accustomed to Roman Law, and with European traditions and aspirations in common. The waves are of people of many colours, with half a dozen very different religions, moral and legal systems; people from countries as far apart and as different from each other as Afghanistan, Laos and Japan, with traditions very different from America, and with very different expectations of America.

The last but one point in the list, the matter of racism, is, of course, an emotional and controversial issue. At the moment there are many people who approve of the kind of society portrayed in Orwell's *1984*, and would very much like thought police to exist with the powers to stop us even considering such things, let alone speaking or writing about them. But refusal to acknowledge its existence will not make it go away. The fact of the matter is that racism has long been an element in American urban society. There was very strong anti-Semitism until the 1950s and the continued attitude of many white people towards black people is self-evident to anyone who will look and see. But racism directed towards those other than black people has been obscured until recently by xenophobia, the dislike of strangers whatever their race or colour. The resentment of Jews from Russia was so similar to the resentment of Catholics from Ireland.

Now, however, one can see that the xenophobia shown by native Americans towards the newly-arrived Asians is often not as strong as the dislike and contempt shown by groups of people from one part of Asia for those from a different part of the largest continent. Thus a new factor is the racism being imported along with the immigration as different Asian groups continue their intolerance of each other in what is, or was, supposed to be the melting pot.

The Burgess model of the concentrated, concentric city showed ethnic areas in a ring round the city centre. By the 1990s this is no longer an accurate model of the elements and functioning of immigrant areas in the American city, nor an adequate explanation of the processes taking place. Ethnic areas are no longer phenomena which start near the centre, move out and disappear as the people Americanise and disperse. Ethnic communities now exist in every part of the continuously built-up-area, suburbs included, and at the moment those communities show every sign of growing, persisting, and being in some measure antagonistic towards each other.

172

A clear example is Los Angeles, one of the major air ports of entry for Asian people crossing the Pacific to America. The major black and Hispanic communities are in the classic locations close to downtown Los Angeles. The ghetto runs southwards, through Watts towards the better areas around Wilmington. The Barrio starts actually in downtown and is growing eastwards rapidly, with some extra spread to the north. To the west, and further from the new skyscrapers of downtown, is a Russian Jewish neighbourhood which is beginning to show signs of dispersing. The fact that the new Asian communities are predominantly suburban now is underlined by the fact that the majority of them are in Orange County rather than Los Angeles County. Some nine or ten tightly clustered Japanese communities are located in Los Angeles, small ones just east and west of downtown, but larger ones out towards Santa Monica and between Gardena and Torrance. To the east, in Orange County, the major Asian communities are located in Garden Grove and Westminster, where the community of 80,000 Vietnamese is referred to as Little Saigon, Koreatown with 30,000 Koreans, and Monterey Park with 30,000 Chinese. Southwards, Long Beach is now home to 40,000 Cambodians, while in the north, around Glendale, a large Thai community seems about to spill over into the San Fernando Valley.

There is conflicting evidence about whether or not these new Asian immigrant groups do or do not disperse; the result of partial views, probably. While it is claimed that the Chinese do not group together, that evidence comes from California, whereas in New York, and Manhattan in particular, the clustered Chinese communities are growing rapidly. The only consistent evidence at the moment seems to be that the Filipinos, among all the Asian groups, are the least likely to keep together in national communities. As for the others, the examples most often quoted of newly-arrived Asian people living singly in the suburbs are the most able and successful professionals and entrepreneurs.

Meanwhile, the white natives are beginning to circle the wagons. The rapid build-up of such large, new, alien communities in the suburbs, such as those noted for Los Angeles and which equal in size the populations of such places as Gainsborough and Grantham, is a process which has not happened before, and which is consequently producing a new reaction. Generations of native-born Americans, familiar with the old slow process of immigrant groups gradually moving into the suburbs and, as often as not, dispersing and Americanising in the process, have been taken by surprise by the spatial behaviour of the new, Asian immigrants. Even when Welsh, Italian and Jewish communities moved outwards but kept together, the slow movement gave time for adjustment and acceptance. Now, successful Asian communities are almost literally dropping out of the skies into psychologically unprepared suburbs and a new phenomenon is producing an age-old atavistic reaction — a defensive attitude.

Activities which once functioned to maintain ties with Europe now function, predominantly, to differentiate the old immigrants from the new. They are used to preserve group identity. There is a revival of interest in European languages which, together with territory, are the strongest forces which bind nations together. White Americans in the suburbs who can trace their origins to Europe are taking an increasing public, group interest in what they call Ethnic Studies. But the studies of each group relate only to the country of origin of that group's particular European ancestors. There are more and more of these ethnic organisations, historical associations, language study groups, and cultural revival groups, each designed to emphasise the neighbourhood's identity, strengthen contacts between members and, inevitably in the process, increase rather than reduce differences with other suburban groups. These associations organise Heritage Days and 'National' (not American but German, Swedish, Greek, etc.) festivals when dress, language, music, paintings, food and old artefacts from the country perhaps their great great grandparents came from are featured and celebrated. Some elements in such occasions suggest it is many decades since these American people visited the old country in question. The costumes and Disneyland-like caricatures are often embarrassing to Europeans, but the activities do serve to bind the communities together in co-operation, and to highlight their separateness from the newcomers, which is a main object of the exercises.

I admit to having been puzzled for a period of years in the past by the apparent great strength of religion in American life, particularly when the Constitution forbids an established religion; even more puzzled by its contrast with religious apathy in so much of the rest of the English-speaking world. Nowadays it seems that the fact that so many middle-class Americans are active members of a church of one denomination or another, attend services regularly, and then behave on the other six days of the week as if religion had never been invented, is part of this identity crisis. Church membership, it would appear, is not just a matter of religion but also of politics, economics, social cohesion — a wagon-circling defence against perceived threats. The political function has been demonstrated by the work of the Southern Christian Leadership Conference. Similarly, membership of a church brings with it business status, as well as useful contacts. Above all, membership identifies the in-group, and differentiates it from the other groups, Baptists from Episcopalians from Jews from

Catholics from Greek Orthodox from Russian Orthodox from Muslim from Hindu. The churches are a matter of neighbourhood identification and protection as much as to support a faith.

It is the same with the newspapers, magazines, local radio stations, local TV stations and the rest. The original argument that such things were to serve the recent arrivals, still dependent on their native languages, no longer holds water. The old immigrant groups are now in their fifth and sixth generations; if the new groups maintain *their* Spanish, Portuguese, Arabic, Hindi, Korean, Bengali, Japanese, Chinese and other Asian languages for as long, then American society will disintegrate. Some of the organisations and media do have an immediate and practical purpose, such as helping refugees from the old country, or for political canvassing, but all of them share two common characteristics in addition to the one proclaimed and perceived: they function to keep each group together, and to keep it separate, different, and therefore isolated from the rest.

Native Americans, then, are reacting in a new way to a new, different type of immigration. That immigration differs in several respects. First, and possibly most important, it is not biased towards the type of people who founded the nation only a couple of centuries ago. Second, it is different in its geographical and spatial characteristics. Immigrants are officially welcome from any part of the globe, but in fact at the moment the largest continental group is from Asian countries. Moving to America — paradoxically for Americans — they arrive from the west and locate in Pacific coast and other western cities much more than the Europeans did. They arrive by air and find locations for their homes in every part of the city, with large numbers going to the suburbs. Equally importantly they are not going through the spatial movement and the socio-economic process which, before 1965, were considered the necessary rites of passage.

Thirdly, the immigration comprises a very wide spectrum of social and economic backgrounds, and while there are poor immigrants from the Third World, the attention seems to be much more on the middle-class people, well-educated and with very high expectations of the American city and the American economy and society. But from the American point of view, they are all seen merely as Asians, and one of the most common complaints comes from Chinese and Japanese who hate each other strongly and are outraged when Americans can not see any difference between them. The many nationalities and religions arriving in the American suburbs have absolutely nothing in common as far as culture is concerned. There is merely the coincidence that all their different societies originated in the huge land-mass labelled Asia as a matter of convenience. The differentiation is

175

made not by the native Americans, but by the 'Asians' themselves as they meticulously keep to their own national, language and religious groups, forming distinct, and often very large, colonies in the urban and suburban areas.

Fourthly, these varied peoples are arriving in an America which is very different from the America which received the last major wave, that of Europeans in the 1920s. Now, the gigantic suburbs not only exist, but contain most of the available work, certainly most of the desirable jobs, as well as most of the housing. The inner cities, once the traditional reception area and springboard for immigrants, are now financially bankrupt, beset with a host of intractable problems, and peopled predominantly by black and Spanish-speaking peoples rather than by hosts with much in common with the immigrants.

White, middle-class Americans are surprised and disturbed when what are to all intents and purposes large Korean, Thai, Arab or Vietnamese towns spring up rapidly in what they thought of as their suburbs. Moreover, the black people and those of Hispanic origin are becoming more and more frustrated and outraged as they witness those Asians who do happen to locate first in the inner city get on to the socio-economic lader, rise up it relatively quickly, and in every sense leave them behind. Hispanics started in the city after the blacks and generally made quicker progress; Asians started most recently of all and in many cases have leapfrogged the other two. Some inner cities are becoming a three-way battleground where blacks, Hispanics and Asians battle for opportunities and jobs in a situation where only a small proportion of them can win. New York again has the worst scenario, where that three-way racial antagonism is aggravated by a renewal of overt anti-Semitism, not helped by the Rev. Jesse Jackson's recent derogative reference to the Jewish neighbourhoods as 'Hymietown'.

Finally, a noticeable result of the new immigration is the reversal of the absorption and the melting-pot effect of the past; the Hispanics and Asians are changing America. The most noticeable and immediate effect is the fact that cities like San Diego, Los Angeles, Houston, Miami and New York are now bilingual; Spanish is almost an official second language. Catholicism is now much more widespread than in the late 1950s when John F. Kennedy seriously thought his religion might prevent him becoming President. On days like George Washington's birthday, the anniversary of Lincoln's Gettysburg Address, and on Thanksgiving, one wonders how much the British roots, British culture, tradition and law mean to the newest Americans now. Are they in America because they subscribe to the ideals of 1776 as well as for the chance of economic success? Do they love that Constitution and realise how lucky they are to live under it? Or will *their* roots, cultures, religions and laws change the American suburbs, and then America, into something else?

The new immigrants are changing American big-city suburban society by their work, their aspirations, their languages and religions, their food, entertainment and their communication media. They tend to look to South America and to the separate countries of Asia rather than to Britain and Europe. The 'Special Relationship' between Britain and America may well be a thing of the past as more and more Americans look westward across the Pacific, and as the Pacific with the United States on one side and Japan and Australia on the other becomes the centre of world economic and political power.

More immediately, in the reaction to their arrival, the new immigrants are the cause of increased racial unrest in the inner cities, and of a closing of ranks and a strengthening of the older neighbourhoods in the suburbs. They are catalysts in producing a separation, rather than a merging, of 'national' territories. The old immigrants from Europe were like new boys in a nineteenth-century English public school. They had no status, they fagged for the prefects, and were abused at first. But as they rose up through the classes they gained privilege and status, became part of the school and jealous of its traditions. In the end they earned the right and the opportunity to become School Captain. In contrast, the new immigrants from Latin America and Asia often come in half-way up the senior school, sometimes very near the top, and appear, as in Miami, to be taking over. Not surprisingly, those who played the old game resent all this and fear the worst: the old school is going to hell on a bicycle. Many of the senior pupils, more politely, believe that if the numbers become too great they will change the ethos of the school. Since 1965 the pecking order of much of American society has been thrown into confusion.

In a major eight-page article in March 1990, *Time* reviewed the situation after a quarter of a century. Among other things, the magazine sampled the native-born reaction to the arrival of millions of Asians. This reaction ranged from the almost friendly labelling of Chinese yuppies as Chuppies, to the stark phrase — echoing the crude language of the Vietnam War — 'Gooks Go Home'. Xenophobia combines with resentment of the *nouveaux riches* to produce much hostility in the suburbs. The hostility is the greater the nearer the Asian neighbourhood. Conversely, some Asians see their progress as difficult, slow and obstructed. A common complaint is that the very top jobs are denied to Asians and, as one Chinese put it, 'the corporate ladder is a broken one for us'. The contrast is with the first-gen-

177

eration Europeans and first-generation black people in the city who would not have expected the top jobs even for their grandchildren. That Chinese speaker might not have felt so frustrated if he had known of the non-escalator slums of despair, possibly in the same city where he complained to the *Time* reporter. The article suggested that the poor Asians are resented in the modern American city, and that the rich Asians are both resented and feared. A further turn of the screw is that white Americans, seeing how Asians have prospered in such a short time, now feel even less of an obligation to help black people. In effect the attitude to poor blacks now is increasingly along the lines of, 'the Asians have made it, so why can't you?'

During that same quarter of a century, of course, immigration continued from Europe and from the rest of the world. Some immigrants continued to locate in the inner-city slums as well as moving to the suburbs. Moreover, many other people wanted to move to America and that, in practical terms, means to American cities; many more than the quotas would allow. Perhaps the rate of immigration is too fast, because as early as 1985 70% of all native-born Americans were no longer in favour of a continued immigration policy: I'm safely aboard, pull up the ladder, Jack.

'How many can America take?'

'Do the advantages outweigh the disadvantages of racial conflict?'

'Are immigrants successful at the expense of the poor and the blacks?'

were the kinds of questions being asked. The majority opinion was summed up in the sentence, 'We don't need immigrants, the country is full now.' America is not full, over-populated, by any stretch of the imagination, but many cities are now too big, and some of the suburban areas do appear to be fragmenting, as unexpected results of the well-meaning Immigration Act of 1965.

9

VIEWS OF THE CENTRE

To attempt to describe and explain the centre of the large American city at the end of the twentieth century is to invite contradiction. The most obvious problem is that, unlike the task attempted in the first chapter, one has not the benefit of hindsight and a fossilising set of agreements on which to draw. Many people now make assumptions about the rapidly-changing centre which are up to thirty years out of date. Moreover, matters of vital concern today may prove to have been of little importance a generation from now. One can only report as accurately as possible using the data and information to hand.

A less obvious problem is that one will be contradicted by several groups of people who 'know' what the centre of the American city is like in the 1990s, each group having its own, distinct view. Residents of the suburbs have a different, partial, understanding from that of residents of small American towns. The Republicans have a view different from that of the Democrats, the sociologists from that of the politicians, the police from those who work in the CBD. Understandably, the black residents of the central cities believe that they are the only ones who can describe what that environment is really like now. But they may well be at a loss to explain it. Moreover, coping with the problems day after day, they are too close to one part of their own city most of the time to have the luxury of being able to sit back and try to comprehend the wider picture.

The British have been to Orlando, Manhattan and Washington, so they know how wonderful the centres of American cities are. American students, on exchange, usually white and always middle class, know better because they live there. That is, they live in, say, the suburbs of New York, as far from the Empire State Building as Nottingham is from Sheffield, drive into the city in an air-conditioned car along urban motorways fenced off from the ghettos, visit the boutiques in the converted fish-market, shop on one avenue, perhaps visit the theatre or an art gallery, then go back to their own country.

Besides being aware of the many partial experiences of the Central City, one needs to be aware that the Central City inside the administrative boundary is at least two kinds of place. Firstly, there is the relatively very small renewed city centre, familiar to suburban visitors and foreign tourists alike, and looking more prosperous than ever. Secondly, there is the huge surrounding inner city, familiar to addicts of violent movies and TV cop shows, to sociologists and the odd geographer, and to the residents themselves. Meeting the contradictions head on, it is suggested that the first of these is becoming a fake, or at least a museum, and that the second is in some danger of degenerating into anarchy. To balance that perhaps too-pessimistic view, one has to admit that the Central Cities have carried on some twenty-odd years since national urban renewal schemes officially ended, although they may be in such slow decline that the rate can now be measured only over longer intervals.

From a distance, the view of each of the largest American cities is more impressive in the last decade of the twentieth century than ever before. As one circles to land at Kennedy airport the twin towers of the World Trade Center and the sloping roof of the Citicorp building punctuate a Manhattan skyline full of tall new towers. The gold, brown and beige solid geometric shapes of cities such as Dallas, the glass tubes and boxes of Los Angeles, and the gleaming white Embarcadero around the Transamerica pyramid in San Francisco are becoming as familiar to tourists as to couch potatoes watching television. From the air, or from Lake Michigan, downtown Chicago looks as shiny, new and perfect as an architect's model.

Once one has driven in from the airport, one finds that the Loop, and the downtown areas of most of the big cities *are* architect's models. They are full-scale, but they are not far from being redundant monuments to a past age and to professional pride. The newest towers are unnecessary additions to the centre which no longer function as the only business and nerve centres of the gigantic urban agglomerations. The towering new buildings are as impressive from close to as they are from a distance, but in a different way. Close to, one is impressed, then disappointed, then confused. The sheer amount of modern and post-modern architecture, good and bad, is impressive. One can not help but be impressed by the amount of capital invested in steel, concrete, glass, granite and marble during urban renewal and the period of urban revitalisation since. Then one is disappointed to find that many of these buildings, of a type once the epitome of the American city, had to be financed by the Japanese and other foreigners. The Americans themselves no longer have much confidence in the long-term financial health of their city centres. The disappointment is compounded at a personal level when one finds that these giants have feet of clay. They meet the sidewalks and plazas not in shops, hotels, bars, cafes, theatres, cinemas, second-hand bookshops or any of the varied features of the vital, crowded concentrated city of the past, but in blank marble, hard granite, locked security doors, dead exteriors. The disappointment is compounded at an intellectual and professional level when, on further investigation, one finds that these examples of magnificent architecture are half-empty (table 9.4), and that most of the big firms occupying those floors which have been finished and furnished usually have to be subsidised by the city authorities — in a sense bribed to stay there. The situation is not unique to America, but it is reaching extremes there. A similar situation much closer to home is to be found on Canary Wharf in London's Dockland.

One turns away to look at the historic area, usually the original docks and the port, for example the Harbor area in Baltimore. Faneuil Hall, the original market and meeting place in Boston is most attractive, as is Ghirardelli Square, the gentrified chocolate factory next to the old docks in San Francisco. Such areas attract masses of people, especially at weekends in summer. But these areas are no more essential to the serious business of greater Baltimore, Boston or San Francisco than Covent Garden and Camden Lock are to London, or the Royal Exchange to the business life of Manchester.

On the way from skyscraper sham to Disneyfied docks one may pass through gentrified residential areas. Some of the refurbished brownstone houses of the north east appear to be most desirable residences. Bill Cosby chose exactly the right setting for his character, the middle-class, black gynaecologist Doctor Heathcliffe Huxtable to emphasise his social status and wealth. The converted factories and warehouses, the so-called lofts, rival city homes to be found anywhere. For nearly twenty years now there has been a desultory but continuing argument in geographical journals as to whether this gentrification, or urban homesteading, as some of it was called for a time, really is bringing wealthy people back into the city or is merely moving round those people who have always been there. If those geographers studying this small corner of urban life after two decades and two censuses can not agree, then clearly the number of people and the amount of money brought into the city has been negligible.

So, who lives in the city centre now? The janitors and the security guards, the gentrifiers, the very rich and the very poor. That needs to be qualified: the janitors and guards work there but probably live in the suburbs; the very rich have other residences elsewhere, so are really only part-timers. But the very poor do live there, in cardboard boxes over the ventilation shafts of the subways and in doorways. That leaves only the gentrifiers with permanent addresses in the city centre now.

So, who comes here day in day out? The answer is, fewer and fewer as time goes on. The fundamental difference from the days of the concentrated city is that the city centre is no longer seen as the best place to make a buck. (see tables 9.2 9.3 9.4) So who does come to work? The city employee, the fireman, the cop, the garbage collector, the workers in the museums, concert-halls, law courts and galleries, and the city bureaucrat. If they work for the city and want to qualify for their pensions they have no option but to come downtown, however unpleasant that may be becoming. Also the office worker whose firm is either so prestigious that Manhattan or the Loop are still vital addresses, or so unaware that they haven't noticed where all the smart operators are going. Then there are two kinds of shop-keeper: the one who sells a single diamond necklace a month, and lives very well off that, and the one who sells basic food, the cheapest clothing, cigarettes, booze, unbelievable videos and magazines and tourist junk. A rapid survey of retail functions in the American downtown, except in a few places like Salt Lake City which to me seemed old fashioned, attractive and safe, will show only the extremes, a few very high-order specialists, and a crowd of very cheap, shabby convenience outlets.

As fewer and fewer businessmen and women work in the city centre, fewer and fewer other people have any reason to come in. If people have to find the offices of firms and professionals in the suburbs anyway, they stay there and do everything else there too. The middle-class Americans one finds out in the open air in the centres of the very big American cities, perhaps with the exception of New York, are more and more like the foreign tourists and the hicks from the sticks with whom they mingle. The American still comes to see the Empire State Building, the boutiques in the Historic Center, Olvera Street, Fisherman's Wharf, Larimer Square, the Trolley Station and so on, but then drives or flies home to the suburbs in his or her own MSA.

On looking through R. Murphy's 1954 list of Central Business District functions, the very things by which the CBD was defined in mid-century, one is hard put to find anything else which is still in the centre *of necessity* and flourishing there because that is the only, or at least the very best, location. The big department stores have gone. The hotels depend on tourists, not people on business. The main railway and bus stations are either almost empty or full of the city's most unfortunate who have nowhere to live. The names Wall Street, Madison Avenue, Hollywood, The Wheat Pit and the rest refer now to functions, not to the actual places where those functions are carried out today. The action is no longer on the streets and in the buildings whose very names epitomised the big bustling city — the City of the Big Shoulders — not so very long ago. The public buildings are still there, but it may shock an American to learn that he or she can no longer see the Liberty Bell in Independence Hall. The city authorities say that the building in which the new nation was founded is closed temporarily; the truth is that it is permanently closed because Philadelphia can not afford to keep that tiny building next to tall new skyscrapers in repair. The vital economic functions of Philadelphia's CBD, the bustle and life of that tiny area of Philly which in the past produced so much wealth — if not actual excitement, according to W.C. Field's gravestone — have gone to places like The King of Prussia examined in the next chapter.

The functions which do hang on, and which can fool the short-stay visitor into believing that the CBD is alive and well and still in the city centre, have moved into the megastructures. These are gigantic, misshapen, ugly structures which house car-parks, shops, offices, restaurants, hotels, convention centres, cinemas, saunas and who knows what else all under one roof and, more importantly, all inside strong walls and defended doors.

There are several reasons for the retreat into the megastructures. The huge buildings themselves are another attempt at that urban renewal by which the city still tries to be seen as the most prestigious part of the whole urban area. They represent the victory of pride over common sense on the part of multinational companies and international architects — the Canary Wharf syndrome again. They demonstrate the need for defence, protection and security on the part of those high-order functions which are taking up a smaller and smaller part of the centre in the rapidly growing and deteriorating slums which comprise so much of the inner cities. They provide the defended space for the suburbanite who perceives the city as a dangerous place and is scared to walk abroad in the centre.

As early as 1984 Linda Blandford in her *Guardian* American Diary put the megastructures in perspective. She picked out four key features of the city of Detroit to exemplify the trend. First, she saw the secure multi-storey car-park as the type of new building which gave the best clue to understanding what the city is becoming. That is where the suburbanites, the vast majority of the population in the urban areas, leave their cars in safety when they venture into the contemporary city centre. Blandford described the defended mega-structure of the Detroit Renaissance Centre, the place the motorists visit, showing it to be Main Street moved indoors. She then juxta-posed this with the dilapidated ghost town of Woodward Avenue, once the heart of Detroit's shopping area, and finally with the unheated homes of the unemployed people in the inner city of once-proud Motown all around. Linda Blandford in an excellent, concise article reduced the elements to car-park, megastructure, defunct outdoor CBD, and inner-city slums. One suspects it may eventually come down to two: defended space and decay. For an American view, at greater length, read what Loren D. Estleman through his character Amos Walker thinks now of his home town, Detroit.

Direct observation and the descriptions one reads tend to make one think more and more of medieval and early renaissance European towns where the palaces of the rich were wall to wall with the hovels of the poor. The palaces of Bologna, Lucca, Florence and many other city states raised their towers in the arrogance of wealth and pride of power in competition with other palaces, some of which were just across the sewage-filled street and others in the next country just across the valley. The towers of Lucca reached ridiculous heights to show off their status as rich residences, but every palace also had to be a fortress, not so much to keep out rivals but to keep out the dis-possessed, the mobs of the poor. Increasingly the defended spaces in the former Central Business Districts of American cities are coming to resemble in essence, if not in appearance, those defended strongholds of European towns just emerging from the lawless Middle Ages.

In 1991 Paul Knox described what he called the Restless Urban Landscape, the contemporary big-city landscape of the United States. Knox chose Washington DC as his case study, admitting that it is atypical in certain respects, particularly in the socio-economic constitution of its population, the concentration of administrative and high-order functions, and the fact that there is now new development in the CBD.

However, the key features which Knox describes are also character-istic of the urban landscapes of many of the other large American cities at the end of this century. With maps, photographs and full descriptions, Knox identifies seven major items of the contemporary MSA:

- The Post-Modern Centre
- The Historic Area
- The Gentrified Areas
- Mixed-Use Developments (MXD)

- Multi-Use Developments (MUD)
- Master-Planned Suburban and Exurban Communities
- High-Tech Corridors.

Some of these have been discussed above. Washington is unusual in having new retail and office development in the centre, and in the large size of its gentrified areas just to the north of the well-known public buildings. Eric Inglefield gives details of the preserved historic areas in Washington and in 49 other cities. Knox's MXDs and MUDs include the megastructures explained above and Washington has variations on this theme. Knox identifies 40 of these in the Washington area, some two-thirds built since 1980, and about two-thirds of them in the suburbs. They include:

- Crystal Plaza
- Crystal Square
- Ballston Metro Centre
- Bethesda Metro Centre
- Dulles Town Centre
- Reston Town Centre
- Tysons II.

Note the repetitive and misleading names appearing once again. Knox refers to these commercial and residential developments as architecturally opulent with lavish interior design and very high-order retail functions. The high-tech corridors compare with the strip developments described by Cervero, as explained in the next chapter. The suburban and exurban master-planned communities also tie in with the next chapter, but will be outlined here to complete Knox's picture of the whole MSA.

If a megastructure can be almost a private CBD, then the suburban master-planned community is almost a private village walled off from the rest of the residential areas in the outer parts of the MSA. Defence and exclusiveness are becoming more and more a part of the American urban landscape. Knox describes the boundary walls and guarded gates around the carefully landscaped acres of very low-density expensive housing interspersed with tennis courts, golf courses and swimming pools. There are clear restrictions on who will be accepted to live in these expensive and exclusive guarded enclaves, each watched over by a community association. A few examples can be traced back to the 1930s but as with MXDs most of the 30-odd communities round Washington have been built, in a variety of post-modern and European period styles, since 1980. Most are in

Montgomery and Fairfax Counties in the northwestern part of the MSA. The most ambitious is Kentlands near Gaithersburg, which has:

- 1600 homes, in nineteenth-century styles
- a 1.2 million square foot shopping mall
- a million square feet of office space
- a preserved 1852 farmhouse and outbuildings
- new buildings styled as 1800s barns, mills, fire station and carriage house but used for cultural activities
- a wetlands environment and 12-acre lake
- churches, a school and recreation centre
- bike paths, jogging trails and equestrian centre.

Knox describes this type of community as 'an upper-middle class vivarium'. He writes, 'the net result is a collage of intensively private worlds, each entered through brick or timber portals in the manner of an English landed estate'. That idea of private worlds will be picked up again in the next chapters which consider the residential pattern of the MSA as a whole.

In the 1950s, about the time Jean Gottmann was alerting the world to the emergence of Megalopolis, James Wreford Watson, using Hamilton in Canada as his example, wrote about the contrast between geographical and social distance. Watson described how, in North American cities like Hamilton, the very rich could be found living within a few yards of the very poor. The geographical straight-line distance was nothing, but the social and economic distance was greater than anywhere else in the world. Not as many people live in the centre now as did in 1950, and the distance between penthouse rich and sidewalk poor may be a few metres more, but the contrast to which Watson drew attention is now self-evident to anyone who lives in, or goes to look at, the inner-city areas beyond the architectural parks of the centre. David Rieff, a longtime resident in New York, and clearly familiar with the state of the inner cities of the north east, makes a convincing case in *Los Angeles, Capital of the Third World* that even the city of dreams is now a place where the white thirty per cent of the population on the west side feel beleaguered by the black, Hispanic and Asian millions, mostly the poor who now outnumber them by two to one. It may also be recorded, but I have not seen, how the poor people feel about this social and economic distance from their side of the divide.

As one goes from the obsolescent CBD of the old Rustbelt city, not on a freeway, parkway or turnpike, but 'on the surface', as the LA phrase has it, along the potholed streets away from the centre, one

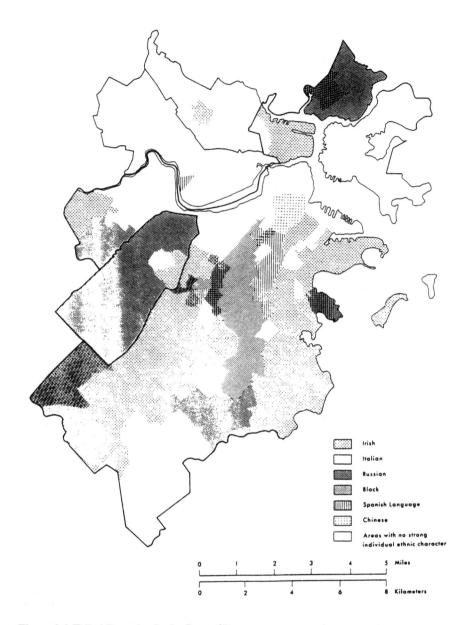

Figure 9.1 Tribal Domains in the Inner City
In the last quarter of this century, protection of turfs, as here in Boston, has included
gang wars and murder, especially by young dealers protecting their small market
areas from rivals
Source: Conzen, M.P. & Lewis, G.K., *Boston*, Ballinger Division, HarperCollins Publishers,
1976, p. 41

187

experiences that greatest contrast between the tiny city centre and the overwhelming sprawl of the streets where the citizens of the Central City actually live. One traverses the slums, then the incipient slums and finally the reasonable outer parts still within the Central City boundary. This large area between the original CBD and the corporate boundary is the part of the urban area where no cosmetic rebuilding has taken place to hide all the losses to the suburbs. It is the area where very few jobs come in and where not enough wealth is created even to maintain the fabric and provide a minimum satisfactory standard of living for the people, never mind growth and regeneration. To compound the overwhelming problems, in those cities where a few self-regarding corporations and gullible foreign companies have been lured into the city, millions of poor whites, blacks, Hispanics and Asians also continue to move in, hoping to find work there, not knowing that most of it has gone and that what does move in is hopelessly inadequate for their needs.

The old immigrants of European origin have largely gone. The manufacturing, retailing, wholesaling and services which once provided work have also largely gone. The temporary fact of world recession should not cloud the issue; the Central City was in long-term functional decline before the depression of the 1990s and has simply been aggravated by that event. There is no longer sufficient production of wealth to maintain the Central City from its own resources and to provide a reasonable income for the millions of people who still live there. As a result the list of urban problems, the social blight, the awful conditions in which those millions of Americans live grows decade by decade.

One sees the problems of one generation creating the extra problems of the next. The poverty of the 1960s, and then the hopelessness after the black riots resulted in millions of dollars being made available not for homes and jobs and schools, but for extra riot gear including armoured cars for the police, aggravated the mass drug addiction of the seventies and eighties. That massive drug market in fact then provided work, income and status for the hierarchy of people from the top financiers to the pushers on the street corners. As things got worse, to the crimes of mugging, robbery and burglary to get money for drugs, were added the gang wars of the late eighties and the nineties. The gangs use machine guns and bombs, in addition to mere pistols, as they continue to fight for control of territory, and hence markets for their drugs.

A common phrase used some years ago to describe the condition of the young unemployed people in the inner city was 'anomie and alienation'. Observers were worried that young black people and immigrants were not accepting Euro-American culture, American values and a WASP way of life. They were alienated from such things, but having little to identify with from elsewhere and little prospect of jobs, careers, families and homes, had little hope or sense of purpose. Nowadays the key phrase is 'role model' and the concern seems to centre on the lack of these for the young in the inner cities. This is pure cant. There are plenty of role models for the young to emulate; the problem is that they are not the kind of role models of which sociologists or suburban society at large approve. The models for young men which used to exist and which would still be preferred were fathers, teachers to whom they could relate, and older men who inducted them into their first jobs or careers. With single-parent families now the norm, schools where the teachers have to be protected from the pupils by armed guards, and very few jobs in which to be shown the ropes, such role models are long gone. Instead there are the millionaire drug barons, the Mafia bosses who defy the government, the local gang leaders, pimps and pushers with expensive clothes, foreign cars and money in their pockets. These are the examples whom the young black men, the Mexican and Korean and Pakistani young men apart from the small number who succeed in sport and entertainment, can realistically hope to emulate. They are the only successful men whom they either see or hear about in their own neighbourhoods and with whom they can identify (see table 9.5). They are the kinds of role models with whom they come in contact. John Wayne, Henry Fonda and Gary Cooper just aren't around any more.

The young people in the inner city are becoming alienated from a society they see only on television. The models implied in the current criticism of inner-city life are those with WASP — or at least ex-European — values and ways of life. The European immigrants to the city at least came into contact regularly with WASPs, long enough to accept or reject such roles as they chose. But the uncomfortable fact is that most of the young people in the inner city no longer get anywhere near the kinds of people they are expected to emulate, even if they wanted to. So they are not going to become the kind of old-fashioned 'American' behind the concept of the melting pot. The inner-city young are too far from the furnace, too far from the warmth and the wealth to melt down and metamorphose into good WASPs.

When anomie and alienation were the acceptable ideas, it seemed that inner-city society was disintegrating. Now, with the new role-models in evidence, one is much more inclined to believe that a society completely different from the suburban version is developing in the inner cities: a sub-society very different and increasingly dangerous. As the young people of the inner-city areas have less and less

189

chance of entering the economy at large, there is less and less chance that they will want to emulate and financially be able to join some 'American' society at large. They are creating a society of their own with the kinds of resources at present to hand. Many people in the inner city are trying hard to continue to make a living and to live a decent life in the decaying areas. But these places tend to be less and less slums of hope as the years go by. Already the reports of crime and gang warfare, which seemed so new and difficult to believe just a few years ago, are being pushed aside by the horror stories of the sheer numbers of homeless people living on the sidewalks of American cities. The depression of the 1980s and 1990s certainly has aggravated this situation but, again, it is argued that any disinterested observer would agree that this is merely speeding up a systemic long-term trend.

Such emotional matters tend to be exaggerated, and given that it is difficult enough to get an accurate census of people in permanent residences, numbers of the homeless are impossible to determine with any degree of accuracy. One distressing result is that politicians and others with some power to do something too often use that fact to deny the existence of the phenomenon when the people with nowhere to live — whatever the accuracy or otherwise of their numbers — are there to be seen on the streets. Given that caveat, one sees responsible estimates of some two million homeless people in US cities, including 20,000 in Washington and 80,000 in New York. One report asserted that this latter figure is tenfold the number counted there in the Depression of the 1930s. The situation to someone not involved is bad enough. But a report by Martin Walker underlined the real horror and distress involved. When one sees able-bodied adult men with bottles of wine, old sleeping bags and cardboard shelters sleeping rough, one may be able to shrug it off. But when one reads an article by an experienced, level-headed journalist describing families, husbands, wives, sons and daughters, being evicted, not in wartime Bosnia, but on to the streets of contemporary Washington DC, New York and other once-wealthy and powerful American cities, that has a different and disturbing effect. Being evicted in the richest country in the world must rub fierce salt into their wounds.

The contrast between the city centre and the inner residential areas is becoming ever more marked. In the 1980s St Louis featured in newspapers and TV documentaries to illustrate the differences over a few miles, another variation on the idea of social and economic distance. By the 1990s East St Louis is being labelled the worst inner-city area in the USA and observers keep coming up with the same explanation — that by city, state and federal authorities alike, it is simply being ignored. This resonates with what has been said about the poorer black people. No conspiracy is necessary; people and places no longer part of the economic or social system are just bypassed and ignored. Similarly a recent review of Pittsburgh, describing a second round of rebuilding, urban revitalisation, following up the first very successful urban renewal in the 1950s, still has to admit the 'devastation' on the South Side of the city in the 1990s. This devastation referred to people on minimum wage or unemployed, unemployment in the ghetto described as 'catastrophic', declining population, crime, drugs, the highest mortality rate in the country, and 'civic neglect'. Remember that Pittsburgh, compared with St Louis, has a legacy of successful urban renewal.

In 1991 Detroit reported 100,000 people homeless. Given the relative sizes of the two cities, this is a much higher proportion of the people of Motown than of the Big Apple. Those names sound a bit sad now. In May 1991 Philadelphia announced that it was in danger of going bankrupt on 1 July, three days before Independence Day. The particular timing may have been a ploy to get extra publicity for the old city, but the financial crisis was real all the same. There is some evidence that the attitude towards the inner cities by the mayors and the city authorities is quite deliberate. For example Houston is one of the richest cities in the USA and, partly as a result of being a Sunbelt city, partly as a result of more local conditions, it has fewer problems about being unable to annexe its suburbs to increase its control and revenue. Yet Houston has exactly the same kind of decaying inner-city areas and social problems as virtually every other major city in the union. These areas are where black Americans and people of Mexican origin are concentrated. If Houston has no long-term financial weakness, and yet its inner city is still as bad as those of Pittsburgh, St Louis and Detroit, as Shelton describes, then this can be the result only of wilful neglect, not financial necessity.

It follows that there are now more items to add to the earlier list of urban social blight. That list was long enough and serious enough, but there are two groups of contemporary problems to add, either new, or now with greater significance.

The first group is:
● the neglect of the infrastructure
● the inadequacy of the public services.

The second is:
● racial tension
● new artificial drugs such as crack
● Aids and HIV

191

- tuberculosis
- homelessness
- lack of any prospect of improvement
- gang warfare.

These, of course, do not involve every single family in the inner city. Only a minority may be actively affected or involved. People who do not want to believe it or who want to shun the responsibility to do anything about it can easily point to neighbourhoods which still look good to the casual eye. The point is that these terrible features are now sufficiently common not just to ruin the lives of the few, but to act to the serious detriment of the majority. All nine of the features listed above tend towards increasing the anomie of a larger and larger proportion of the people. They become alienated from the society which ignores them in this plight, and they are developing a very special type of society of their own to try to cope with it. They are in non-escalator slums of despair now.

That this can seem over-exaggeration to anyone who does not pay attention to this least accessible part of the urban area is well illustrated by an article in the *Sunday Telegraph* in January 1992. John Hiscock reported that two Welsh ladies from Cardiff, on holiday in Los Angeles, decided to go to see the hand- and footprints of the Hollywood film stars pressed into the cement outside Mann's Chinese Theatre on Hollywood Boulevard. The half-page article details the horror and shock of the two lady tourists when they found themselves in a slum surrounded by winos, drug addicts, beggars, prostitutes and muggers. ' "Oh dear! It's nothing like one is led to expect!" said Indegwynne Jones. "It's all so distasteful!" ' If 'distasteful' were the only problem, it could soon be solved. But one wonders and wonders just what they were led to expect in 1992, and by whom?

Pittsburgh managed to attract enough capital for a second round of revitalisation, but spent nothing on the black people and poor whites on the South Side. Detroit apparently has abandoned its inner-city areas. Los Angeles is going to tidy up the *place* in Hollywood, so that the tourists will no longer find it distasteful, but there are no plans to do anything for the people.

At the time of the black riots of the 1960s all but a few American cities had white administrations. By the end of this century most Central Cities have black mayors and administrations, but one of the inescapable facts is that these mayors have not achieved much for the centres, the inner cities or for black people themselves. One reason is that few have had the resources, but there are also indications that some have not had the political will either. After sixteen years in power, Tom Bradley was re-elected Mayor of Los Angeles at the turn of the decade. When first elected in 1973 Bradley promised to revive the decaying city centre and turn it into an international city with a growing economy. Some of his promises were fulfilled: the new sky-scraper CBD has been built in his time, Los Angeles hosted the Olympic Games, and the city is now considered an important part of the international economy of the Pacific Rim. But on the down side are the other facts: pollution the worst of any US city, the freeways jammed solid most of the time, giving us the new word gridlock; and the urban rail system promised in 1973 has not been started. Mean-while, the gangs murder some 500 people each year and the drug trade, poverty and homelessness escalate. In this context Christopher Reed wrote in the *Guardian*: '[That] the city's burgeoning poor are in a desperate plight is largely overlooked... Critics claim that he [Bradley] has become complacent, frequently taking pleasant foreign trips rather than grappling with the city's immense problems.' The old city machines of the Irish and the Italians may have gone, but some black mayors have picked up the idea. 'Yet Mr Bradley thrives' — Reed again.

While American suburban dwellers and foreign visitors rarely go into the inner cities, there is much academic debate about what is happening there. One argument is about whether the total population is in long-term decline or not. At first sight many derelict and aban-doned properties in the old Rustbelt cities suggest that it is. Certainly those who can get out do so as quickly as possible. But so many poor white people, Hispanics, Asians, immigrants from literally all over the world at the same time are moving in. There is a massive transient population, changing an unknown number of times between censuses. Moreover, those moving in from Third World countries tend to have higher birth rates than the more successful ones moving out. It is all but impossible to be sure of numbers, rates of change, decline or growth.

Another argument is about crime and the extent of the drug culture. Each city tries to minimise what is going on and to cover up as much as possible in order not to damage its precarious economy further. Again, facts about crime, drug abuse, drug trafficking, prostitution, illegal activities, illegal immigrants, gang wars and the like are by defi-nition impossible to obtain in any complete and reliable form. But the sheer number and variety of reports and studies, including the most recent and alarming which suggest that the drug/crime culture is spreading to the suburbs of Midwestern cities, tend to confirm that the problem is growing. Some suggest that the situation has deterio-rated far enough to be in danger of destabilising communities in the inner cities. When people in those areas receive no help to reduce unemployment and to combat crime which seems almost out of control in some cities like Atlanta, Miami, Newark and St Louis, either because of lack of funds or because of simple indifference, it is no surprise that they become alienated from the rest of American society. But cause and effect are so interrelated, and the start of trends so lost in the past, that for every observer who sees perennial victims of crime and the drug culture becoming alienated, there is a critic who sees alienated people turning to drugs and crime.

Learned opinions and predictions are divided. On one side is the argument — perhaps more a belief or a hope — that most people will move out of the inner city. The unstated implication is, of course, that somehow they will, in the process, leave all the ills behind. As if social problems appertained to *place*, whether inhabited or not, rather than to *people*. On the other side is the prediction that social blight will spread. A few determinedly optimistic geographers argue that market forces will continue to operate as they have done before. They point out that property prices and land values are now incredibly low in the inner city. Therefore, they argue, it is only a matter of time before the move to the suburbs completely reverses direction, and capital and people start moving in the opposite direction from that of the last seventy years. They may well do so; one sees the argument. But as with what has happened to London's Dockland, it will change the place; and it will not help the particular people living there at this moment. If people somehow escape the inner city without finding work, they will take their social characteristics with them. If the inner city is rejuvenated by market forces, it will see the influx of middle-class people from the suburbs, not suddenly and magically create jobs for all the uneducated and untrained inner-city poor who live there now. The centre may well thrive again in time; but where will the present residents be then?

In the American city one group of people seems most unlikely to get out. Of all the racial, ethnic, national and religious groups which have passed through the areas which now form the inner cities, those with the smallest proportion of their total numbers to have made it to the suburbs are the black people. There are middle-class black people in the suburbs, but census returns show both that some three-quarters of all urban black residents are in the Central Cities, and that in many Central Cities sixty, seventy, even eighty per cent of the total population consists of black people.

Their position *vis-à-vis* the old immigrant groups of Europeans, and then the new immigrant groups of Hispanic peoples and Asians has also been a matter of emotional argument, like that over their politi-

194

cally correct name. But one sees an undeniable trend. For whatever reasons, the Europeans, the Latin Americans and now the Asians have been more successful economically, and therefore more successful socially, and they have tended to leave a large proportion of the black people socio-economically, and geographically, behind. As other peoples come and go in the inner city, it is arguable just who are the most permanent residents, but as the decades have dropped away since the time of the First World War, one can see that the permanent elements of Central City populations have become predominantly those of black Americans. In the meantime, the Hispanic and Asian elements have come, and are now going.

In the past, when the ghetto was only part of the Central City, notwithstanding the red-lining in the back offices of Savings and Loan companies, the ghetto had an indefinite boundary. Now, when the population of many American Central Cities is 70% or 75% black, the poor black community does have an official boundary; it is the city boundary. In February 1992 Kurt Vonnegut, one of the century's most original and socially aware American writers, put into words a concept half-formed in my own mind at the time, but which I voiced then only when I felt up to an emotional brawl. Vonnegut was well ahead of me, and put it so eloquently in a detailed exposition.

I have long argued that there was, and is, no conspiracy against black people in the American city in the twentieth century. From all my studies I believe that they are just forgotten, neglected and put out of mind by the rest of the people — WASP, European, Hispanic, or Asian — whenever possible. Vonnegut, in his tired, resigned acceptance of how things are, goes further. In an honest, clear-sighted and devastating article, he states that he sees the poor black people within the boundary of the Central City as being exactly like the American Indians of the recent past. To all intents and purposes, within the city boundary, the black people are out of sight and out of mind, on the reservation.

Table 9.1 City Revenue From Government Sources 1990. $Millions

New York	12,334	Indianapolis	257
Washington	1,306	Virginia Beach	253
Baltimore	802	Norfolk	220
Chicago	752	Denver	205
Boston	746	San Diego	195
San Francisco	740	Nashville	183
Detroit	673	Newark	174
Philadelphia	611	Atlanta	166
Memphis	469	Albuquerque	162
Buffalo	441	St Paul	156
Los Angeles	439	Jacksonville	143
Rochester	317	Cleveland	130
Phoenix	314	New Orleans	127
Anchorage	278	Tucson	120
Milwaukee	277	Honolulu	116
		Charlotte	104
		Cincinnati	100

Source: Statistical Abstract of the US 1992

Table 9.2 City Debt Outstanding 1990 $Millions

New York	26,005	Dallas	1,750
Los Angeles	6,278	Tulsa	1,451
Chicago	4,298	Detroit	1,450
Jacksonville	4,297	San Diego	1,406
San Antonio	4,035	Denver	1,266
Philadelphia	3,796	Albuquerque	1,264
Houston	3,611	Baltimore	1,257
Washington	3,423	Tampa	1,217
Austin	3,188	New Orleans	1,128
San Francisco	2,392	Oakland	1,110
Nashville	2,331	Columbus	1,072
Phoenix	2,062	Atlanta	1,069
Minneapolis	1,980	San Jose	1,043

Source: Statistical Abstract of the US 1992

Table 9.3 City Employees per 10,000 Population 1990

Washington	776	Seattle	204
New York	537	Indianapolis	202
Buffalo	397	Philadelphia	194
Baltimore	387	Atlanta	192
Boston	361	Colorado Springs	186
Virginia Beach	359	St Louis	183
Nashville	352	New Orleans	181
San Francisco	351	Cincinnati	170
Norfolk	343	Minneapolis	165
Memphis	327	Albuquerque	164
Denver	241	Cleveland	158
Austin	206	Newark	156
Detroit	204		

Source: Statistical Abstract of the US 1992

Table 9.4 Percentage of Offices Vacant 1990

New Orleans	29	Washington	19
Dallas	26	Philadelphia	18
Houston	25	Chicago	18
Denver	24	Charlotte	16
Milwaukee	23	Los Angeles	16
Indianapolis	21	New York	16
St Louis	21	Pittsburgh	16
Boston	20	San Francisco	14
Baltimore	20	Kansas City	14
Atlanta	19	Seattle	12

Source: Statistical Abstract of the US 1992

Table 9.5   Crime Rates per 100,000 Population 1990

1	Atlanta	19,236
2	Miami	19,024
3	Tampa	17,125
4	Newark	16,256
5	Dallas	15,520
6	Fort Worth	14,977
7	St Louis	14,671
8	Kansas City	12,953
9	Seattle	12,601
10	Charlotte	12,594
11	San Antonio	12,477
12	New Orleans	12,436
13	Baton Rouge	12,384
14	St Petersburg	12,289
15	Detroit	12,192
16	Tucson	11,879
17	Boston	11,851
18	Austin	11,714
19	Stockton	11,503
20	Houston	11,338
21	Birmingham	11,262
22	El Paso	11,239
23	Portland	11,101
24	Rochester	11,039
25	Oakland	10,906

Source: Statistical Abstract of the US 1992

10

THE SUBURBS ARE THE CITY

We are approaching the time when we will need a new name and a new complete model to identify and formalise the new kind of American city which is coming into existence. It is no longer accurate, nor realistic, to call the urban areas where most of the people live and where all of the vital functions are located the 'suburbs'. The Bureau of the Census has faced this already, but the term Metropolitan Statistical Area will never have the same ring in everyday use as the word city had in the past. Nor will the models of Burgess, Hoyt or Harris and Ullman continue to provide a satisfactory description and explanation in the twenty-first century. American cities are now like old but impressively vigorous trees with hollow centres. Those centres were vital in the past; now they are preserved with decreasing importance and function. The new outer growth is where most of the life and most of the vital functions are located, and it is because of this that we need a new name and a new model. The present, inadequate word suburb now refers to the kinds of areas and the kinds of functions once implicit in the word city.

Table 8.1 shows the percentages of the populations of the 25 largest urban areas now living beyond the boundaries of the Central Cities. In the Phoenix area this is still only 54% and in greater New York it is only 60% — but that is already nearly two-thirds of the population outside the city proper. For San Francisco, Boston, Atlanta, Cleveland, Minneapolis, St Louis and the like, one is looking at over eighty per cent of the population of the built-up-area in what increasingly are misnamed suburbs. The suburbs are no longer just the quiet residential areas where the well-heeled live; they are where the action is. And if the concept of the city is defined as the place where the action is, then the suburbs are now, *de facto*, the city.

Having described how people from all levels of society, and how every kind of manufacturing and CBD function have relocated to the former suburbs, the substance of earlier chapters will not be repeated here. If the following list is familiar, it will serve to emphasise the point:

New York	Stamford, Conn.
Chicago	Schaumberg, Ill.
Los Angeles	Costa Mesa
Washington	Tysons Corner, Va.
Philadelphia	King of Prussia, Penn.
Dallas	North Dallas
Atlanta	Dunwoody, Ga.

If the list is not familiar, it will point up the fact that one needs to learn the new names for Wall Street, the Loop and the other original financial centres, because these places in the suburbs of these cities are the locations to which the highest-order financial functions — the very essence of Murphy's definition of the Central Business District — have now transferred, or are transferring. As for new names, Stamford may never have the same ring as Wall Street, but King of Prussia, a suburb of Philadelphia, might.

Thus one argues that the enormous low-density built-up urban areas where the majority of the people now live and work in the complete range of city functions, from lowest to highest order, need an appropriate name which will shake us out of the now-obsolete habit of thinking of them as mere suburbs, *sub urbs* — bits on the edge of, very different from and less important than, the city. The reality today is that the urban areas beyond the boundary of the Central City are very little different from what the Central City itself used to be at mid-century. The differences are in appearance and density rather than function. The centre is a place of decline, abandonment and obsolescence, while the contemporary suburb is the place of growth, in-migration, constant renewal, with high-order city functions increasing in number and variety all the time. Perhaps an old but vigorous hollow tree is not the best analogy. In that most of the functions and up to ninety per cent of the people have moved, leaving the buildings and a relatively small proportion of functions and population behind, it is perhaps more like a snake casting off its old skin and moving away as it grows.

Some few functions have remained in the centre and this, of course, varies from city to city, with places like New York and San Diego at one end of the spectrum and St Louis at the other. Some of the highest-order functions hang on in the centre: prestige entertainment such as shows, opera and the largest orchestras, galleries and museums, the city administrations and the administration of justice.

Most retail functions of any significance are now suburban. Most manufacturing is now suburban, if not actually rural, as Brown and Wardlow appear to argue. Wholesale functions, the professions, education, much art and entertainment and the host of interesting odds and ends which made up the exciting variety of the big city in the past have followed. Finally, the heart of the CBD has moved out, forming a separate hierarchy of centres in the suburbs. In this context there are two more useful acronyms, SEC and FIRE.

FIRE stands for Financial, Insurance and Real Estate functions, which are now much more characteristic of the suburbs than of the CBD. Moreover, so many of these functions — once the essential residents of the skyscrapers of downtown — are so numerous, and located in so many different suburban areas, that the abbreviation SEC has been formulated for the convenience of those geographers, urban analysts, regional students and planners who constantly need to refer to these Suburban Employment Centres. Somehow the terminology given by academics never has quite the ring of names given by city dwellers; Suburban Employment Centre hasn't got the magic of downtown either in name or fact.

Unfortunately for the WASPs who fled to the suburbs in the 1950s and the hopeful others who followed them later, the transfer of city-centre characteristics to the former residential areas does not stop there. That is because the economic functions, desirable in that they at least provide work, have been followed by the features which few people want: pollution, noise, crime, litter, drug abuse, racism and, in urban life, the worst disaster of all, traffic congestion. Read David Rieff's recent book on Los Angeles and you will find a thread of preoccupation with freeway gridlock. Robert Cervero's *America's Suburban Centres* describes the elements and functions in great detail, but the aim of his extremely useful book is to start to help with solving what is becoming *the* suburban nightmare — one complete traffic jam with cars bumper to bumper (fender to fender) as commuters try to drive across the gigantic suburban areas in every direction of the compass. Start collecting magazine, journal, newspaper and other reports and articles on American suburban traffic problems and you will soon need an extra office. So, almost everything, including the bad and the hopeless, the very things which people started moving away from only half a century ago, is now in, and characteristic of, the suburbs. There has been considerable change within these environs during this half century. They are now nothing like the suburbs of the 1960s; and the suburbs now, complete as they are with the high-order functions including high finance, are not exactly what downtown was fifty years ago.

201

Four major processes have been in operation to bring about this change. In the first place has been the growth in area of the suburbs, so that now they cover a vastly larger surface than the original Central City. In many cases they have engulfed smaller cities and towns, so that what is referred to as the large American city now is what in Britain we would call a conurbation. There are also some half-dozen cases now of these conurbations growing and joining to form the Megalopolises, the very, very big cities — more correctly urbanised regions.

Secondly, since the 1950s many of the older, inner suburbs have been torn down and rebuilt, in some instances two or three times. Within the American urban timescale, so short by European standards, many suburbs are mature, even old now. They have been established, re-arranged, added to, consolidated then rebuilt to meet the requirements of third- and fourth-generation occupiers and residents.

Thirdly, residential mobility has continued as a major characteristic. Over the decades, however, the pattern has become more complex than the simple continuous outward movement described by Burgess and accepted as the norm by most lay people. Some of the mobility still is the outward movement, as those who can afford to do so move into the newer areas on the fringe as the non-residential features push them out more and more. Americans move home much more often than most western Europeans, not only from suburb to suburb but from city to city. Increasingly, however, there seem to be lateral movements, and some observers claim to have identified even inward movements. With immigrants to the United States now just as likely to find their first location in the suburbs as in the inner city, the pattern of residential movements within and between suburban areas is now more complicated than at any time in the past. As a result, it is no longer accurate to think of simple concentric or sectoral arrangements of residential areas based on economic criteria, even round one city centre. When one remembers that the very big cities, the objects of study of this book, are in fact conurbations of many former towns and cities, then the residential pattern of one complete built-up-area is complex indeed.

Fourthly, difficult as the layout of any one continuously built-up-area around any one Central City or group of Central Cities may be to comprehend — even for the residents, whose mental maps seem to be very partial — the suburbs do now have a structure of very complex and sophisticated hierarchies of different kinds of commercial, retail, professional and business centres. There are separate hierarchies, not one for each built-up-area, as there was for each

202

concentrated city. That hierarchy from the CBD at the top down to the local family-run shops on the corner was symbolised by the diagram of the exterior of a large circus tent held up (inaccurately) by one tall pole in the centre representing the CBD and rings of smaller and smaller poles further and further out, holding the folds of canvas lower and lower near the outer wall, representing the secondary, tertiary and lower-order functions further from the CBD. The Ma and Pa grocery stores were tiny bumps in the canvas which represented the relatively simple economic surface of the concentrated city, the peaks where the poles pushed up were the commercial nodes at major cross-streets and the like.

A circus tent model will not do for the suburbs because there there are several different kinds of poles. Further, they are not located as neatly as the focal points in the concentrated city where the gridiron street plan gave a substructure. The suburban centres have a much more irregular distribution and, probably, in the end we may have to conceive of more than one layer of canvas, each representing a different type of activity surface. Very large and very important commercial centres now exist in the suburbs in large numbers (the maps, lists, photos and descriptions in Robert Cervero's book are very useful in this regard), but their characteristics, locations, and hierarchies are different from, and more complex than, what used to exist in the Central City.

Retail, manufacturing, wholesale, sports and entertainment, cultural and business centres have developed at a variety of nodes in the vast field of the total built-up-area. In the nineteenth-century city the grid-iron plan of streets and avenues provided cross-street locations for such development at a range of distances from the CBD and on a variety of scales. In the suburbs not only has the variety of potential locations been greater, but the unplanned nature of the man-made environment has resulted in a less regular distribution, apparently less logic in the juxtaposition of the different functions, and a wide range of motoring (as opposed to walking) distances between them.

Road junctions are still the most common and important sites for all kinds of suburban centres, and away from the east coast the network of east–west and north–south lines left by the land survey tends to offer a rectangular base in some areas. But even where this existed it was often soon changed by the construction of the freeways and tollways which both radiate from the old centres and ring them at various distances, often joining up with the rough grid of the Inter-state system. When one adds to this the fact that the residential areas were deliberately laid out differently from the city, copying the irregular layouts of the avenues, lanes, circles, closes, crescents and the rest in Britain, then the pattern of available nodes becomes much less regular, even haphazard.

Other natural and artificial nodes presented themselves: river crossings, a few railway junctions, airports galore — unbelievably numerous to British observers — golf courses, race courses, country clubs, lakes, the occasional farm, a hill or a valley. As the suburbs spread tens, and then scores of miles from the original city centre, settlements of all sizes were engulfed and naturally provided nodes for further rapid commercial expansion. The whole range of former separate settlements has been swallowed, from crossroad gas stations through small service centres (the nearest America ever had to market towns) to major towns and even formerly independent cities.

Mention of golf and race courses is not frivolous. The layout of many modern SECs is deliberately rural, with grass, lakes, woods and jogging tracks. Sports and recreational facilities are logical choices for developers who lay out their commercial developments in a style often described as campus-like, in order to help attract the most able and ambitious people into the suburban high-tech businesses. Erickson and Gentry add Government Facilities to this list, and suggest four stages in the development of commercial nodes in the suburbs:

1950s initial development:	residential, wholesale
1960s industrial and commercial expansion:	retail and manufacturing
1970s speculative development:	services and multistorey development
1980s redevelopment:	highest order functions now coming in to the suburbs; older property filtering down to lower order functions

Cervero also suggests four stages:

1950s: bedroom communities
1960s: independent manufacturing and retail added
1970s: catalytic growth; offices added
1980s onward: high-rise buildings and high technology.

Both these early attempts are probably too simple to classify such complex developments in such a short time, but they do confirm and help to emphasise some characteristics which are relatively recent and so not widely known, understood and accepted abroad:

- the high-rise building in the 'suburbs';
- the rebuilding, replacement and redevelopment already common;
- the establishment of the high-order financial, typically 'city', functions in the outer suburbs now.

While stressing the variety of different types of focal points for commercial development in the suburbs, however, and their spatial irregularity, one can not over-stress the importance of road junctions, airports and former separate settlements as the three most effective types of node. The developments at these points are not all the same size, and hierarchies of commercial centres have been developed in the suburbs. The retail hierarchy resembles, in its major respects, that which once existed in the concentrated Central City. There, one large, high-order Central Business District was surrounded by, say, half a dozen second-order centres at major focal points, a dozen or so third-order centres spread all over the city, on down through the five, six or seven ranks, according to the size and importance of the city, to the lowest-order centres, the innumerable clusters of corner shops within walking distance of the homes.

In the suburban retail structure now, some of the characteristics are seen again, but with important differences. A hierarchy of retail centres has certainly emerged with, in each major MSA, two or three huge, very high-order regional shopping centres at the top of the retail hierarchy. There are two or three, as opposed to one centre for the concentrated city, strategically located in the suburbs to avoid the necessity of crossing the huge built-up-area from one side of the Central City to the other if there were only one. There can no longer be one, obvious focal point. For most people, using one of these regional centres still involves a long journey by car, but the size, variety and high order of shops justifies the cost and time of travel, just as the shopping centre of a big city did in the past. Further down the suburban shopping hierarchy one finds a larger number of smaller centres with fewer services and lower-order, less specialised shops. These centres are therefore easier to reach for the majority of shoppers, but meet their needs most of the time. However, for several decades one feature of the concentrated city was missing from the suburban retail hierarchy: the equivalent of the little shop just round the corner. Just as the low density of residences could never support public transport, it seemed in most suburban areas for a long time that neither could the low-population densities support convenience shops — until the Asians arrived. In mentioning a few names in current use there is no intention here of attempting a definitive hierarchy. The rapid growth and change in the suburbs means that the real world is still too dynamic, and the labels which students of the phenomena currently use are rather too cumbersome. The present aim is simply to convey the idea.

At first the shopping centres were called malls (a name which could be misleading to anyone who has walked towards Buckingham Palace on a rainy day with some of the Household Cavalry clattering past leaving steaming piles of manure for the royal roses). American malls keep out the weather, the horses, and, for that matter, everything else undesirable. Then there were regional malls, mega-malls and many permutations on the term.

The largest malls, whatever name may stick for the top of the range in the long run, are sterilised town centres put indoors. They are gigantic, purpose-built, one- or two-storey structures, suburban and exurban megastructures. Places like Tysons Corner in Virginia, Galleria in Houston and Roosevelt Field on Long Island typically contain:

- two or three department stores
- 200–300 shops
- up to 25,000 employees
- up to 500,000 visitors per week
- half a dozen cinemas
- scores of restaurants
- two or three hotels
- a bowling alley or ice-rink.

All of these could be found at one time in any medium-sized British city. But these modern replacements for Main Street are roofed in and the visitor arrives and leaves through doors. It is like going to a hygienic Nottingham via a guarded entrance. Some things have been added to the old-fashioned, outdoor shopping street: air-conditioning, piped music, surveillance cameras, private police forces, public broadcasts and announcements. Other things have been taken away (or, more correctly, never let in): beggars, undesirables, bars, porn shops, street traders — except Disneyland type fakes — demonstrators, rain, steep hills, shade trees; in short, the things which made downtown an exciting and unpredictable place to be, a breath of fresh air.

When one has been inside one of these completely artificial worlds for most of a day, it can be a shock to go outside again. One does not leave what appears to be a big city centre via a multi-storey car-park and a drive through the inner city, or via the bus station, or even a walk home. One comes out into nothing. Well, acre upon acre of flat car-park stretching over the horizon, and that sinking feeling that one can not remember in which part of Kazakhstan one left the car...

That is one extreme, which will be looked at shortly. One can go down the suburban retail hierarchy to smaller and smaller structures, more common, closer together, usually although not exclusively older, until one comes to the uninspiring local mall — for want of a better specific name — with shoppers' goods in convenience stores. David Rieff identifies a new type of retail facility which is emerging in the suburbs and which does not seem to have got into the learned journals yet. Strangely for an independent spirit, Rieff is conditioned into referring even to this as a mall; one begins to suspect that to Americans now the word is just a synonym for shops. Rieff describes what he calls the mini-malls which are now regarded as the saviours of civilisation in the enormous suburban sprawls of places like Los Angeles. It seems that as suburban population grows, as a higher and higher proportion of that population goes *everywhere* in cars, not only are the freeways blocked, but when one manages to reach a genuine mall the goddam car-park is full too.

Asians have saved western society. They have opened what Europeans — remembering what such things look like — would call shops on bits of waste ground, known locally as vacant lots. These clusters of a few shops, out in the smog-filled open air, sell TV meals, canned foods, instant coffee, toilet rolls, kleenex, condoms, bread, Coke: all the things you find you have run out of only when you get back from the super regional tri-state Baltimore-all-under-one-roof Multimegamall. So you drive a few yards on an ordinary street and find a place to park in front of the little shop run by a Pakistani, Iranian, Thai or Korean; and believe once again in American free enterprise.

Rieff describes these retail outlets as a manifestation of what he calls the Third World economy of the poorest immigrants. Many suburban white, middle-class residents hate the ugliness and the ubiquity of these mini-malls, but they use them gratefully, and ubiquity is the key to their success.

One reason for stressing the plurality of hierarchies in the suburbs is that, while the super regional mall may well have all the retail and entertainment functions once found in the city centre, it does not contain most of the business functions, the FIRE functions which formed the big-city CBD. Robert Cervero has produced a very useful account of one of these separate financial hierarchies in the suburbs, which he calls Suburban Employment Centres. The name is as ill-thought-out as most others in such research. Cervero means white-collar tertiary and quaternary types of employment in financial services. Malls are also employment centres, certainly when they can employ up to 25,000 people, but clearly he does not include these. For the moment, however, SEC will have to serve as a convenient short-hand.

Items three and four in Cervero's classification of the business centre hierarchy, the SECs, have been rearranged in order to proceed more logically from the smallest which he identifies to the largest. Smallest, then of the SECs in Cervero's classification of suburban centres is

1. THE OFFICE PARK

This is an area of some 1,000 acres, planned as a single coherent development with a single dominant business function. The office park is a low-density area of low-rise buildings, not more than four storeys, laid out in grounds with grass, trees and water in the so-called campus style. There may be a small retail unit, but there is definitely a number of large car-parks which, combined, cover more space than the office buildings themselves.

2. OFFICE AND CONCENTRATION CENTRES

Though again the name tends to confuse rather than clarify, one will stick to Cervero's labels. By 'concentration' it seems he means the accumulation of other functions in addition to the offices.

These centres are larger and at a higher density than Type One, and have not been planned as one coherent whole. However, the business function still predominates and the rural-style landscaping is still the main visual characteristic.

3. MEDIUM MIXED-USE DEVELOPMENTS

These, like Office Parks, are typically of the order of 1,000 acres. FIRE functions are the important business element, but they have acted as the magnet for retail functions, wholesaling, some light manufacturing, and perhaps some residential development.

4. LARGE MIXED-USE DEVELOPMENTS

These can be up to three or four square miles in area, archetypal suburban sprawls. Some are linear, along major road routes through the suburbs, others are large enough to be major retail centres while containing the financial, wholesale and industrial functions which define them.

5. SUB-CITIES

Not only are these the largest SECs Cervero identifies, but they are also the fewest in number, the furthest apart, and feature the widest variety of high-order functions. But, for the moment, perhaps before they become indistinguishable in the twenty-first century, one should note that at present they are seen as different from the super regional malls in that a significant proportion of their functions and employment is provided by the kind of financial and business activity which once was characteristic only of places like Wall Street and the Loop.

6. LARGE-SCALE OFFICE CORRIDORS

This type of development does not fit neatly into the classification of SECs but Cervero appends it for completeness. In this case there is neither planning, landscaping nor a particular site, but as the corridors can be as much as 20 miles long they are of considerable significance. The main road or the urban motorway provides the access to an unplanned accumulation of a large variety of commercial functions. These have been built at very low densities on cheap suburban land strung along the road, with large car-parks for the absolutely essential car transport. Again, by definition, the office corridors contain a high proportion of tertiary and quaternary FIRE and related functions as well as other things which either benefit from association, or derive trade from the business people concentrating in the area.

With the necessary proviso that one finds a variety of sizes and mixtures of functions, some key characteristics of these Suburban Employment Centres can be highlighted. This hierarchy is distinguished from others (as is the retail hierarchy) by having a single predominant type of use, in this case office buildings for business. Whereas all the shops in a retail mall are close together so that a shopper, having parked the car, can walk from one to another, the office blocks can be considerable distances apart and too much walking would be involved. At present most of the buildings are less than five storeys high, but the glass, or horizontally striped glass and concrete office buildings extend over large tracts of land. (Some of the buildings are, in fact, large enough to have been referred to as horizontal skyscrapers.)

The grounds in which these office buildings sprawl, widely separated, are landscaped with grass, bushes, trees, ponds or even lakes, and such things as jogging tracks for the staff. There is a deliberate attempt to make SECs look more like a rural campus than like a busy city centre from which their functions derive. However, some of the largest, most prestigious SECs now have skyscrapers of 20 or 30 storeys sticking up like beacons above the trees and the residential areas.

Not only are the SECs entirely dependent on the car both for the employees to get to and from work, and for anyone who needs to do business face to face, but they are also usually so dispersed on their sites that some employees drive when moving from one building to another. Much has been written about white-collar workers staying at home and working via telecommunications, but for the great majority that state of affairs is still some way off. In the SECs 93% of the workers are dependent on the car, and 1,300 square feet of car parking space is provided for every 1,000 square feet of office space. The lowest-density SECs have one-third of their land built on and two-thirds landscaped or used for car-parks — a far cry from the days when the Sky-Angle Laws were needed to admit daylight between downtown office buildings.

Some of the larger mixed-function SECs with skyscrapers do have higher densities than this, but at the moment employees still drive from one building to another. In addition to the distances involved, two reasons given for using the car rather than walking are: one, that there are no functions such as shops, cafes, newsstands, etc. on the outsides of the buildings at ground level; and, two, where there are pavements, they don't necessarily go anywhere, or rarely where pedestrians would want to go. Some of the largest developments are just beginning to think about putting in a few shops and laying out pavements which have more purpose than just to add the final touch to the architectural model. Above all the short, separate bits of pavement need to be joined up so that one does not have to walk across a car-park, say, then though some bushes, round a pond, along a jogging track, past a blank-faced building and through a trash dump to get from Marketing to Accounts.

If the super regional mall has replaced downtown for all retail functions, so that the resident of the suburbs need never go into the Central City for that purpose, then the so-called Sub-City is fast replacing what is left of the old CBD for purposes of business. That Americans are beginning to realise this is shown in the names which have been given to the largest SECs, the suburban business centres; names such as Urban Village, Satellite City, Suburban Downtown, Uptown and Megacentre. The names reflect the growth, the features, plus the fact that no one name is in general use yet.

Urban Village is downright misleading; it is the kind of name once given to places like Greenwich in Manhattan — sentimental at best, but way off the mark. Satellite City is better, in that it points up the city-type functions. But these are no longer satellites separate from the city. They are right in there, in the matrix of the continuously built-up-area. Suburban Downtown is both unwieldy and a contradiction in terms; if downtown has moved into the suburbs, they are definitely not suburbs any more. The single word Megacentre can too easily confuse these centres beyond the city boundary now under discussion, with the megastructures built in the city centres to try to prevent or reverse this very kind of dispersal. Of the names on offer, the name Uptown seemed best for a time, but that can be confused with uptown Manhattan and other parts of other cities. A real name is needed, the kind that is unambiguous, accurately descriptive, and specific. Until it is found, we will have to bear with Cervero's term Sub-City.

Cervero, in calling them Sub-Cities, puts them second down the hierarchy, with the Central City CBD still at the top. In discussing specifically the area outside the city boundary, it is more logical to place each Sub-City at the top of its own separate hierarchy in its own part of the urbanised area which surrounds the Central City. If one refers to Murphy's list of the functions which defined the downtown CBD:

I RETAIL
A Automotive
   AA - AD

V Variety Stores
   VA - VD

M Miscellaneous
   MA - MH

F Food
   FA - FG

H Household
   HA - HE

C Clothing
   CA - CF

P Parking

II Service, Financial & Office
B Financial
   BA Bank
   BB Personal loans
   BC Insurance, real estate
   BD Stock broker

T Service
   TA Personal service
   TB Clothing service
   TC Household service
   TD Business service
   TF Newspaper publishing
   OA Headquarters office
   EA General office

R Transport
   RA Railway
   RB Bus
   RC Air
   RD Trucks

it is clear that enough have now transferred for the Sub-City to be regarded as the equivalent in functions of the CBD at the top of the hierarchy in a new location in part of the urban region outside the Central City. (If not in all American cities yet, it is certainly the case in more and more as the present forces continue to operate.)

Admitting the variety from Seattle to Long Island, and emphasising that these Sub-Cities are in a condition of growth and change, consider the following snapshots of some characteristics. The new Sub-City centres are some 18 miles from the old downtown. They cover an area of the order of five square miles, and have around 5,000,000 square feet of office space each. While offices predominate, justifying claims that these are emerging as the replacements for the CBD, the Sub-Cities have the largest variety of mixed functions, giving what one observer described as 'a downtown feel'.

This has been strengthened already by the construction of a handful of 20–30 storey skyscrapers in some Sub-Cities and plenty of high-rise buildings rather closer together than in the first office parks. However, they are not as densely packed as in the old Walking City and so transport between them is essential. Unlike the old Walking City, and competing directly with results of urban revitalisation in the Central Cities, the Sub-Cities have megastructures housing super regional malls, conference centres and the like. If their purpose is not to be defeated then, of course, the new Sub-Cities have to be as accessible as possible by car. So the provision of a very large number of parking spaces in multi-storey car-parks is another characteristic which makes them even more like downtown centres.

A few of these Sub-Cities already employ around 50,000 people — more than the entire population of a British market town of some standing. Such numbers can mean over 20,000 office workers when one sees that the mean proportions of employment are:

clerical	22%
technical	20%
administrative	15%
management	14%
manufacturing	13%
sales	12%
other	4%

The appearance of manufacturing in Cervero's figures may be surprising, but the major proportion of the work is clearly white-collar. The addition of some very expensive and exclusive residential property and the newness of most of the buildings certainly help to maintain the

212

upper middle-class WASP atmosphere which characterised the areas back when they were brand-new suburbs.

So, the CBD has almost caught up with the first escapees, but not quite. The 'suburban' Sub-City is similar to the former downtown, but some differences are very important. Moreover, there are contrasts among the present Sub-Cities themselves. The comparison of a few features of two of them will point up these variations. Ten Sub-Cities already well established are:

Sub-City	State
Central Bellevue	Washington
Central Stamford	Connecticut
Central Towson	Maryland
Denver Technical Centre	Colorado
N. Dallas Parkway	Texas
Perimeter Centre	Georgia
Post Oak-Galleria	Texas
S. Coast Metro	California
Tysons Corner	Virginia
Warner Centre	California

In giving instant names to these new centres the developers very clearly have been preoccupied with emphasising centre, central, centrality, etc. until they have tied themselves into a linguistic knot and come up with the apparently ultimate absurdity: Perimeter Centre. Yet that is what they are — the types of urban area we used to identify with the centre, now out near the perimeter.

Bellevue, in the suburbs of Seattle east of Lake Washington, has been called the 'archetypal suburban city'. But it is small; the feature or features which earned it its name do not include size. Bellevue is 350 acres, has 8,000,000 square feet of office space, and some 20,000 workers. What has made it so like a downtown area is the re-designing and rebuilding since 1980 which have made it more and more of a place for pedestrians.

Bellevue is small, with a high density by SEC standards. There is a variety of functions including a super regional mall and high-rise office buildings of 25 storeys — thus combining the retail and financial functions. The re-fashioning for pedestrian use has included the provision of walk-in functions on the outsides of the massive buildings at street level, the connecting up of formerly pointless short stretches of sidewalk, the reduction of car parking spaces and the relocation of remaining car-parks underground. These are very early days yet, but this is a reversal of so many of the key features of the original suburban set-up. We will have to wait to see whether this really is the beginning of the introduction of concentrated city layout to the suburbs, as well as merely the functions. Most important in Bellevue for this kind of change has been the building of the Transit Centre, which combines a bus station with a rail station tying Bellevue into Seattle's rapid transit Metro system.

The greatest contrast with this is Post Oak, six miles west of downtown Houston. Post Oak at present is the largest Sub-City in America, and the first to be called an Uptown. But while its sheer size and range of different types of function make it a clear rival for a downtown CBD, its layout makes it a very different kind of place in which to work or to carry out any of the purposes for which others used to venture to the old downtown.

Post Oak has 25,000,000 square feet of office space and nearly 80,000 workers. The complete range of retail, business, service and entertainment functions, in type, order and number (attributes and variates) are in direct competition with downtown. Some see Post Oak as second in the hierarchy in greater Houston, but it can also be argued that it is at the top of the 22 suburban centres of various types and sizes in the sprawling built-up-area around the city. The building of the 65-storey Transco Tower and other, lesser skyscrapers shows that the business community aspires to just that. Post Oak is now more often referred to as Post Oak-Galleria since the addition of the large and high-order Galleria shopping centre in this SEC. This is an example of items in two of the separate retail and business hierarchies being built very close together; so close together, in fact, that they become thought of as a single unit and resemble even more an alternative CBD.

However, in spite of all its functions, prestige buildings and claim to pre-eminence, Post Oak-Galleria is not an old-style city centre transferred to, or rebuilt in, the suburbs. The densities are much too low for that. Post Oak, the largest Sub-City, is an area of such low building density (in contrast to the old concentrated cities such as Chicago or Philadelphia) that cars are absolutely indispensable for workers, shoppers and business people to get around. Without a car in Post Oak, one is like a pedestrian whose legs have been amputated. Many of the widely separated blocks have no sidewalks and in the cases of those which have, the short stretches of sidewalk do not connect up and don't go anywhere in particular.

There is little to see and less to do outside these new, enormous buildings. As Cervero says, the buildings are designed only for 'vehicular access'. If you are not in a car you are criminal, or crazy; there

214

is no strolling up the equivalent of Broadway and Times Square here. Fifty thousand free parking spaces were available in the early 1990s, most located so that workers had 'zero distance' to walk to work. Check, zero distance. If one arrives early, one can park next to one of the guarded doors of Galleria, which is very convenient. But one can not, having finished in Galleria, leave one's car there and just walk to the next building; it is too far away and too difficult to get to in a Sub-City designed only for the car. Post Oak may be a downtown for the twenty-first century, but it is a car-user-friendly, a vehicular-access-only, a zero-walking downtown.

Joel Garreau has also investigated in detail these suburban centres, and he has given more exhaustive consideration to the names than in Cervero's book or here. Garreau has, after the study of nine MSAs, named the Sub-City Edge City, using the name for the title of his 1991 book on the subject.

Edge City has a double meaning. Like Periphery Centre it emphasises that these new features are the equivalent of downtown in the outer suburbs. But Garreau explicitly uses edge in another sense; this type of location is now where the entrepreneurs have the edge or advantage over the stick-in-the-muds in the old centres:

'I have come to call these new urban centres Edge Cities. Cities, because they contain all the functions a city ever has, albeit in a spread-out form that few have come to recognise for what it is. Edge, because they are a vigorous world of pioneers and immigrants, rising far from the old downtowns, where little save villages or farmland lay only thirty years before.'

Garreau has studied the same phenomena as Cervero from a slightly different point of view. His Edge Cities are Cervero's Sub-Cities, multiple urban cores in the suburban sprawl, which Garreau sees as having passed through three stages of development since the Second World War:

1. the suburbanization of America — the movement of homes out of the city;
2. the Malling of America — the movement of retail in the 1960s and 1970s;
3. the Rise of Edge City — 'today we have moved our means of creating wealth, the essence of urbanism — our jobs — out to where most of us have lived and shopped for two generations.'

Garreau gives a five-part definition of Edge City, although this must change since the phenomenon is still growing and changing:

215

1. 5,000,000 square feet of office space
2. 600,000 square feet of leasable retail space
3. more jobs than bedrooms
4. perceived as a (central) place
5. in 1990 under 30 years old.

The book *Edge City* consists of an introductory essay; detailed studies of nine major urban areas: New Jersey, Atlanta, Southern California, Boston, Phoenix, San Francisco Bay Area, Detroit, Texas, Washington DC and region; extensive lists of all the Edge Cities/Sub-Cities Garreau has identified; very clear maps; a glossary of the new jargon; a chapter of definitions; and a valuable reading list. Towards the end Garreau moves beyond Cervero's brief to consider the people involved. He looks at what Edge Cities mean to the majority of American citizens who now depend on them the way Central City dwellers depended on downtown in the past. He has many ideas which could lead to much debate and plenty of argument, and all are worth consideration. For the moment, one short quotation from the beginning of his book which is appropriate towards the end of this book. Referring to the people he writes, 'the more you will find them grappling with ever more profound and wonderful questions — about identity, and community, and civilization, and soul, and all the other attributes of the good life for which we yearn. For that is the most interesting and challenging task — of really penetrating our latest attempt at Utopia.'

Now that the majority of big city residents live in what were the suburbs, now that most of the wealth-producing and population-serving functions are in the areas which used to be the suburbs, now that the former suburbs are the *de facto* important part of the total built-up-area, we may need a new name for these 'suburbs'. But before a sensible, everyday label can be applied, we need to be clear about what the original low-density, semi-rural, residential WASP areas have become. Two key characteristics of what we, for the moment, have to continue calling the suburbs, are low-density land use and multinuclear form. While a range of different kinds of people and functions are now located in these misnamed suburbs, reflecting almost the whole range of peoples and functions of the old Central Cities, the suburbs are very different from the compact, concentrated, single-centre cities. People and functions have moved and their location and distribution are now very different. It is not simply a case of relocation in the same form. The city has moved, grown, and changed almost out of recognition.

When moving outside the administrative boundary the city became lower in density and, more significantly, separated out into its different

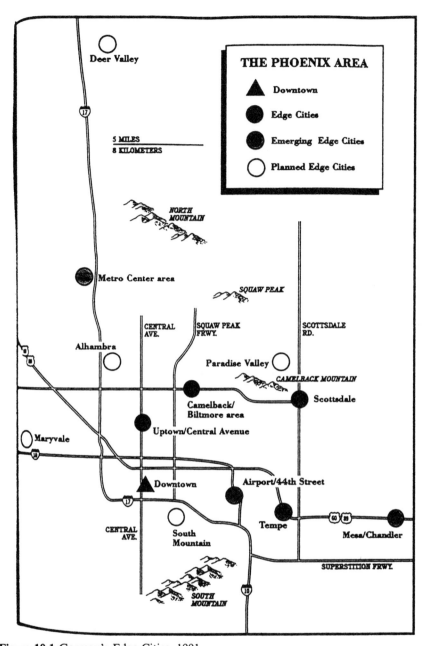

Figure 10.1 Garreau's Edge Cities, 1991
Examples of Detroit from the rustbelt and Phoenix from the sunbelt show that
Garreau identifies some half-dozen rivals in each case to the old downtown.
From *Edge City* by Joel Garreau. Copyright 1991 by Joel Garreau. Used by permission of
Doubleday, a division of Bantam Doubleday Dell Publishing Group, Inc.

217

Auburn Hills/I-75

Troy/Big Beaver Rd.

Farmington Hills/
I-696

I-696 & Telegraph Rd. area

Prudential Town
Center area

Northland Mall area

8 MILE RD.

8 MILE RD.

GRAND RIVER AVE.

GRATIOT AVE.

Ann Arbor/
Rte. 14

MICHIGAN

Lake
St. Clair

Downtown Detroit

Dearborn/Fairlane Village

Downtown Windsor

ONTARIO

Detroit
River

THE DETROIT AREA

▲ Downtown

● Edge Cities

● Emerging Edge Cities

5 MILES
8 KILOMETERS

components. There are SECs with retail, business, manufacturing and other functions, but more common at the moment are single-function office parks, industrial estates, shopping malls, leisure facilities, educational campuses and the like, each in its own planned landscape. The suburbs are multinuclear in the sense that these several separate hierarchies of functions are still usually on their own separate sites. They range in size and sophistication from small and simple to the large, complex and high-order, to the extent that within the suburban area, somewhere, the service exists. So, in function if not in convenience of finding and of access, the suburbs are not really dependent on the Central City and the CBD in many MSAs any more.

In the concentrated city most of these functions could be found mixed together, or in nuclei side by side. They were served by trams, trolleys, buses, subways or elevated railways, as well as by taxis and cars. There are some commuter rail lines in some suburbs, but even when they do exist they focus on the obsolescent CBD, not on one of the Sub-Cities. Some Sub-Cities are connected to new Metro systems, but not many. There are bus services but the low residential densities make it difficult to generate enough passengers on any but a few routes, and, by the same token, make such services inconvenient for commuters. The suburbs were either designed for, or grew up as the result of, people using cars. The residents are now dependent on cars. As the suburbs continue to grow, and as SECs proliferate, the cross-commuting produces more and more potential for gridlock.

The suburbs have their problems no less than the Central Cities, but they are of a different order and some are of different kinds. The suburbs in their entirety are not short of revenue but, as they are fragmented into townships and other administrative units, some parts of the suburbs are in financial difficulties. Moreover, exactly the same type of problem faces the authorities when it comes to matters of coordinating services and development over the whole suburban area. The problems of transport coordination, water supply, policing and so on, discussed in an earlier chapter, get more intractable as time goes on, as the suburbs become more complex and as positions harden.

Other problems stem from features characteristic of the suburbs such as the low densities, the relative newness, the unplanned nature of much development, or strict zoning in other areas. Provision of any type of infrastructure in low-density areas is, by the fact of the users being that much further apart, much more expensive than in densely built-up cities. This means that European visitors are often surprised to find that apparently wealthy suburbs have no pavements, rely on septic tanks and are supplied by power via unsightly and not very safe-looking bundles of overhead wires. If they knew how sparse the police coverage is, and how far away public fire and private ambulance services can be, they might value their own services much more.

The traffic situation epitomises the kind of problem characteristic of the suburbs. It stems from successful private enterprise, as virtually everyone over fifteen and still in control of their faculties drives his or her own pickup, four-wheel-drive or car. But this depends now on local government at some level to keep it running and to solve the problems deriving from that very success. Homes are built by private enterprise, cars are purchased privately, factories, malls, offices and the rest are paid for and developed privately. Often the power, water and security are provided by private companies. But it all has to be coordinated and the circulation kept healthy, the traffic kept moving. Attitudes of 'me first and the devil take the hindmost' are then counter-productive.

That last sentence may seem too provocative here, but the people and the residential patterns of the suburbs will be examined in the next chapter. So long after the European immigrants arrived in the Central Cities, located near the docks, entered the socio-economic system and started to go up the ladder and move out to the suburbs, the melting pot has had time to turn them into Americans. Now that the suburbs are so mature that one can at least suggest that they now constitute the city, competition has had time to work itself out. The successful suburbanites have reached what they aimed for: they have achieved the American Dream. They all want to drive their Nissans, Hondas and Toyotas to work, to the mall, to the baseball and to the burger joint. There can't be any conflict, can there?

11

SEPARATE STRANGERS

Cities attract people — let's state the obvious first. But the majority of people hate cities, at least if one believes what they say, and gives credence to much of creative and investigative literature. Thus it should be no surprise that there have been, and still are, continual stresses and tensions in the processes producing the residential structure of American cities no less than cities in other countries. In the United States the urban centres have attracted hundreds of millions of people in just two or three centuries, to produce some of the largest cities in one of the most highly urbanised countries in the world. The resulting residential patterns are both highly complex and constantly changing. Moreover, they rarely seem to be satisfactory for more than a small number of people for more than a short length of time.

In the United States those hundreds of millions have been attracted to New York, Chicago, Seattle, Los Angeles, St Louis, Atlanta and the rest, and then have soon directed their efforts to getting away from the very docks, factories, warehouses, offices, theatres, libraries and shops which proved such a powerful magnet in the first place. A few people choose city centre penthouses or lofts, and many poor Americans are unable to get out of the inner cities, but the majority, by the 1990s, have had the opportunity and the will to get out again. The paradox is that people want much that only the cities can provide, without having to live in the wretched things.

One major process, then, has been a centrifugal movement away from the old centres to what were the suburbs, then from the old suburbs to the new suburbs, then often to even newer suburbs as the non-residential functions followed behind. But another process is supposed to have been going on in the American city at the same time. America set itself up to be the land of the free and then, rather later, recognised officially what it seemed to be becoming at one stage — the melting pot in which people from many other countries and cultures could fuse together and be poured out in the American mould. One could debate endlessly just how free those migrating to American have been, with all the legal, social and moral pressures put on them; and one could similarly debate to what extent America ever has been the land of free enterprise, in the face of so many farming subsidies and government contracts for the industrial-military complex. But the point here is that for some 150 years at least, American society has seen itself as the crucible within which foreigners ultimately become Americans.

Now, as the vast majority of immigrants over that period of time have been attracted to the cities rather than to the farms, and as there has been, this century, massive rural depopulation with millions of native-born Americans also moving into the cities, then the city has been the very place where that melting or fusing has, or should have, taken place. For the moment the three processes — urbanisation, sub-urbanisation, and Americanisation — are underlined as central to the theme of this concluding chapter. By urbanisation is meant the increasing proportion of the population in cities; by suburbanisation the attempt to get away from other urban functions, and by Americanisation the becoming of a citizen in the mainstream of the host society.

Another belief about American society — widely held by many Europeans — is that it is a classless society. That results either from ignorance or from wishful thinking. American society is indeed class-less — but only if one defines class in the particular way we do here in Britain; but not if it is defined in one of several other possible ways, such as by economic status. Even in communist countries there was a minimum of three classes: the masses, the party members and the bosses. So, one begins to see the different groups of people making up the complex of American urban society: urban-born and former rural, native-born and foreign, white-collar worker, blue-collar and unemployed, ex-European, ex-Latin American and ex-Asian, white, black and yellow, Christian, Muslim, Hindu and Buddhist, communist and fascist and everything in between.

Some of the many variables in such a society are considered more important than others by geographers, sociologists and demographers, often to the exclusion of all the rest. Others are considered of vital importance by the people themselves in their daily lives. For example, some academics try to play down the factor of race, but for a Japa-nese and a Korean, little could be of greater significance. To people with brown and yellow skins watching the endless video re-runs of four white policemen savagely beating up black Rodney King minutes after he had given himself up in Los Angeles in May 1992, race seems

222

to be the only factor of any importance for survival in that particular corner of American society.

For Burgess, economic status seemed the key to the urban residential pattern, with people moving outwards to zones further from the city centre as they got richer. He and Park detailed the immigrant quarters near the centre of Chicago, with the assumption at the time that they would disappear in the melting pot soon, reappear as 'Americans', go up the American-style class ladder — that is the economic ladder — and move outwards to suburban nirvana.

For Homer Hoyt, again economic status was all-important. Not surprisingly, as he had been commissioned by the Federal Housing Agency to identify the poor areas of the city. The FHA wanted to know exactly where the middle-income middle-class lived so that it could guarantee their mortgages with safety. In the late 1930s the FHA needed to be sure where the poor lived so that it could deny mortgage guarantees to those who wanted to set up new houses but who were poor risks for repayment. Against all conventional wisdom Hoyt claimed that the different economic classes were *all* moving out from the city centre, each class along its own sector, each along its own slice of the American apple pie. Hoyt saw the rich moving out along their tree-lined sector, the middle class along their slightly less desirable sector, and the poor along the industrial canals and railway lines — all this before the Second World War. Hoyt did not say much about immigrants or any other way in which the people were differentiated.

Since the classical times of Burgess et al. with their archery target pattern, Hoyt with his dartboard pattern, and Harris and Ullman with their checkerboard — all three rather too simplistic — most modern models of urban residential patterns have derived from some more objective research by Shevky and Bell. They studied many more American cities than Burgess and Co., who looked *only* at Chicago; even more than Hoyt, who looked at a number to avoid anomalies. Shevky and Bell, in a study of most of the large American cities in the 1950s, pointed out that in the study of something as complex as US city residential patterns, dividing people by only one factor — income — is much too simplistic. They looked at three factors: income, family status and ethnic origin.

Compared to the earlier Burgess, Shevky and Bell are almost forgotten now. In fact, in many applications of their methods to the study of European cities, their names are never mentioned. Some deny that Shevky and Bell are important any more, but the names of the people who did the pioneering work will be used as a convenient label here, consistent with the use of names of the authors of the other

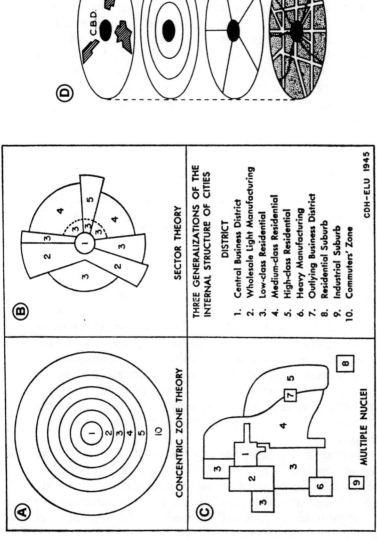

Figure 11.1 Four Models of the American City

A. The Concentric Model, Park, Burgess and McKenzie, 1924. B. The Sector Model, Homer Hoyt, 1939. C. The Multiple Nuclei Model, Harris and Ullman, 1945. D. Social Area Analysis, Shevky and Bell, 1955

Each of the models A and D sees all cities as having essentially the same pattern. Model B allows for the arrangement of sectors to vary from city to city. Model C is just one example of the innumerable possible spatial arrangements of the nuclei.

Source: Herbert, D., *Urban Geography*, David & Charles, 1972, p. 183 Mayer H.M. & Kohn, C.F., *Readings in Urban Geography*, The University of Chicago Press, Chicago and London, 1959, p. 281

classic models. In the first of the three factors — economic status — they found the same pattern as Hoyt, namely a sectoral pattern. If one considers only income, isolated from everything else which influences where people choose, and are able, to live, then the sectoral, dartboard pattern emerges.

But Shevky and Bell also divide people into five stages in the life-cycle. These are: rising young families, mature established families, aged declining households, young footloose cosmopolites, and blue-collar working-class families. Clearly their labelling is not consistent: the last item lets economic class creep back into the picture. But when people are divided into phases on the eternal stages of life — birth, raising families, old age and death — then a different spatial pattern emerges. As they progressed through the age-old process, Americans, as observed in a large sample of cities by Shevky and Bell, moved further and further from the centre, forming a zonal, archery-target type of pattern. The young footloose cosmopolite, unmarried, lives near the downtown area where most of the action was in the 1950s. When two of them marry and start to raise children they move out a short distance to somewhere quieter and safer, but not too expensive. As Dad gets promoted to executive level in the furniture factory and each teenager demands his or her own room and a car, they move further out to a bigger home. Shevky and Bell claimed that after the kids had been thrown out of the nest Mom and Dad moved back to a smaller house again near the city centre. As few middle-class Americans in their right minds would move back to the centre now, it is more probable that the old people who Shevky and Bell did undoubtedly record in the inner rings were people who had never made it out in the first place. Much more common is the case of the couple who, so relieved to get the kids off their backs at last, feel they can afford to buy their dream house out in the real, almost rural, newest suburbs.

When they examined people by ethnic origin, Shevky and Bell found that the different ethnic communities formed clusters, nuclei in the matrix of the city. But their diagram does not repeat the diagram of Harris and Ullman completely. The Harris and Ullman multiple nuclei checkerboard pattern has only nuclei and nothing else. The nuclei all touch each other like tiles made of irregular polygons which somehow all manage to fit together. But Shevky and Bell often found ethnic communities separate from each other, so the nuclei on their diagram are scattered about to reflect this real pattern. But say one was a middle-income, footloose young cosmopolite of German origin; did one live in a concentric zone, a middling sector, a German neighbourhood, or in Milwaukee? That piece will be left in a threatening position in the corner of the chessboard for the moment.

225

Two things need to be emphasised at this point in the argument. First, that all the models of urban residential areas are about process just as much as they are about pattern. Second, however much one may disagree with any one model, all of them are based on a demonstrable truth when one is trying to understand where people live and why: *that like groups with like.*

On the matter of process, the concentric Burgess model incorporates movement outwards from zone to zone. The sectoral Hoyt model also incorporates outward growth, although in this case by the addition of similar people at the outer end of the sector. The Harris and Ullman model is based on an illogical mixture of income, jobs, origin and the location of non-residential functions, but it also involves the accumulation of people into the many nuclei. The derivatives of the original Shevky-Bell model have all three patterns, concentric, sectoral and nucleated, at the same time, like a three-tiered cake, but they also describe movement outwards during the family cycle, outwards along the sectors, and in towards the nuclei.

On the second matter, rich people like to live with rich people. White people prefer to live with white people. Jewish people group together to maintain their religion. Mexican people live together and communicate in Spanish. English people stick together to play cricket, complain about the weather and to look down on the natives. One finds Mom and the 2.4 kids on the kind of estate where all the other moms have 2.4 kids and all the dads have the same kind of car. It is a complex of social characteristics the people have in common which makes them cluster together, not just income. More fully, people group together where they feel most comfortable. They try to live in a neighbourhood where the others look the same, behave in a similar way, have similar backgrounds, similar life styles and similar hopes and expectations. Living apart from people of different colours, with different languages, religions, levels of income and life styles helps greatly to minimise day-to-day tensions. Admittedly, in America and in other countries the black people who live with other black people, and the poor who live with the poor may have very little choice in the matter, but the different forces operating in these cases still result in like being grouped with like.

People move about — like groups with like — and some kind of pattern results. But not the simplistic pattern seen by Burgess or by Hoyt. This is true of many other cities in many other parts of the world. But America has an extra ingredient deriving from the fact that it encourages immigration from every part of the world and that it has some idea of being a melting pot in which all those people will eventually become Americans. Throughout the world the evidence is

226

that different groups keep themselves apart, but in the American city they were expected to mix. So there are four themes for the understanding of present residential patterns in the total built-up-area of the big American city:

- movement of people
- grouping of like with like
- Americanisation
- the merging of cities into MSAs.

In the previous chapter some of the major contemporary problems of the suburbs were mentioned briefly. One of these — increasing racial strife — was not stressed, partly because it is only incipient in the suburbs at the moment, but more importantly because it is germane to the examination of urban society in this chapter. Given that newspapers and television may well be exaggerating some events, their sheer number leaves little doubt that friction, tension, open hostility and occasional violence are increasing between the many ethnic and racial groups in American cities. The word racial is used as a shorthand here for the differences of nationality, ethnic background and religion, as well as of race, which residential groups in American cities perceive among themselves. This perception, in addition to the resulting violence, appears to be working in the same direction as other forces in the residential areas to increase the separation between groups, in direct opposition to the traditional melting pot ideal.

The situation should not be over-dramatised, but it does exist. A tiny sample of cases from the turn of the decade will serve to illustrate the point.

OCTOBER 1989

In Bensonhurst, Brooklyn, a gang of young Italians gunned down a young black man who had come into Little Italy to buy a second-hand car. This was 1989, remember, not Chicago in 1929. In the same month David Dinkins, black candidate for Mayor of New York, and Jesse Jackson, one-time presidential candidate, referred to New York with its large Jewish population as 'Hymietown'. As the *Guardian* said at the time:
'During the election campaign, the great legend of New York as an ethnic melting pot has become a sad farce, and the pot's contents have congealed into its tribal and mutually suspicious parts.'

MAY 1990

Again in Brooklyn, black people boycotted Korean shops for four months. A Korean shopkeeper, seen as white by the blacks, prosecuted a black woman for shoplifting. The black community turned this into a mass, long-term racial confrontation. A Vietnamese was almost beaten to death when the black protesters mistook him for a Korean. The *Guardian* reported:
'In the tightly packed (inner) suburbs of east New York where Asians, Africans, Jews and Italians live close together, where a dwindling economy has left many blacks out of work and crack is rife, race relations have become an acute problem. It is here that the "gorgeous mosaic" of New York's ethnic groups, which the city's new black mayor, David Dinkins, likes to refer to, is falling apart.'

OCTOBER 1990

David Dinkins announced the biggest-ever expansion of New York's police force. With the city in debt, there must have been compelling reasons for that move. *Time* magazine polled New Yorkers: 60% said they would leave the city if they could. By the turn of the last decade of the twentieth century New York was described as 'marked out in primitive territorial squares', meaning racial territories, no-go neighbourhoods for people of other colours, religions, national origins or languages. The *Guardian* again in a detailed, very useful article, Cracks in the Melting Pot said:
'Recently, several ethnic groups, from well-ensconced WASPs and Jews to come-lately Koreans, have fastened on a single crime against their ethnic group as evidence that they are all under threat. These murders, rapes and robberies turn into media campaigns and become indications of the level of racial tension in the city.'

APRIL–MAY 1992

Los Angeles experienced severe racial riots — said to be worse than those of the 1960s — when four white policemen were acquitted by a white jury of the charge of battering a black man, Rodney King. Black people had every reason to be angry. An amateur video, broadcast many times in Europe as well as all over America, showed 56 baton blows to King's body after he had given himself up and been pushed to the ground. My file of newspaper and magazine articles on the incident runs into August editions, showing how much outrage at the crime and alarm at the evidence of racial vindictiveness was generated. In April 1993, two of the officers were convicted after a re-trial and the danger of more riots was averted.

JULY 1991

A black youth escaped from apartment 213, Oxford Apartments, 924 North Twenty-Fifth Street, Milwaukee, and the police were called for the second time. On this occasion they arrested Jeffrey Dahmer, a German-American. Subsequently he was tried and convicted for killing 17 young men, mainly black, Laotian, or Korean, in that very apartment.

This was horror enough. But the racial element, which caused consternation and much soul-searching in liberal Wisconsin, was the incident the first time the police were called to North Twenty-Fifth Street. It was learned that on that first occasion Konerak Sinthasomphone had managed to escape Dahmer, but had been taken back into the murder apartment by three white Milwaukee policemen. There he was slaughtered and disembowelled in May.

Konerak, a 14-year-old Laotian boy, escaped to get help. The police talked to Jeffrey Dahmer in the street and let him take Konerak, whom he said was his gay lover, back inside. Barbara Reynolds wrote in *USA Today*, in August:

'In response to a neighbour's complaint, police find a blond, blue-eyed boy, on a quiet suburban street, naked, crying, disorientated and bleeding from the rectum. They listen sympathetically to a black man who explains not to worry, it's only a homosexual spat; they hand over the bruised merchandise and leave.

'Not on your life would this ever happen. Not in the movies. Not in your wildest nightmares.'

Barbara Reynolds was right. But it was a black-haired, brown-skinned, brown-eyed kid, and it was a white man who soft-talked the white police into letting him take Konerak back inside, where he was killed as soon as the door closed.

In Don Davis's excellent, objective, unsensational analysis of these seventeen serial killings, *The Milwaukee Murders*, he quotes Dr Ashok Bedi, an Asian psychiatrist working in Wisconsin:

'I should say, as an Asian-American myself, that Milwaukee is not so much racially prejudiced as psychologically unprepared to integrate. There is not prejudice, but [there is] fear of what this integration is going to do.'

For people who would never pick up a book on real-life murder, let alone one on serial racial killings, the whole book, and Chapters 16–

18 and 21 in particular, are recommended as extremely useful for the insight they can offer into contemporary urban America.

Racial conflict has been an element in American urban life since the middle of the nineteenth century, when Irish immigrants started to flood in and, a few decades later, black people began to move out of the South. But the antagonism towards European immigrants eventually died down and in the 1970s and 1980s a question was, why were black people no longer rioting as they had done in the sixties? Everything seemed to be quietening down.

Those types of conflict were largely two-way, WASPs against foreign-born, or whites against blacks. But the conflicts which are now on the increase in the Central Cities and which threaten to spread to some suburbs involve three or more groups, and in any one particular case WASPs are not necessarily one of the groups. For a long time the received wisdom has been that racism is a uniquely white sin. When Asians fight Hispanics, and black people attack Vietnamese because they look like Laotians, then a very complicated and dangerous situation of racial conflict is developing, and we see that blacks, Asians and Spanish-Americans can be as guilty of prejudice, intolerance and mistrust as anyone else.

One now sees Jews and other people of European origin drawn into the conflicts. As explained in an earlier chapter, while some European groups tried to keep their identity, most slowly Americanised. But now the trend may be reversing and people born in America who twenty years ago were Americans now call themselves Irish-American, Italian-American, Polish-American: the hyphenated American has been resurrected in opposition to the newcomers. In his seminal article on black people, Kurt Vonnegut announced, with resignation, that he is a German-American, clearly deploring the trend he can do little to prevent.

I believe xenophobia to be one of the basic elements of human nature, but its effects can be minimised for centuries, given favourable conditions. It seems that the conditions in American inner cities and in some suburbs are such that racial attitudes are being stirred up vigorously now. Sometimes the trigger seems trivial to someone not involved, not irritated to the point of lashing out, as with the small events which triggered the race riots of the 1960s. But that, in fact, is a measure of how tense the situation has become in some areas.

Illegal immigrants from Mexico and, by association, most Hispanics, are seen by other groups — black and white — as responsible for much of the drug traffic. The Cubans are resented for having taken over Miami, much as the Irish were resented for taking over Boston and Chicago in the past. The Spanish language is now essential for business in Miami, and is becoming so in New York and Los Angeles. Old people who came from Greece, Poland and other countries with languages very different from English, and who had to learn English to survive, often bitterly resent this 'babying' of Hispanics. Two languages, or ethnic division — or both — could split urban society along new lines of weakness.

There is conflict over behaviour and morals, conflict over language, conflict over religion, but most of all there is resentment aggravated by the perceptions of economic position, of wealth and relative success. As immigrants Americanised in the past, they had to embrace, and most came to believe in, such things as the Constitution, the school system, cut-throat competition for jobs, the English language, the political machine and the then apparently fair, and apparently immutable arrangement whereby the last to arrive not only stepped on to the land of the finest nation on the face of the earth, but also on to the bottom rung of its social ladder. Germans, Irish, Italians, Poles and Russians all did that; they played the game. But then the black people put a foot on the bottom rung, and the rules changed. Very few black people were allowed their turn to climb. Then Latin American Spanish-speaking people started to arrive in significant numbers and quickly many of them had climbed up the socio-economic ladder to be ahead of many of the blacks. When, during the last two decades, Asians arrived in America in large numbers and often started in American society apparently half-way up the socio-economic scale, most blacks and many others believed that one of the time-honoured American systems had collapsed, that the Dream was over and that it is now every man, woman and gang-member drug-dealing child for himself.

There is much argument at the moment about whether Hispanics or Asians have leap-frogged over the black people furthest in the socio-economic system. Anecdotal methods can point to destitute Asians just as easily as to a few black millionaires. The question is about the majority here. One important point is that the conflict has grown to vast proportions. The struggle between Poles, Estonians and Letts for jobs in the slaughter-houses of Chicago involved a few hundreds of people. The struggle between blacks, Asians and Hispanics in most American cities is a conflict of a completely different and very serious order now.

Another major factor is at work in both vastly increasing the numbers involved and in increasing racial conflict, rather than tending to reduce it as time goes on. This is that, while the struggle between the Irish, the Italian and the Pole took place in the old concentrated city – which was expanding, had plenty of work, and often was short of manual labour — the present racial conflict, becoming a fight for survival between black, white, yellow and brown, is taking place in the bankrupt inner cities where the jobs have gone and everything is in decline. Europeans settled into the inner city at a time of prosperity and growth, while many of the new immigrants are having to adjust in an environment of recession and neglect.

As indicated in the extracts from the press above, even a minor crime, when perpetrator and victim are from different nations, or speak different languages, worship different gods, or are slightly different shades of brown, is viewed as a racial attack on the whole of the victim's group, and as such requires group revenge. Reports from journalists that all the minorities in the city seem to be inciting violence against all the others are becoming commonplace and repetitive. More original, at the moment, are reports of conflict within the major groups too: Puerto Ricans in conflict with Cubans in conflict with other Hispanics from mainland South America; black gang against black gang. Perhaps this is more surprising than reports of Iranians in conflict with Koreans in conflict with Thais. WASPs see them all as Asians but they are perhaps further apart culturally than were Irish Catholics and Russian Jews.

Increasingly one reads in the press of conflict, of separation, of groups establishing turfs and defending neighbourhoods. In this context the words mosaic and tiles are being used more and more frequently, not only by journalists, but by geographers and sociologists trying to describe and explain the social and residential patterns now emerging in the total built-up-area of the MSA. The journalists write in magazines and speak on television of the residential areas as a mosaic of many different colours, shapes and sizes of tiles. This is not just careless purple prose, but a genuine and sensible attempt to give an accurate account of the true state of affairs. The concept of a variety of different sizes and colours of tiles, loosely fitting into a rough mosaic, does this very well. Each tile of a particular shape, size or colour represents a residential area where like groups with like, middle income with middle income, Buddhist with Buddhist, Korean with Korean, young Peruvian couple with young Peruvian couple. But as each tile becomes more homogeneous and more distinct, by that very fact it becomes different from, and potentially antagonistic to, the tile in the next block over. Two phrases from Americans already quoted above are relevant here:

'tribal and mutually suspicious parts';
'psychologically unprepared to integrate'.

There was a period up to the end of the 1950s when, the longer immigrants had lived in the American city, the more they integrated with those already there. The mechanism of the melting pot seemed to be working and Americanisation seemed to be progressing. But that period deserves closer analysis; perhaps it was an aberration. Perhaps there were special conditions which no longer obtain. Perhaps the idea of the melting pot meant different things to different people. The immigration up to the fifties was predominantly of people from Europe covering just over a century in the history of the whole world. Given the social variations over Europe, those people were white, and the majority were young, intelligent and either middle class or aspiring strongly toward it. There was a bewildering array of languages, but most were rooted in Latin and Greek. There were strong religious differences, but the religions were all part of the Judaeo-Christian tradition. In short, white, able, ambitious, mainly Christian Europeans were crossing the Atlantic to join people of the same origin and similar social, religious, economic and cultural backgrounds. The differences which caused friction for a time may now be seen as superficial in comparison with all that they had in common but which was very much taken for granted, and in comparison with the differences between all the present various groups of Latin Americans and Asians.

The European immigrants were expected to Americanise. Primary education in America was organised to that end. The newcomers were expected to learn English, embrace the Constitution, dress like Americans, speak like Americans, live like Americans, later, drive cars, watch TV and raise their children, not like Americans but *as* Americans. Mass-produced goods, mass-produced houses, the mass media of the cinema, radio and then television all helped towards the same end. National and religious differences declined in importance as the old languages fell out of use and as most people of European origin went up the same socio-economic ladder and moved to the suburbs.

This process is often referred to as the melting pot which, if it existed, was located and operated in the inner residential areas of the American city. Consider the analogy: one has copper melting in a pot in a bright, hot furnace. One adds zinc and it melts into the copper. One adds tin, and it too melts to join the alloy. One adds lead, iron, gold, silver, platinum, aluminium, nickel and tungsten. All these metals melt down and merge. But in that melting pot do they all melt down and become exactly like the native, original, resident copper? Or, if one started with gold as the original item in the pot, do all the other metals become gold as they melt down and merge in the pot? If they do, the alchemists of old went badly wrong somewhere.

No; each new ingredient, as it melts down and merges, changes the original single metal into something new. Copper and zinc become brass, copper and tin become bronze, tin and lead become pewter. The melting pot, when ingredients are added, does not produce more of the same stuff already there. It produces a completely new metal, a new alloy. The new additions change the original, just as the original changes them — providing that the new additions are the kinds of things which will combine in the first place. So, the analogy holds even when one extends it to represent the new immigration of greatly contrasting elements. There comes a stage when so many different metals and other chemicals have been thrown into the pot that they just will not combine, the process will not work any more, and a satisfactory alloy will not emerge.

But for a time it seemed that the masses of Europeans going to America before the very strict quotas were applied in the 1920s were, over two or three generations, becoming the kind of Americans already there in the beginning. But the fact is that they could not become WASPs, most were not Anglo-Saxon and many were Catholics. However, for a time the differences and the changes were not too great. The society which resulted consisted of white, European Judaeo-Christians with the legacy of legal, political and economic systems in common, many of them originally British, all of them European. The native Americans had been changed during the process of immigration, just as the copper is changed in the analogy, but the relatively few additions to that melting pot had demanded, *in world-wide terms*, relatively easy changes for both immigrants and Americans.

Let us return to the example in which some ingredients will not combine. It may be that for a short time the melting pot process worked under very restricted and special conditions where Europeans were combining with Europeans. But it may not be the case that the melting pot system will work when every possible kind of people from every country on earth is casually expected to combine with no more trouble than those Europeans experienced, in particular when no official provision is made to facilitate that process once the newcomers have been admitted. Then, in addition to combining, there is the matter of Americanisation. It has been suggested that what was regarded as American was changed as much as what was regarded as immigrant. WASPs of 1960 were very different from those of 1830, just as brass and bronze are very different on close inspection. From 1965 onward it may turn out to be the case that Americans have entered a longer or shorter period of change when what is now regarded as American could be changed out of all recognition by the influx and combination of so many different peoples from every part of, and from every other culture in, the world.

234

In this light it may be impossible to over-state the fundamental long-term importance of the 1965 Immigration Act for American society in general and the American city and suburbs in particular. There are restrictions on the numbers which can enter America in any one year, but there are very few restrictions on where the people come from, and there are none on colour, language, or religion. Even if the melting pot process did work, then many elements never witnessed before have been coming into that pot for thirty years. The kind of alloy, the kind of society, which can result from such a wide range of contrasting ingredients, is problematic. How it will change America, Americans, the city and the suburbs is anybody's guess.

Since 1965 native-born Americans have written less and less about the melting pot but more and more about a relatively new idea: the Salad Bowl. The key analogy has changed from that of metals in a white-hot crucible to one of vegetables and fruits in a cool bowl. The new analogy has been used to illustrate the growing belief that the many different immigrant groups, plus the varied groups already established in the city and suburbs, are no longer melting, merging and combining, but remaining clearly separate. If pieces of lettuce, tomato and cucumber represent WASPs, black people and those of recent European origin in the city before 1965, then pieces of green pepper, chinese leaves, kiwi fruit, apple, carrot, cabbage, guava, papaw, yam, banana and celery, items like grapes, olives and brazil nuts represent people of every colour, every nation, every continent, every social background, every religion, every language and from every type of political and legal system (or lack of system) moving into American society and into the city.

Neither integration nor Americanisation is taking place at the speed once expected and the residential areas stay as a bowl of multicoloured salad or a floor of different coloured tiles. But perhaps a different time scale from that used for the old immigrants *is* needed. Give the new immigrants enough time, over several generations, and a new kind of integration and the future type of American will evolve. People do interact and influence one another, even if not in the way foreseen and intended. The danger is that they may only react against one another, as different peoples who once lived together apparently peacefully for a long time have done recently in Yugoslavia. People do not live side by side like inert tiles, but neither do they necessarily get on with each other, and the process could be one of conflict and balkanisation just as easily as integration.

Inevitably questions remain at this stage in time. How quick or slow are the social interactions now? Which is the dominant group or

235

groups? Who is changing most, newcomer or host? What are the implications for the Central City and the suburbs? What does this mean for the residential patterns? The three-ring circus will be putting on a fascinating show in the next few generations.

With the vastly increased numbers of immigrants to the USA each year since 1965, and the arrival of people from every continent, country and culture, the balance of society in the American city is changing rapidly and may well change beyond the recognition of people who knew the city in the 1950s. While one can predict the inevitability of rapid change with confidence, the particular type of society which will result, and the type of cities in which the new Americans will live, is very much a matter of conjecture. If present trends continue, the racial balance in the city will change, with both blacks and whites becoming minorities. Racial conflict is likely to increase for two reasons. One, people from South America, Africa and the many parts of Asia have shown themselves to be no less prejudiced and ready to argue than Europeans. Two, as newcomers, with no history in North America, they do not have that feeling of guilt towards the black people which WASPs have. Nor, for that matter, have they any sense of obligation towards the whites or any of the native-born.

The change in the socio-economic balance could be much more complex. There are many people moving to America primarily to escape conditions of one kind or another, but the vast majority are moving to gain economic opportunity. At first this means an over-supply of people willing to start in any kind of work. But these ambitious people intend to go up the ladder to the top and out through the built-up-area to the best suburbs. Rockefellers, Kennedys and Carnegies will be replaced by Jamarillos, Koyus, Lees, Sinthasomphones, Patels and so on. Many immigrants now come from economies as different from the American version as it is possible to find. But they soon learn the American way, as black people overtaken on the ladder by Colombians and Koreans are finding out to their cost.

But many immigrants also come from countries and cultures with political and legal systems fundamentally different from those of America; where democracy is not understood and trial by jury is unknown. These people will be making their contributions to American society and expressing their opinions in the twenty-first century, and they have brought their own cultural baggage with them, very different from European backgrounds. Too often people support the idea of democracy if they win the election, and seek to subvert it if they do not. Probably those who approved of the inscription on the Statue of Liberty did not foresee Sicilian ways prevailing in Chicago

236

and later in other parts of the country, and one wonders whether those who framed the 1965 Act foresaw the possibility of Islamic law replacing Roman in the New World one day.

Less fancifully, one may pertinently ask which language will prevail in the American city two hundred years from now? Who would have predicted the spread of Spanish with any confidence half a century ago? English might just survive, but it will not be the English of Thomas Jefferson, Ben Franklin and Tom Paine. Similarly, a few decades ago, Americans debated whether a Catholic could ever be elected to the presidency. A few years ago they wondered whether Michael Dukakis, a Greek, could make it. It may not be long before a second-generation born-in-America Catholic Mexican-American is running for president, with massive support in the Spanish-speaking urban areas. Is it then really so absurd to foresee a Muslim Asian-American running towards the end of the next century? Some observers, perhaps prematurely, feel the balance in American society — more precisely the balance in American suburban society — is changing from white, European Protestant, to latino-Hispanic-Catholic; and it is not impossible, providing that present trends do continue, for that balance eventually to move to brown, Asian Islamic, Buddhist or Hindu. The Constitution forbids an established religion in the United States of America, but there is a predominantly Christian ethic at the moment, and the Great Seal of the United States announces 'In God We Trust'. Could that god's name be Allah one day?

'The country is full, we don't need immigrants.'
'How many can America take?'
'Are immigrants successful at the expense of the poor and the blacks?'
'Do the advantages [of immigration] outweigh the disadvantages of racial conflict?'

These are the kinds of phrases heard more and more as time goes on. Translated, these four become:

'Close the gate, I'm in.'
'America is full.'
'Immigrants cause racial trouble.'
'There are no advantages to immigration any more.'

A straw poll in 1985 suggested that over 70% of Americans were against further immigration; in July 1993 a Gallup poll found 65%. Things had changed so much that those people had had enough. There was open resentment of Asian success, and a more secret fear of Hispanic illegal immigration. Much more common, at the level of the vast silent majority, much harder to quantify but which, if sustained, is of much more fundamental significance, is the tendency for white Americans to become defensive, separatist and exclusive. Perhaps this does not amount to being hostile, but they are not really welcoming any more. David Rieff tellingly describes how even as a journalist he had difficulty meeting people during a long stay in Los Angeles. He describes his peers, white, middle-class people, as always in defended space — not always hiding, as that might sound, but always in protected space of one kind or another. This took different forms, the private defended space of home, school, work, or car — and they all seemed to spend a depressing amount of time in the car — or in defended commercial space: the shopping mall, the office complex or the sports/entertainment facility. Malls have become the equivalent of medieval walled towns, and the middle-class homes protected by private security firms have become the moated, defended manor houses. Rieff augments the analogy of the Old West recognised by Kurt Vonnegut. Kurt likened the black people to Indians isolated on the reservation; David likens the residents of the white suburbs to the old settlers, and he tells us that each different group is now circling the wagons to take up defensive neighbourhoods, turfs, tiles, with the people inside each defensive circle warily eyeing all the others.

Rieff's analogy is telling in two respects. It indicates the separating-out of the different groups in the suburbs, like grouping with like, but it indicates an important new feature too. Not very long ago, American residents in the suburbs, faced with the perceived encroachment of other social groups thought not to be compatible, would simply have moved on, further out. According to Burgess, they would have gone to another concentric zone even further from the centre. According to Hoyt, they would have extended their sector even further into exurbia. But now, apparently, they huddle together, circle the wagons and stay put; there seems to be nowhere else to go. An important factor in this perception is the fact that nowadays new immigrant groups can, and do, take up their very first locations in America, and in the city, not just in the inner rings, but more or less anywhere in the total built-up-area. The suburbs may well continue to grow, but in the future by a new process. Instead of rich, middle-income and then poor following each other in order further and further outwards, in future the location of all types of groups, classified in a variety of different ways, may locate seemingly at random as far as the spatial pattern of the built-up-area is concerned, with some immigrant groups locating beyond long-established wealthy communities.

A description of the extreme of this trend has been given by Michael Lind in his book *The Next American Nation*. In writing of the increasing gap between the richest twenty per cent of society and the rest of the people, the 'Brazilianisation', Lind describes the overclass which he claims is becoming an hereditary elite. This is the professional and managerial class commanding huge salaries and fees as a result of brain power and exclusive education. Moreover, the wealth and education are not merely the means by which power is exerted, they are also the means by which others are excluded and the class of the cognitive elite is perpetuated. Huge sums of money are required to put their children through four years of Ivy League college, where some fifth of the places may be reserved for the children of alumni, then three years of expensive professional training. Lind describes such people as living discreetly in the outer suburbs, in fortified neighbourhoods he calls 'desiccated ghettos'. Such places, of course, are the opposite of black ghettos, where the people are kept in; these are ghettos where other people are kept out. Lind claims, however, that the potential leaders of the black and Hispanic communities have been co-opted to reduce the danger of a populist rebellion. According to him this elite favours low taxes, free trade to keep prices and workers' incomes low, and unrestricted immigration to maintain the flow of cheap labour for this New Feudalism.

Increasingly, then, one is seeing a residential pattern of nucleations. Nucleations or neighbourhoods in residential areas are by no means new, but now we are witnessing these becoming the predominant arrangement of residential areas in the suburbs, with marked contrasts and separation between them. Harris and Ullman recognised residential nuclei fifty years ago. Less often stated in so many words is the fact that many of the concentric zones recognised by Burgess and Park were subdivided into the immigrant nuclei and parts of the black belts. Study of Homer Hoyt's diagram will show that he also divided his sectors into shield-shaped nuclei. This is not a claim that these models were other than as presented; it is a reminder that the nuclei were incipient at the times the models were made. When one then adds and considers the full Shevky-Bell-type model, with all three layers of zones, sectors and nuclei superimposed, then the residential pattern is a set of nucleated areas.

If the nuclei were incipient then, we have seen the multiple-nuclei become the norm in the American suburbs since the 1960s. The present reality is much more complex than those early models envisaged, and the nuclei are differentiated by dozens more factors than the economic and ethnic criteria alone used by those investigators. If one remembers that the Harris and Ullman model allows for a differ-

239

ent pattern of different sized and shaped nuclei in every city, then their diagrams (plural because a different pattern of nuclei can develop in each city), give the pattern, while the several layers of factors in the Shevky-Bell derivatives begin to approach the complexity.

Immigrants still tend to keep together, but rather than a score of European countries of origin we now see people of almost every country in the world taking up residence in the American city. The very rich and the very poor form the two extremes of separation, but the gigantic suburbs now contain an immeasurably wide range of neighbourhoods based on the finest gradations of scores of factors. One can collapse these for the purposes of study, but that does not mean that the real people in the real houses suddenly cease to notice things which, until the computer started its number-crunching, they considered of vital importance in shaping their lives in the city.

So the people in a residential area identify themselves as a group, and see themselves as different from others, by means of a particular permutation of income, social class, colour, religious sect, age, family status, language, country of origin, history, national or regional culture, moral and legal codes, political beliefs and attitudes towards America in general and the city and the suburb in particular. Some observers, commenting on the trend, have labelled these tiles in the mosaic of the suburbs 'National Neighbourhoods'. When one remembers that there are some forty nations in the lands loosely referred to as Asia, one begins to see the complexity of the situation. When one further remembers that one 'nation' can have Sri Lankans and Tamil Tigers at one another's throats, Christian against Muslim, Chinese against Tibetans, Sikhs against Hindus and so on, the potential for mutual misunderstanding, mistrust and continued separation is infinite. As the British have found in cities such as Bradford and Bedford, immigrants do not leave these divisive feelings behind when they migrate. Studs Terkel has produced a number of books about American society, including *Division Street: America* (1967) and *American Dreams Lost and Found* (1980). His collection of interviews with ordinary Americans on the subject of work was published in 1974. In 1992 he published *Race*, another collection of interviews with, and views of, ordinary people on what he and they saw to be one of the main concerns in the early 1990s in America.

Without in any way being alarmist, David Rieff reports the kinds of situations which have resulted in Los Angeles.

'The LA public school system has its institutional hands full trying to educate the new immigrant population whose children make up the majority of people under eighteen in the county. In a district where instruction has to be offered in eighty-two languages from Spanish to

Hmong, the problems of (white) middle-class kids are bound to seem secondary.'

Not only are newspapers published in many of these languages, but newspapers in the major languages, English and Spanish, now each have many sub-editions, each targeted at a particular group of people in a particular neighbourhood. With broadcasts in several languages, imported films from India and Latin America and the like, the press, radio, TV and the successor to Hollywood are no longer the all-American unifying factors they were half a century ago.

But the separation is beginning to go further than this. Differentiation is one thing, isolation and defence are something else. Continuing the paragraph quoted above:

'racism plays a part, of course... In 1989 a Long Beach high school had to erect a wall around its playground to protect its students from gang-related drive-by shootings; the case was hardly untypical' and; 'neighbourhoods like Brentwood were a sea of barred windows and octagonal signs planted in shrubbery or rose gardens that read "Westec Security: Armed Response".'

That suggests a possibility of what the salad bowl might turn into. '...the melting pot conception of assimilation no longer worked in an era when the new arrivals were bringing with them "profoundly dissimilar languages, religions, folkways and arts, and a deeply ingrained pride in maintaining their cultural identity". What was missing, of course, was an acknowledgment (in LA's plans for the future) that these profound dissimilarities might pose any impediment at all to harmonious relations between all these disparate groups.' We shall have to wait and see.

Several concepts, each of which has some bearing on the others, can become confused and perhaps misunderstood in situations like these — concepts such as One Nation, and/or One Society; the difference between immigrants becoming Americans, and Americans and immigrants merging to become a group with a third, new identity; the ideas of one nation or separate societies within one country, or multicultural and pluralist societies.

It seems that the old idea of Americanisation may have gone. Probably it could never have worked in any complete and extreme form of a one-way process. The evidence is that European immigrants changed those already in America as much as they were changed by the Americans. But the idea of one nation, one society, is still there. Moreover, the idea of one group of people, with one language, one culture, one set of ideals across the continent is still strong, and an idea which from this side of the Atlantic seems to be well worth pursuing. As Czechoslovakia, Yugoslavia, Russia, India and other

241

nations break apart, it is evident that the idea that any randomly assembled group of people will unite to form a nation is by no means a given. When one sees what is being lost in those countries, then the preservation of a flourishing nation seems to be worth a great deal of effort and self-sacrifice on the part of all the citizens, new and old alike. Everyone needs to be made to feel that he or she has a stake, belongs, and is valued. Neglecting a major group of people or, in effect, consigning another to a *de facto* reservation, negates any hope of a melting pot or of Americanisation.

The ideas of pluralism and of multicultural societies are familiar enough these days, and to many people they are acceptable, even desirable, But can anyone point to any genuine pluralist, multicultural state which has existed and flourished for any credible length of time under any type of rule but that of a virtual dictator, and say, *that* is the ideal? Tolerating other cultures seems to be so reasonable, so intelligent, so liberal, so very much what responsible people ought to be doing in the third millennium. But what happens when a nation becomes a genuine multicultural, many-cultured, piece of the earth's surface, with no single culture dominant? It may hang together, but where will it being going? Will it need a Tito to lead it and collapse when he dies?

One may not admire the urban culture of America in the late nineteenth and early twentieth centuries, but the City of the Big Shoulders, hog butcher for the world, tool-maker, stacker of wheat, player with railroads, bareheaded, shovelling, wrecking, planning, building, breaking, rebuilding, knew where it was going, and all-comers had to join in.

There is the evidence that many disparate groups of people merged together in the American city in the past. Thus the odds are that in time the present residents of the salad bowl will also merge and form a single society rather than a pluralist one. The only certain thing is that whatever American society emerges from such a process, it will be very different from the one that exists now. Just as American cities have grown and changed so much more rapidly than their European counterparts, American society is also changing at a much quicker rate.

In the early 1980s P.O. Muller attempted a description of the mosaic of the suburbs. He identified three types of other nuclei inside a matrix of middle-class suburbs which themselves were already beginning to subdivide into tiles of finer grades of differentiation. Within this main mosaic of middle-class subdivisions Muller identified first the exclusive, affluent areas, containing the kind of people who had originally moved out of the city first. These now account for

242

many more people in many types of locations, not only in large detached houses but in exclusive apartment blocks and expensive condominiums. Such rich neighbourhoods, of course, occupy the most attractive and desirable sites in almost any part of the built-up-area.

Second were the lower-income blue-collar areas, appearing in the suburbs as successful manual workers followed both the jobs and the middle class beyond the city limits. Muller identified many of these blue-collar areas as still recognisably of ethnic origin, mainly European. Whereas the rich people in the affluent areas reinforced their nucleations through the ties of the church, country club and private schools, the poorer areas relied much more on the extended family, followed by their churches and what Muller called taverns for cohesion. Thirdly, he identified cosmopolitan groups, suggesting that these are less localised than the others. The identification of professional people, intellectuals, students, artists and writers as a group, or groups, in the suburbs dots the i's and crosses the t's of the suburbanisation of all the key characteristics of big-city life. Muller found such people not in Manhattan, Greenwich or Georgetown, the equivalents of the old Montmartre, Bloomsbury and the rest, but out in the suburbs, united by their community of interests in the new theatres, concert-halls, galleries, restaurants, university campuses and so on which are now themselves scattered all over the built-up-area.

Muller, too, showed like grouping with like to maintain similar interests and lifestyles, but he also showed that particular location in any one part of the suburbs is no longer an identifying characteristic. In the concentrated city the new immigrants, for example, tended always to locate near the centre, for identifiable reasons. Now, in the suburbs, a particular socio-economic group still forms a nucleus or nuclei in each city, but may well locate in different relative positions in different particular cities. The grouping persists but the choice of locations in much larger areas with weaker and more varied structures is obviously more difficult to explain.

David Clark, in his book *Post-Industrial America*, shows the widening gaps between the different elements of suburban society, and he refers to the greater diversity of the features which distinguish one nucleus from another. The trend, clearly, is not at the moment to a single cohesive American population forged in the heat and the pressure of the concentrated inner-city melting pot, but towards a pluralistic society adding more and more different ingredients to the salad bowl, and spreading and separating them out in the increasing isolation of the low-density suburbs.

Muller, Clark and others agree on two characteristics of the suburbs now, although they differ on the details. First, that the residential groups, differentiated by an increasing array of variables, are as separate now as ever they were. Second, that while the pattern of distribution varies from city to city, and the trend has gone further in some cities than in others, that pattern is predominantly one of multiple nuclei. This is definitely not an attempt to go back to the days and ideas of Harris and Ullman, but a case of using that apposite, well-known and well-understood descriptive label for a modern pattern of many more nuclei. These nuclei of residential neighbourhoods now vary not only in size, but in shape, composition and, in different cities, in relative location. In the residential areas the idea of a concentric pattern is now a thing of the past. There is a crude division between the predominance of poor people and black people in the Central City, and of the well-off and of white people in the suburbs, but the differentiation beyond that simple dichotomy is now becoming of greater significance.

This development of the multiple nuclei pattern of residential areas is underlined when one remembers that it is increasingly difficult not just to study a single city, but actually to find one large American city all by itself separate from any others. In fact, if one could specify such a city now, any study would be marginal and atypical: MSAs, PMSAs and CMSAs are today's norms. Burgess's and Hoyt's models had some reality when Chicago and Boston could be considered each as a separate city focused on one centre. Now that over 150 of the largest cities in the USA are parts of the agglomerated Metropolitan Statistical Areas, one has to face the fact that most of the large cities have grown until they have each merged with at least one other large city, with several towns, and with scores of original separate small central places. As a result the total built-up-area of any one MSA now has perhaps a dozen major focal points made up of these former free-standing cities and towns. Thus the residential pattern of any one continuously built-up-area can not form concentric zones or radiating sectors centred on one single point. The patterns round each of the dozens or even scores of centres interfere with each other like the ripples from hailstones plunging into a pond, producing an extremely complex pattern of residential nuclei. Thus single-centred models are no longer appropriate for multi-centred metropolitan areas anywhere.

Others go further still. In the conclusion to his description of Washington in 1991, Paul Knox writes: 'The examination of new urban landscapes in the Washington metropolitan area lends support to the notion of a new urban geography, with a radically different form and ecology from that of the classic American city depicted by factorial ecologies and explained, with varying degrees of success, by bid-rent theory, theories of residential mobility, Weberian theory, and neo-Marxist theories. The spatial patterns associated with the landscape elements described in this essay do not fit comfortably within the sectors, zones or mosaic patterns that have been the focus of academic debate surrounding the classic American city. Fragmentation, multinodality, fluidity, plurality and diffusion are more in evidence than homogeneity, nodality and hierarchy. Vance recognised these qualities some time ago in his survey of Bay Area urbanisation, suggesting that "We are witnessing the birth of a new complex urbanism in which the specialized social districts have begun to replace a synoptic pattern (of land rent) in shaping the morphology of settlement." Pierce Lewis coined the phrase "galactic metropolis" to capture a new urban geography in which "The residential subdivision, the shopping centres, the industrial parks seem to float in space; seen together they resemble a galaxy of stars and planets, held together by mutual gravitational attraction, but with large empty areas between the clusters."' Vance, Lewis, Knox and others recognise and describe this strange new landscape of the contemporary American city but are not yet at the stage of achieving a new model and a coherent, unifying explanation.

* * * * * * *

The aims of this book do not include either prediction or advice to planners. Prediction is not part of Geography, and planning is a separate profession. But some conclusions are in order about the stage which has been reached in the structure of the American city and the distribution of its citizens.

Although the concentrated city became too large and too congested, it had a logic in its time. There was logic in its elements, in the way it was arranged spatially and in the way it worked that is not so apparent in the structure and functioning of the sprawling MSAs. The concentrated city was not really planned, but it might have continued to work in America if many more medium-sized centres had been founded in the very short period of city generation in the United States. In the event, an enormous and rapidly growing population concentrated on what turned out to be too few centres for the numbers of people involved. Demonstrably, the MSA sprawls have not been planned either, and far from being able to see any naturally occurring logic in the layout and operation, one sees a creaking system which is neither entirely satisfactory to the citizens, nor indicative of any future stability. To admit that one can not identify an overall logic is not, of course, to say that none is there, but it seems

245

more likely that the logic is local, within individual parts of the con-tinuously built-up-area, rather than in the supercity as a whole.

Just as prediction is futile, there is no sense in harking back to a past Golden Age of the American city which probably never existed outside one's imagination. The concentrated city had fundamental problems which had to be resolved in one way or another. The expe-dient proved to be flight to the suburbs, avoiding the problems rather than facing them. Similarly, the present arrangement of multi-centred multiple nuclei MSAs has characteristics which make it unlikely that it can continue to exist in its present form for any length of time. Change is inevitable anyway, but in the American city it seems to be a necessity at the moment.

At the end of the twentieth century the geography of the large American city has five features which most observers might agree are unsatisfactory. First, the political and financial arrangements are tending to leave large areas of poverty and slums in the inner rings of the Central Cities. Secondly, the same arrangements in combination with the present socio-economic attitudes which prevail tend to con-centrate the poor in very high-density areas. One might include the black people in point two, but as racial prejudice gives their condition an extra dimension, this is made a third, separate point.

Fourthly, the way the built-up-areas, the so-called suburbs which it has been argued are really the main part of the whole urban area, have an extremely inefficient layout. The panics of the petrol shorta-ges of the 1970s gave an illustration of this. If, for any reason, as in Cuba in 1993, petrol becomes unavailable, the suburbs will not work. In the fifth place, without over-stressing the liabilities at the old centres, the American MSAs are in danger of becoming some of the largest and most complex urban areas in the world with inadequate focal points and, infinitely more seriously, inadequate government for the whole urbanised area.

Finally, the matter of immigrants has to be mentioned separately because it could be argued that the other major features described in this book would be much as they are with or without such a whole-hearted immigration policy. At one time ethnic areas in the Amer-ican city were referred to as 'anthologies of Europe'. As immigration was opened up again, some people started to see America not as one nation, but as a 'nation of nations'. In Los Angeles, at least, by the 1990s many observers were giving up trying to see foreign neigh-bourhoods as exception in the sea of WASP suburbia. Instead, Don Harrison called Los Angeles 'Collage City' as the hundreds of sepa-rate, differentiated and potentially isolated groups balkanised the suburbs.

246

It may be too much to predict that this will happen in the suburbs of all the other large American cities. But for the moment, this is what many residents *perceive* to be happening. More to the point, many white people fear that this is becoming the norm; they fear it, and so they try to prepare against it, in the process making assimilation and integration that much harder. Ideas of Americanisation and/or the melting pot may now be things of the past. The salad bowl and the mosaic are now the accepted state of affairs. Fortunately they are accepted by many in a spirit of optimism that there will be wealth, enterprise and cultural richness generated by such ethnic diversity. But this pluralism, the Collage City which is rapidly becoming an anthology of the whole world, could embody mankind's deep divisions as well as the hope for a better life — which, in the first place, brought so many different peoples into America, and into the American city.

12

A PERSONAL CONCLUSION

Different commentators on the American urban scene express, and have expressed, a variety of reactions, ranging from sadness through arrogance to optimism. In the last chapter of *The Great Gatsby*, Scott Fitzgerald's Nick Carraway is looking back on the end of Gatsby's dream. Among other important matters he contrasts the city, where we believe Gatsby started, with Gatsby's progress out to the exclusive suburbs on Long Island Sound. First, on page 182 of my tattered Penguin, he gives a vivid glimpse of the old concentrated city, Chicago at Christmas, in the days when one travelled by train:

'One of my most vivid memories is of coming back West from prep school and later from college at Christmas time. Those who went farther than Chicago would gather in the old dim Union Station at six o'clock of a December evening, with a few Chicago friends, already caught up into their own holiday gaieties, to bid them a hasty good-bye. I remember the fur coats of the girls returning from Miss This-or-That's and the chatter of frozen breath and the hands waving overhead as we caught sight of old acquaintances, and the matching of invitations: "are you going to the Ordways'? the Herseys'? the Schultzes'?" and the long green tickets clasped in our tight gloved hands. And last the murky yellow cars of the Chicago, Milwaukee and St. Paul railroad looking cheerful as Christmas itself on the tracks beside the gate.'

Then, within the last three short paragraphs, Fitzgerald shows that it was not only Gatsby who failed to find whatever he believed was in the future, in the suburbs:

'He had come a long way to this blue lawn, and his dream must have seemed so close that he could hardly fail to grasp it. He did not know that it was already behind him, somewhere back in that vast obscurity behind the city, where the dark fields of the republic rolled on under the night.

248

Gatsby believed in the green light, the orgastic future that year by year recedes before us. It eluded us then, but that's no matter — tomorrow we will run faster, stretch out our arms further... And one fine morning — '

I feel that Fitzgerald is making a profound statement here, the subtext of his book, marginally about the city, centrally about the Republic itself, and the new people with a new start in new cities in a new continent.

'...for a transitory enchanted moment man must have held his breath in the presence of this continent, compelled into an aesthetic contemplation he neither understood nor desired, face to face for the last time in history with something commensurate to his capacity for wonder.'

It seems to me that Fitzgerald, with gentle resignation, is sadly saying what could be bluntly stated as, 'they had it — and they blew it.' Perhaps not.

At one time I was in tune with that kind of idea, but then the very changes continued to stimulate the old interest. If one is to sum up the themes in the American city likely to continue to be dominant into the next century, then they seem to be: an increasing diversity between cities; the changing effects of the new immigrants; the precarious financial arrangements for the Central Cities and for vital services in the suburbs; and a need to understand the very structure of the suburbs which are now Edge Cities. There is much of interest, much to study and to understand, much which will go on changing, maintain one's interest, pose an intellectual challenge and renew one's optimism.

In the preceding chapter a call was made for a new model of the urban residential structure, as a minimum requirement for our continued understanding of the phenomenon. As already mentioned, Paul Knox goes one further, and in his article in the *Annals of the Association of American Geographers*, makes a call for a new urban geography. There is a touch of arrogance here. Just as one deplores the blinkered approach of Positivists in applying American models to British and European cities whether they are appropriate or not, one has to smile ruefully at Knox's statement that because we certainly are in a process of constantly updating our understanding of the American city, a 'new urban geography' is needed. They might be a bit surprised about that in Capetown, Alma Ata, or even Florence. The present urban geography will serve very well now that it is shaking off the Positivist strait-jacket, provided it is prepared to develop and incorporate new models, instead of regarding Burgess and his contemporaries much as the ancients regarded Plato and Moses. Flexibility and open-mindedness are what is required.

Open-mindedness is the refreshing quality I found in Joel Garreau's work on Edge City. I knew and loved *The Great Gatsby* even before starting to study the American city, and that is too long ago to contemplate. *Edge City* came to hand a couple of years ago as this final draft was being made. Joel Garreau's optimism gives me the quotation for the conclusion of this work, and a challenge to the next generation of geographers.

'But the farther toward the back of the book you are, the more you will find [Americans] grappling with ever more wonderful and profound questions — about identity, and community, and civilisation, and soul, and all the other attributes of the good life for which we yearn. For this is the most interesting and challenging task — of really penetrating our latest attempt at Utopia. And of trying to gauge how far along we are.'

REFERENCES

CHAPTER ONE

1. Girouard, M., *Cities and People*, London, 1985.
2. Bromfield, E.T. (Ed.), *The Land We Live In*, New York, 1891.
3. Warner, S.B., *The Urban Wilderness*, New York, 1972.
4. Knos, D., *Distribution of Land Values in Topeka*, Lawrence, Kansas, 1962.
5. Ward, D., *Cities and Immigrants*, New York, 1971, (Chap. 5).
6. Yeates, M. and Garner, B., *The North American City*, New York, 1971, (Chap. 12).
7. Mayer, H.M. and Wade, R.C., *Chicago*, Chicago, 1969.
8. Pred, A.R., 'The Intrametropolitan Location of American Manufacturing', *Annals of the Association of American Geographers*, Vol. 54, pp. 165–180.
9. Park, R.E., Burgess, E.W. and McKenzie, R.D., *The City*, Chicago, 1925.
10. Sandburg, Carl, *Harvest Poems*, New York, 1960.

CHAPTER TWO

1. Lewis, Sinclair, *Babbit*, London, 1922.
2. Jackson, K.T., *Crabgrass Frontier*, New York, 1985.
3. Fitzgerald, F. Scott, *The Great Gatsby*, New York, 1925.
4. Chandler, A.D. Jr., *Giant Enterprise. Ford, General Motors and the Automobile Industry*, New York, 1964.
5. Berry, B.J.L. and Horton, F.E., *Geographical Perspectives on Urban Systems*, Englewood Cliffs, NJ, 1970.
6. Royko, M., *Boss*, London, 1972.

CHAPTER THREE

1. Miller, Z.L., *The Urbanisation of Modern America*, New York, 1973.
2. Alexander, L.M., *The Northeastern United States*, Princeton, 1967.
3. Gottman, J., *Megalopolis*, New York, 1961.
4. Dyckman, J.W., 'Transportation in Cities', *Scientific American*, Vol. 213 No. 3, Sept. 1965, pp. 162–177.
5. Schaeffer, K.H. and Sclar, E., *Access For All*, 1975.

251

6. Smith, D., *Report From Engine Company 82*, 1974.
7. Walker, T., *Fort Apache*, 1977.
8. *Time*, 20 October 1975, p. 42.
9. Davies, S. and Fowler, G.L., 'The Disadvantaged Urban Migrant in Indianapolis', *Economic Geography*, Vol. 48, No. 2, April 1972.

CHAPTER FOUR

1. Wright, D.R., 'Pittsburgh — City With An Ailing Heart', *Geographical Magazine*, Vol. XLII, No. 3, Dec. 1969, pp. 177–187.
2. Jacobs, J., *The Death and Life of Great American Cities*, 1964.
3. *The Official Bicentennial Guidebook*. Published by E.P. Dutton, Boston, 1975.
4. Munzer, M.E., *Planning our Town*, New York, 1964.
5. Mayer, H.M., and Wade, R.C., *Chicago*, Chicago, 1969.
6. Glazer, N., 'The Renewal of Cities', *Scientific American*, Vol. 213, No. 3, Sept. 1965, pp. 194–208.

CHAPTER FIVE

For Toronto, see:
1. Brunn, S.D. and Williams, J.F., *Cities of the World*, New York, 1983.
2. Guinness, P. and Bradshaw, M., *North America*, 1985.
3. Yeates, M. and Garner, B., *The North American City*, New York, 1971.
4. Starbird, E.A., 'Canada's Dowager Learns to Swing', *National Geographic*, Vol. 148 No. 2, Aug. 1975 pp. 190–215.

For Los Angeles, see:
5. Banham R., *Los Angeles*, 1971.
6. Nelson, H.J. and Clark, A.V., *Los Angeles*, Cambridge, Mass, 1976.
7. Weaver, J.D., *El Pueblo Grande*, Los Angeles, 1973.

For New York in this context see back issues of the *Guardian*, *Newsweek*, *Daily Telegraph* and *Time*; especially in the 1970s.

CHAPTER SIX

1. Jones, M.A., *The Limits of Liberty*, New York, 1989.
2. Bryan, P.W., *Man's Adaptation of Nature*, 1933.
3. Ward, D., *Cities and Immigrants*, New York, 1971.

4. Riis, J.A., *How the Other Half Lives*, New York, 1971.
5. Stokes, C.J., 'A Theory of Slums', *Land Economics*, Vol. xxxviii, No. 3, August 1962.
6. Burgess, E.W. 'Residential Segregation in Cities', *Annals of the American Academy of Political and Social Science*, 140, pp. 105–115.
7. Jakle, J.A. and Wheeler, S., 'The Dutch in Kalamazoo, Michigan', *Tijdschrift Voor Economische en Sociale Geografie*, 1969, July–August, pp. 249–254.
8. Doeppers, D.F., 'The Globeville Neighborhood in Denver', *Geographical Review*, Vol. VII, 1967, pp. 506–522.
9. Jones, E., *Human Geography*, 1966.
10. Mayer, H.M. and Wade, R.C., *Chicago*, Chicago, 1969.
11. Feininger, A. and Simon, K., 1964, *New York*, 1964.

CHAPTER SEVEN

1. Freed, L., *Black, in White America*, New York, 1967.
2. Osofsky, G., *Harlem: The Making of a Ghetto*, New York, 1963.
3. Morrill, R.L. and Donaldson, O.F., 'Geographical Perspectives on the History of Black America', *Economic Geography*, 48.1, 1972, pp. 1–23.
4. Williams, J., *Eyes on the Prize*, New York, 1987.
5. Finer, S.E. (Ed.), *Five Constitutions*, Harmondsworth, 1979.
6. Morrill, R.L. 'The Negro Ghetto: Problems and Alternatives', *Geographical Review*, Vol. LV, 1965, pp. 339–361.
7. Davies, P., *The Metropolitan Mosaic*, British Association for American Studies, 1980.
8. Warf, B., 'Deindustrialisation, Service Sector Growth, and the Underclass in the New York Metropolitan Region', *Tijdschrift Voor Economische en Social Geografie*, 1990, Vol. LXXXI, No. 5, p. 332.
9. Stafford, H.A. and Watts, H.D., 'Abandoned Products, Abandoned Places', *T.E.S.G.*, 1990, Vol. LXXXI, No. 3, p. 162.
10. Gould, P. and White, R., *Mental Maps*, Harmondsworth, 1974.
11. Smith, D.M., *The Geography of Social Well-Being in the United States*, New York, 1973.
12. Johnston, R.J., *Urban Residential Patterns*, Chapter 6, 1971.

CHAPTER EIGHT

1. Shelton, B.A. et al., *Houston: Growth and Decline in a Sunbelt Boomtown*, Philadelphia, 1989.
2. Chua-Eoan, H.G., 'A Promised Land?' *Time*, Vol. 135, No. 10, 5 March 1990, pp. 34–41.

3. Special issue of *Time*, 'We The People', *Time*, Vol. 130, No. 1, 6 July 1987.
4. Evans-Pritchard, A., 'Uncle Sam's Open Door Threatens to Disunite the States', *Sunday Telegraph*, 2 April 1995. Also draws attention to Peter Brimelow's book *Alien Nation*.

CHAPTER NINE

1. Warf, B., 'Japanese Investments in the New York Metropolitan Region', *Geographical Review*, Vol. 78, No. 3, July 1988, p. 257.
2. Daniels, P.W., 'Foreign Banks and Metropolitan Development', *Tijdschrift Voor Economische en Sociale Geografie*, Vol. LXXVII, No. 4, 1986, pp. 269–287.
3. Jackson, P., 'Neighborhood Change in New York. The Loft Conversion Process', *T.E.S.G.*, Vol. LXXVI, 1985, p. 202.
4. Murphy, R.E., *The Central Business District*, 1972.
5. Banham, R., *Megastructure*, 1976.
6. Blandford, L., 'Detroit', *Guardian*, 19 Dec. 1984.
7. Estleman, L.D., *Sugartown, The Glass Highway, Motor City Blue*, etc., published variously by Papermac and Penguin, 1982ff.
8. Girouard, M., *Cities and People*, New Haven & London 1985.
9. Knox, P., 'The Restless Urban Landscape', *Annals of the Association of American Geographers*, Vol. 18 No. 2, June 1991, pp. 181–209.
10. Watson, J.W., 'The Sociological Aspects of Geography', in: Taylor, G., (Ed.), *Geography in the 20th. Century*, Chapter XX, 1951.
11. Gibbs, N., 'Homeless, U.S.A.'., *Time*, Vol. 136 No. 26, 17 Dec. 1990, pp. 40–45.
12. Tisdall, S., 'Poverty Timebomb Ticking On', *Guardian*, 16 February 1990.
13. Walker, M., et al., 'US Cities in Crisis', *Guardian*, 16 February 1990.
14. Hiscock, J., 'Hollywood Begging Bowls Take Shine Off Tinseltown', *Sunday Telegraph*, 26 January 1992.
15. Smith, N., 'Gentrification and Uneven Development', *Economic Geography*, Vol. 58 1982, pp. 139–155.
16. Vonnegut, K., 'One Hell of a Country', *Guardian*, 27 February 1992.
17. Evans-Pritchard, A., 'U.S. Right Seeks a Cultural Revolution', *Sunday Telegraph*, 26 February 1995.

CHAPTER TEN

1. Brown, D.L. and Wardlow, J.M., *New Directions in Urban-Rural Migration*, New York, 1980.
2. Yeates, M. and Garner, B., *The North American City*, New York, p. 252, 1971.
3. Erikson, R.A. and Gentry, M., 'Suburban Nucleations', *Geographical Review*, Vol. LXXV 1985, pp. 19–31.
4. Rieff, D., *Los Angeles, Capital of the Third World*, 1992.
5. Cervero, R., *American Suburban Centres*, Boston, 1989.
6. Murphy, R.E. *The Central Business District*, 1972.
7. Garreau, J., *Edge City*, New York, 1991.
8. Evans-Pritchard, E., 'U.S. Overclass Has Decadent Overtones', *Sunday Telegraph*, 18 September 1994.
9. Laurence, C., 'John Brown is Dead, Now Randy Weaver Marches On', *Daily Telegraph*, 30 May 1995.

CHAPTER ELEVEN

1. Park, R.E., et al., *The City*, Chicago, 1925. This is the model usually referred to as Burgess.
2. Hoyt, H., *The Structure and Growth of Residential Neighborhoods in American Cities*, Washington, DC, Federal Housing Administration, 1939.
3. Harris, C.D. and Ullman, E.L., 'The Nature of Cities', *Annals of the American Academy of Political and Social Science*, 242, 1945, pp. 7–17.
4. Shevky, E. and Bell, W., *Social Area Analysis*, California, Stanford University Press, 1955.
5. Abler, R., Adams, J.S. and Gould, D.P, *Spatial Organisation*, Englewood Cliffs, NJ. 1971.
6. *Guardian*, see editions from October 1989 onwards.
7. Davis, D., *The Milwaukee Murders*, 1992.
8. 'U.S. Murder Capital Police Beg For Help in Drug War', *Guardian*, 13 March 1989.
9. Great Seal of the United States: ANNUIT COEPTIS, more precisely rendered as: God has favoured our undertakings.
10. Brown, J., *The Unmelting Pot*, [about Bedford, UK] 1970.
11. Peach, C., Robinson, V. and Smith, S., (Eds.), *Ethnic Segregation in Cities*, 1981.
12. Davies, H., 'America Poised to Reject More Huddled Masses', *Daily Telegraph*, 9 June 1995.

13. Lind, M., *The Next American Nation*, Free Press, Bowker, New York, 1995.
14. Applebaum, A., 'Hit the Hispanic Button: English Isn't Spoken Here', *Daily Telegraph*, 31 January 1995. One of a superb series on the United States by Anne Applebaum.
15. Sandburg, C., *Harvest Poems*, New York, 1960.
16. Muller, P.O., *Contemporary Suburban America*, Englewood Cliffs, NJ, 1981.
17. Knox, P., 'The Restless Urban Landscape', *Annals of the Association of American Geographers*, Vol. 18 No. 2, June 1991, pp. 181–209.

CHAPTER TWELVE

1. Fitzgerald, F. Scott, *The Great Gatsby*, 1925; published in Britain in 1926 and still in print.
2. Garreau, J., *Edge City*, Doubleday, New York, 1991.

BIBLIOGRAPHY

Abler, R. (Ed.), *A Comparative Atlas of America's Great Cities*, Minneapolis, Univ. Minneapolis Press, 1976.

Abler, R. et al., *St. Paul-Minneapolis*, Cambridge, Mass., Ballinger, 1976.

Albaum, M., *Geography and Contemporary Issues*, New York, Wiley, 1973.

Alexander, L.M., *The Northeastern United States*, Princeton, NJ, Van Nostrand, 1967.

Amory, C., *Boston*, New York, Dutton, 1975.

Andrus, A.P. et al., *Seattle*, Cambridge, Mass., Ballinger, 1976.

Baldwin, J., *The Fire Next Time*, Michael Joseph, 1963.

Banham, R., *Los Angeles*, Penguin, 1971.

Banham, R., *Megastructure*, Thames and Hudson, 1976.

Bell, C.S., *The Economics of the Ghetto*, Pegasus, 1970.

Bennett, L., *Fragments of Cities*, Columbus, Ohio State Univ. Press, 1990.

Bernardi, R.C., *Great Buildings of San Francisco*, Constable, 1980.

Berry, B.J.L. et al., *Chicago*, Cambridge, Mass., Ballinger, 1976.

Berry, B.J.L., *The Human Consequences of Urbanisation*, Macmillan, 1973.

Berry, B.J.L. and Horton, F.E., *Geographical Perspectives on Urban Systems*, Englewood Cliffs, Prentice-Hall, 1970.

Billingsley, A., *Climbing Jacob's Ladder: The enduring legacy of Afro-American families*, New York, Simon and Schuster, 1992.

Black, M., *Old New York in Early Photographs*, New York, Dover, 1973.

Blair, T.L., *The International Urban Crisis*, Hart-Davis, 1974.

Blumstein, J.F. and Walter, B., *Growing Metropolis*, Nashville, Vanderbilt U.P., 1975.

Bollens, J.C. and Schmandt, H.J. *The Metropolis*, New York, Harper, 1970.

Boston Society of Architects, *Architecture Boston*, Boston, Mass., 1976.

Bourne, L.S., *Internal Structure of the City*, New York, O.U.P., 1971.

Bourne, L.S., *The Form of Cities in Central Canada*, Toronto, Univ. Toronto Press, 1973.

Bromfield, E.T. (Ed.), *The Land We Live In*, New York, Worthington, 1891.

Brook, S., *New York Days, New York Nights*, Hamish Hamilton, 1984.

Brown, H.C., *Valentine's City of New York*, New York, Valentine, 1920.

Brunn, S.D., *Geography and Politics in America*, New York, Harper and Row, 1974.

Brunn, S.D., *Cities of the World*, New York, Harper, 1983.

Brunn, S.D. and Wheeler, J.O., *The American Metropolitan System: Present and Future*, Arnold, 1980.

Bryan, P.W., *Man's Adaptation of Nature*, Univ. London Press, 1933.

Butler, E.W., *Urban Sociology*, New York, Harper and Row, 1976.

Cameron, R., *Above San Francisco*, San Francisco, Cameron, 1969.

Carey, G.W., *New York–New Jersey*, Cambridge, Mass., Ballinger, 1976.

Cavallo, P., *The Lower East Side. A Portrait in Time*, New York, Crowell-Collier, 1971.

Cervero, R., *America's Suburban Centres*, Boston, Unwin Hyman, 1989.

Chudacoff, H.P., *The Evolution of American Urban Society*, Englewood Cliffs, Prentice-Hall, 1975.

Clark, D., *Post-Industrial America*, New York, Methuen, 1986.

Cleaveland, F.N., *Congress and Urban Problems*, Washington, Brookings Institute, 1969.

Cohen, S.B., *Problems and Trends in American Geography*, New York, Basic Books, 1967.

Coles, R., *Still Hungry in America*, New York, New American Library, 1969.

Collier, P. and Horowitz, D. (Eds.), *Second Thoughts About Race in America*, Lanham, Madison Books, 1991.

Colter, C., *The Amoralists*, Penguin, 1991.

Conduit, C.W., *Building, Planning and Urban Technology*, Chicago, Univ. Chicago Press, 1974.

Conzen, M.P. and Lewis, G.K., *Boston*, Cambridge, Mass., Ballinger, 1976.

Cox, K.R., *Conflict, Power and Politics in the City*, New York, McGraw Hill, 1973.

Cox, K.R., *Location and Public Problems*, Blackwell, 1979.

Daniels, R., *Asian America: Chinese and Japanese in the U.S. Since 1850*, Seattle, Univ. Washington Press, 1988.

Daniels, R., *Coming to America: A history of immigration and ethnicity in American life*, New York, Harper, 1990.

Davies, P., *The Metropolitan Mosaic*, British Association for American Studies, 1980.

Davies, W.K. and Herbert, D.T., *Communities Within Cities: An urban social geography*, Belhaven, 1993.

Davis, D., *The Milwaukee Murders*, Virgin, 1992.

Davis, M., *City of Quartz: Excavating the Future in Los Angeles*, Verso, 1990.

Dawson, J.A., *Shopping Centre Development*, Longman, 1983.

Didion, J., *Sentimental Journeys*, Harper-Collins, 1993.

Dinnerstein, L. and Reimers, D.M., *Ethnic Americans*, New York, Harper-Row, 1988.

Editors of Sunset Books, *Los Angeles*, Menlo Park, California, 1968.

Edsall, T.B. with Edsall, M.D., *Chain Reaction*, New York, Norton and Co., 1992.

Federal Writers' Project, *New York City Guide*, New York, Random House, 1939.

Feininger, A. and Simon, K., *New York*, Thames and Hudson, 1964.

Fellows, D.K., *A Mosaic of America's Ethnic Minorities*, New York, Wiley, 1972.

Fitch, R., *The Assassination of New York*, Verso, 1993.

Fox, K., *Metropolitan America: Urban Life and Urban Policy in the U.S. 1940–1980*, Macmillan, 1985.

Freed, L., *Black, in White America*, New York, Grossman, 1967.

Gamio, M., *Mexican Immigration to the U.S.*, New York, Dover, 1971.

Garreau, J., *Edge City*, New York, Doubleday, 1991.

George, L., *No Crystal Stair: Afro-Americans in the City of the Angels*, Verso, 1992.

Gidley, M., *Modern American Culture*, Longman, 1993.

Gilbert, B.W., *Ten Blocks From the White House*, Pall Mall, 1968.

Gilliam, H. and Palmer, P., *The Face of San Francisco*, Garden City, N.Y., Doubleday, 1960.

Ginzberg, E., *New York Is Very Much Alive*, New York, McGraw Hill, 1973.

Glazer, N. and Moynihan, D.P., *Beyond the Melting Pot*, Cambridge, Mass., M.I.T. Press, 1963.

Godfrey, B.J., *Neighborhoods in Transition: San Francisco's Ethnic Communities*, Berkeley, Univ. California Press, 1988.

Goodall, L.E., *The American Metropolis*, Columbus, Charles E. Merrill, 1968.

Goro, H., *The Block*, New York, Random House, 1970.

Gottlieb, D. and Heinson, A.L., *America's Other Youth*, Englewood Cliffs, Prentice-Hall, 1971.

Gottmann, J., *Megalopolis*, New York, M.I.T. Press, 1961.

Gottmann, J. and Harper, R.A., *Metropolis On The Move*, New York, Wiley, 1967.

Gould, P. and White, R., *Mental Maps*, Penguin, 1974.

Green, C.M. *The Rise of Urban America*, H.U.L., 1966.

Greer, S.A., *Urban Renewal and American Cities*, Indianapolis, Bobs-Merrill, 1965.

Hacker, A., *Two Nations: Black and White Separate, Hostile, Unequal*, New York, Ballantine, 1992.

Hall, P.G., *The World Cities*, Weidenfeld, 1966.

Halpern, K., *Downtown U.S.A.*, Architectural Press, 1978.

Handlin, O., *Boston's Immigrants*, Cambridge, Mass., Belknap, 1959.

Handlin, O., *The Newcomers, Negroes and Puerto Ricans in a Changing Metropolis*, New York, Anchor, 1962.

Harrington, M., *The Other America: Poverty in the U.S.*, Baltimore, Penguin, 1963.

Harris, B., *Chicago*, New York, Crescent Books, 1983.

Harris, B., *Boston*, New York, Crescent Books, 1984.

Harris, C.D. and Ullman, E.L., 'The Nature of Cities', *Annals of American Academy of Political and Social Science*, 242 7–17, 1945.

Harris, F.R. and Lindsay, J.V., *The State of the Cities*, New York, Praeger, 1972.

Hart, J.F. (Ed.), *Regions of the United States*, New York, Harper and Row, 1972.

Hart, J.F. (Ed.), *Our Changing Cities*, Baltimore, Johns Hopkins Press, 1991.

Hartshorne, T.A. et al., *Atlanta*, Cambridge, Mass., Ballinger, 1976.

Hartshorne, T.A., *Interpreting the City*, New York, Wiley, 1980.

Hicks, D.A., *Urban America in the Eighties*, New Brunswick, Transaction Books, 1982.

Hitchcock, H.R. et al., *The Rise Of An American Architecture*, Pall Mall, 1970.

Hoag, E., *American Cities*, Philadelphia, Lippincott, 1969,

Holli, M.G., *Detroit*, New York; Franklin Watts, 1976.

Holli, M.G. and Jones, P.D'A., *The Ethnic Frontier*, Grand Rapids, Eerdmans, 1977.

Hoover, E.M. and Vernon, R., *Anatomy of a Metropolis*, New York, Anchor Books, 1962.

Hoyt, H., *The Structure and Growth of Residential Neighborhoods in American Cities*, Washington, DC, Federal Housing Administration, 1939.

Hughes, R., *Culture of Complaint: The Fraying of America*, New York, O.U.P., 1993.

Inglefield, E., *Cities of America*, Hamlyn, 1984.

Jackson, K.T., *Crabgrass Frontier: The Suburbanisation of the United States*, New York, O.U.P., 1985.

Jackson, K.T. and Fairbanks, R.B. (Eds.), *Essays on Sunbelt Cities and Recent Urban America*, Arlington, University of Texas Press, 1990.

Jacobs, J., *The Death and Life of Great American Cities*, Pelican, 1964.

Jacobs, J., *The Economy of Cities*, Cape, 1969.

Jacobs, P., *Prelude to Riot: A View of Urban America from the Bottom*, New York, Random House, 1966.

Jankowski, M.S., *Islands in the Street: Gangs in American Urban Society*, Berkeley, Univ. California Press, 1991.

Johnson, J.H., *Urbanisation*, Macmillan, 1980.

Johnston, R.J., *Urban Residential Patterns*, Bell, 1971.

Jones, E., *Towns and Cities*, Oxford Univ. Press, 1966.

Jones, E., *Readings in Social Geography*, O.U.P., 1975.

Kogan, H. and Wendt, L., *Chicago, A Pictorial History*, New York, Dutton, 1958.
Kramer, J., *North American Suburbs*, Berkeley Cal., Glendessary Press, 1972.

Lapham, L.H., *Money and Class in America*, 1989.
Larsen, L.H., *The Urban South*, Lexington, University Press of Kentucky, 1990.
Lee, J.F.J., *Asian Americans*, New York, New Press, 1991.
Leinwand, G., *The Negro in the City*, New York, Pocket Books, 1968.
Leinwand, G., *Governing the City*, New York, Pocket Books, 1971.
Leinwand, G., Carter, W. and Hancock, B., *Poverty and the Poor*, New York, Pocket Books, 1970.
Leinwand, G. and Collins, E., *The Slums*, New York, Pocket Books, 1968.
Lemann, N., *The Promised Land*, Macmillan, 1991.
Lewis, P.F., *New Orleans*, Cambridge, Mass., Ballinger, 1976.
Ley, D., *A Social Geography of the City*, New York, Harper and Row, 1983.
Lind, M., *The Next American Nation*, New York, Free Press, Bowker, 1995.
Ling, P.J., *America and the Automobile*, Manchester Univ. Press, 1990.
Longbrake, D.B. and Nichols, W.W. (Jr.), *Miami*, Cambridge, Mass., Ballinger.
Lubove, R. (Ed.), *Pittsburgh*, New York, Franklin Watts. 1976.
Ludwig, E. and Santibanez, J. (Eds.), *The Chicanos*, Penguin, 1971.
Lyford, J.P., *The Airtight Cage*, New York, Harper and Row, 1966.

Maldonado, L. and Moore, J., *Urban Ethnicity in the United States*, Beverly Hills, Sage, 1985.
Masotti, L.H. and Corsi, J.R., *Shoot-Out in Cleveland: Black Militants and the Police*, July 1968, New York, Praeger, 1969.
Massey, D.S. and Denton, N.A., *American Apartheid. Segregation and the Making of the Underclass*, Harvard University Press, 1993.
Mayer, H.M. and Kohn, C.F., *Readings in Urban Geography*, Chicago, Univ. Chicago Press, 1959.
Mayer, H.M. and Wade, R.C., *Chicago: Growth of a Metropolis*, Chicago, Univ. Chicago Press, 1969.
McAlary, M., *Crack War*, New York, Putnam, 1990.
McElvey, B., *The Urbanisation of America*, New Brunswick, NJ, Rutgers, 1963.
McElvey, B., *The City in American History*, Allen and Unwin, 1969.
McElvey, B., *The Emergence of Metropolitan America*, New Brunswick, NJ, Rutgers, 1968.

261

Miller, Z.L., *Boss Cox's Cincinnati*, New York, O.U.P., 1968.

Miller, Z.L., *The Urbanisation of Modern America*, New York, Harcourt Brace, 1973.

Moore, J.W. and Cuellar, A., *Mexican Americans*, Englewood Cliffs, NJ, Prentice-Hall, 1970.

Morales, R. and Bonilla, F. (Eds.), *Latinos in a Changing U.S. Economy*, Newbury Park California, Sage, 1993.

Morris, J., *The Great Port*, Faber, 1970.

Muller, P.O., *Contemporary Suburban America*, Englewood Cliffs, NJ, Prentice-Hall, 1981.

Muller, P.O. et al., *Philadelphia*, Cambridge, Mass., Ballinger, 1976.

Murphy, R.E., *The Central Business District: A Study in Urban Geography*, Longmam, 1972.

Muth, R.F., *Public Housing: An Economic Evaluation*, Washington, D.C., American Enterprise Institute for Public Policy Research, 1973.

Nelson, H.J. and Clark, W.A.V., *Los Angeles*, Cambridge, Mass., Ballinger, 1976.

Olson, S., *Baltimore*, Cambridge, Mass., Ballinger, 1976.

Osofsky, G., *Harlem: The Making of a Ghetto*, New York, Harper and Row, 1963.

Oxford Regional Economic Atlas, *The U.S. and Canada*, O.U.P., 1975.

Park, R.E., Burgess, E.W. and McKenzie, R.D., *The City*, Chicago, Univ. Chicago Press, 1925.

Passoneau, J.R. and Wurman, R.S., *Urban Atlas: Twenty American Cities*, Cambridge, Mass., M.I.T. Press, 1966.

Peach, C., (Ed.), *Urban Social Segregation*, Longman, 1975.

Peach, C., Robinson, V. and Smith, S. (Eds.), *Ethnic Segregation in Cities*, Croom Helm, 1981.

Philpott, T.L., *The Slum and the Ghetto*, O.U.P., 1978.

Polenberg, R., *One Nation Divisible: Class, Race and Ethnicity in the U.S. Since 1938*, Penguin, 1980.

Putnam, R.G., Taylor, F.J. and Kettle, P.G., *A Geography of Urban Places*, Toronto, Methuen, 1970.

Rainwater, L., *Behind Ghetto Walls*, Allen Lane, 1971.

Rieff, D., *Cuba in the Heart of Miami*, New York, Simon and Schuster, 1993.

Rieff, D., *Los Angeles: Capital of the Third World*, Cape, 1992.

Riesenberg, F., *Golden Road*, New York, McGraw Hill, 1962.

Riis, J.A., *How the Other Half Lives*, New York, Dover, 1971.

Rischin, M., *The Promised City*, Cambridge, Mass., Harvard Univ. Press, 1962.

Rose, A., *The Negro in America*, New York, Harper, 1964.

Roe, H.M., *The Black Ghetto*, New York, McGraw-Hill, 1971.

Royko, M., *Boss: Mayor Richard Daley of Chicago*, Paladin, 1972.

Rutledge, P.J., *The Vietnamese Experience in America*, Bloomington, Indiana University Press, 1992.

Schaeffer, K.H. and Sclar, E., *Access For All: Transportation and Urban Growth*, Penguin, 1975.

Schlesinger, A.M., *The Disuniting of America*, New York, Norton, 1991.

Scientific American, *Cities: A Scientific American Special*, Penguin, 1967,

Schwartz, J.E. and Volgy, T.J., *The Forgotten Americans*, New York, Norton, 1992.

Shelton, B.A. et al., *Houston: Growth and Decline in a Sunbelt Boomtown*, Philadelphia, Temple Univ. Press, 1989.

Sherman, R.B., *The Negro and the City*, Englewood Cliffs, NJ, Prentice-Hall, 1970.

Shevky, E. and Bell, W., *Social Area Analysis*, Stanford, Cal., Stanford Univ. Press, 1955.

Sinclair, R. and Thompson, B., *Detroit*, Cambridge, Mass., Ballinger, 1977.

Sleeper, J., *The Closest of Strangers: Liberalism and the Politics of Race in New York*, New York, Norton, 1991.

Smith, D., *Report From Engine Company 82*, Millington, 1974.

Smith, D.M., *The Geography of Social Well-Being in the United States*, New York, McGraw-Hill, 1973.

Smith, N. and Williams, P., *Gentrification of the City*, Allen and Unwin, 1986.

Terkel, S., *Working*, Wildwood House, 1975.

Terkel, S., *Race*, Sinclair Stevenson, 1992.

Theodorson, G.A., *Studies in Human Ecology*, Evanston Ill., 1961.

Thernstrom, S.A., *Harvard Encyclopedia of American Ethnic Groups*, Cambridge, Mass., Harvard Univ. Press, 1980.

Thomson, J.M., *Great Cities and Their Traffic*, Penguin, 1977.

Tunnard, C. and Reed, H.H., *American Skyline*, New York, Mentor, 1953.

Uroff, M.D., *Becoming a City*, New York, Harcourt-Brace, 1968.

Urofsky, M., *Perspectives on Urban America*, New York, Anchor, 1973.

Walker, S. (Ed.), *Stories From the American Mosaic*, St. Paul, Greywolf Press, 1990.

Walker, T., *Fort Apache* [in the Bronx], Tandem, 1977.

Ward, D., *Cities and Immigrants*, New York, O.U.P., 1971.

Ward, D., *Poverty, Ethnicity and the American City: Changing conceptions of the slum and the ghetto*, New York, Cambridge University Press, 1989.

Warner, S.B., *The Private City* (Philadelphia), Philadelphia, Univ. Pennsylvania Press, 1968.

Warner, S.B., *The Urban Wilderness: A History of the American City*, New York, Harper and Row, 1972.

Watson, E.B. and Gillon, E.V. Jr., *New York Then and Now*, New York, Dover, 1976.

Watson, J.W., 'The Sociological Aspects of Geography', in Taylor, G. (Ed.), *Geography in the 20th. Century*, Methuen, 1957.

Watson, J.W., *Social Geography of the U.S.A.*, Longman, 1979.

Weaver, J.D., *El Pueblo Grande* (Los Angeles), Los Angeles, Ward Ritchie Press, 1973.

Weston, G.F., *Boston Ways*, Boston, Beacon Press, 1957.

Wheeler, J.O., *The Urban Circulation Noose*, North Scituate, Mass., Duxbury Press, 1974.

Whitehill, W.M., *Boston: A Topographical History*, Cambridge, Mass., Belknap Press, 1968.

Williams, J., *Into The Badlands*, Paladin, 1991.

Wilson, J.Q. (Ed.), *Urban Renewal*, Cambridge, Mass., M.I.T. Press.

Wirth, L., *The Ghetto*, Chicago, Univ. Chicago Press, 1928.

Woodiwiss, A., *Postmodernity U.S.A. The Crisis of Social Modernism in Postwar America*, Newbury Park California, Sage, 1993.

Yeates, M. and Garner, B., *The North American City*, New York, Harper and Row, 1971.

— *Greater New York Illustrated*, Chicago, Rand McNally, 1897.

— *Los Angeles Birdseye View*, Los Angeles, Orbis, 1972.

U.S. Bureau of the Census, 'Statistical Abstract of the United States 1992', Washington D.C., Superintendent of Documents, U.S. Government Printing Officer, Washington D.C. 20402, 1992.

INDEX